Social Security: Visions and Revisions

The Twentieth Century Fund is an independent research foundation that undertakes policy studies of economic, political, and social institutions and issues. The Fund was founded in 1919 and endowed by Edward A. Filene.

Social Security: Visions and Revisions

A Twentieth Century Fund Study

W. ANDREW ACHENBAUM

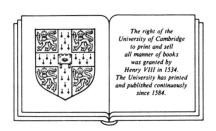

The right of the
University of Cambridge
to print and sell
all manner of books
was granted by
Henry VIII in 1534.
The University has printed
and published continuously
since 1584.

CAMBRIDGE UNIVERSITY PRESS

Cambridge
New York   New Rochelle
Melbourne   Sydney

Published by the Press Syndicate of the University of Cambridge
The Pitt Building, Trumpington Street, Cambridge CB2 IRP
32 East 57th Street, New York, NY 10022, USA
10 Stamford Road, Oakleigh, Melbourne 3166, Australia

First published 1986
First paperback edition 1987

Printed in the United States of America

Library of Congress Cataloging-in-Publication Data
Achenbaum, W. Andrew.
Social security.
"Twentieth Century Fund study."
Bibliography: p.
Includes index.
1. Social security – United States – History.
I. Title.
HD7125.A34   1986   368.4'3'00973   86-4145
ISBN 0 521 32866 7 hard covers
ISBN 0 521 35766 7 paperback

British Library Cataloging-in-Publication applied for.

Contents

To Emily and Laura

Only where love and need are one,
And the work is play for mortal stakes,
Is the deed ever really done
For heaven and the future's sakes.

Robert Frost,
"Two Tramps in Mud Time"

Foreword

It has seemed in recent years as if the nation's social security system is in a state of permanent crisis. But from its very beginnings almost fifty years ago, when it was a very different system, it has been under stress. Over the years, it has been gradually reshaped – expanded, broadened, and strengthened – to meet changing conditions and needs. Today, it enjoys a large measure of immunity from political attack. In fact, when the system was in the midst of yet another crisis just a few years ago, a bipartisan commission recommended new reforms that, once again, saved the system. In the last presidential election, both of the leading candidates made solemn vows to maintain its benefits.

So the system survives. Yet it is clear that its long-term solvency is far from assured. Indeed, the resort to short-term tinkering to shore it up means that facing the basic funding problem of the system has once again been postponed rather than resolved. For that reason, the Twentieth Century Fund decided that what was needed was a searching examination of how the system has evolved, an examination of its economic and social development and the ways in which it has managed to transform itself from a controversial political idea into a permanent – and still growing – institution with widespread support.

The Fund has had a long and continuing interest in the problems of security for retired Americans. Its first study in the area, *The Townsend Crusade,* looked at the movement that dramatized the plight of the aged during the Depression. It was followed by *More Security for Old Age,* a 1937 book that commended the "immense social advance marked by the passage of the Social Security Act," and evaluated various plans for carrying it out. Then, in the mid-1950s, the Fund, "in the face of still unresolved economic problems of aging and retirement," embarked on another investigation that reexamined the system and its problems. Our own history suggests that the quest for a permanent solution is elusive. But it also suggests that there is something to be learned from each new study.

Certainly that is the case with our latest effort, this book by W. Andrew Achenbaum. He brings the special skills of a historian to bear in his analytical account of how and why the system has developed in the ways that it has. In doing so, he has squarely faced the major difficulty in achieving effective and permanent reform, which is just accepting the fact that the system has become a form of welfare rather than a means of insurance. As such, it has attained the status of a political sacred cow.

We think Achenbaum's intriguing historical treatment is a major contribution to understanding the system, which after all is essential to its reform. His recommendations for change are also worthy of consideration. We at the Fund are grateful to him for his thoughtful and thorough study of the system in the context of the sweeping changes that have taken place in the past half century. We think the public, politicians, and policymakers should be too.

M. J. Rossant, Director
The Twentieth Century Fund
November 1985

Acknowledgments

I owe an enormous debt of gratitude to the Twentieth Century Fund, especially for the opportunity to collaborate with three historians in the writing of this book. James A. Smith, my program officer, nurtured the project from beginning to end. With his steady encouragement, I gained a deeper appreciation for the powers of historical analysis and narrative in addressing contemporary social issues. William L. Bischoff showed me how a supportive but tough-minded editor can enable a writer to find his voice. Edward D. Berkowitz shared archival gems and offered good advice while doing his own research. I also wish to thank M. J. Rossant for keeping faith; Wendy Mercer for keeping me fiscally sound; and Marcia Bystryn, Ron Chernow, Nettie Gerduk, and Beverly Goldberg for their help. Frank Smith and Russell Hahn at Cambridge University Press greatly expedited the actual publication of this Twentieth Century Fund Study.

I also received considerable support from people at other institutions. A National Endowment for the Humanities fellowship underwrote a year of research. Administrators, professors, librarians, and students at Carnegie-Mellon University provided resources whenever I asked for them. Pamela Holcomb, Brian Wells Martin, Michael Santos, and Forrest Jewell were tireless research assistants. I particularly benefited from criticism and suggestions made by receptive audiences at the University of Michigan and the Chautauqua Institution, by participants in Yale University's social security seminar, and by those mentioned in the endnotes to Chapter 4. I am grateful to Alan Pifer and Lydia Bronté of the Carnegie Corporation of New York for inviting me to serve on the advisory council of their Aging Society Project; I gained far more than I contributed to the success of that important venture.

Friends assisted in important ways. Peter N. Stearns, Lenore Epstein Bixby, and Robert J. Myers at different times read drafts of the work in progress; they caught many factual errors and tried to spare me from intellectual blunders. Louisa Cunningham, William Kelly, Jan Lewis,

Daniel A. Nichols, and Tom Ramsay offered me hospitality and food for thought on my research sojourns. As always, members of my family helped me to keep the truly important dimensions of social policy uppermost in mind.

Introduction

Social security – the nation's largest, costliest, and most successful domestic program – has reached a critical juncture in its development. As its creators anticipated, nearly every wage earner now pays taxes into the system. In principle, all citizens may be eligible for "entitlements" at some point in their lives. Yet social security no longer enjoys solid popular support. Senior citizens worry that their benefits will be cut; younger Americans are skeptical – if not cynical – about their own benefits upon retirement. Social insurance, once viewed as an institution whose importance transcended politics, is now at the center of partisan debate in the United States.*

Social security's basic orientation has not changed much over time. It continues to alleviate the financial miseries that threaten everyone in a modern society – from family tragedies that might reduce a wage earner's income to the economic uncertainties that accompany old age. Despite the program's continuity of purpose, "rights" to social security are not contractual; benefits are subject to alteration in light of changing economic conditions, legislative priorities, and judicial wisdom. From the perspective of seasoned experts, this is how the system *should* operate.

---

*Most Americans think that social security outlays cover only retirement pensions for the elderly, but technically, social security (OASDHI) maintains four separate trust funds – one for old-age and survivors benefits (OASI); one for disability insurance (DI); and two for Medicare entitlements, hospital insurance (HI), and supplementary medical insurance (SMI). Aid to Families with Dependent Children (AFDC), along with Medicaid and Supplemental Security Income (SSI), evolved as part of social security's framework, even though they are financed through general revenues. Similarly, some authors use "social security" and "social insurance" interchangeably. There are good historical reasons for this convention: Social security was enacted to complement self-help, private philanthropy, corporate benevolence, and other nonfederal sources of aid to the unfortunate. My use of the terms is somewhat different: Social security is indeed the cornerstone of American social insurance, but "social insurance" in the full sense here embraces public and private institutionalized responses to the risks of everyday life, which are financed by employee and/or employer contributions as well as by taxes. As will become evident, such precision in terminology is indispensable if we are to grasp the complexity and confusion that surround social security.

From the beginning, social security was intended to harmonize individual ambitions with civic responsibilities. It was born of the Great Depression, a crisis that proved once and for all that socio-economic forces beyond individual control could result in mass unemployment, hunger, and familial disruption even in America. Pressed to alleviate such problems as quickly as possible, Franklin Delano Roosevelt and his advisors started with a vision of social insurance that compensated for many lacunae in the way society protected itself against risks. They pieced together a strategy that built on familiar institutions to make nascent welfare-state policies palatable to Americans. Politicians endorsed this program as the embodiment of "Progressive" ideals. It was a pragmatic, if limited, solution to contemporary ills.

Today Americans tend to think of social security primarily as a program for the elderly. But the men and women who laid its foundations perceived the problem of old-age dependency in the context of the family and the passage of generations. By addressing the problems of the oldest members of society first, policymakers hoped to relieve hardship among the young and the middle-aged as well.* In addition to the indirect relief these groups would derive from socially guaranteed aid for the elderly, they themselves would benefit directly; they, too, would have pensions upon retirement. Meanwhile, they could count on other social services provided by the 1935 law, including aid to dependent children, expanded state-level unemployment compensation programs, assistance to the blind, and augmented public health services. As the system gained acceptance and was adapted to meet changing needs, expanding a "safety net" from cradle to grave became a distinct possibility.

But neither time nor funds were available to pursue such an ambitious agenda in the 1930s, nor was there commitment or a clear-cut strategy for doing so. Social security had to address immediate woes and hazards. It did not try to solve the underlying causes of unemployment or pauperism. The 1935 act straddled the fence between "welfare" – whose guiding criterion was the *ade-*

---

*Throughout this book, various subgroups among those involved with social security are designated as follows: "Policymakers" includes anyone who develops, administers, or evaluates social security measures. "Lawmakers" refers to elected officials to the executive or legislative branch of government. "Officials" typically hold elected or appointive federal-level positions. "Bureaucrats" refers to men and women with high-level responsibilities in directing programs. "Experts" are presumed to know how the system operates, unless the context in which the word is used suggests otherwise; they may be legislators, bureaucrats, or outsiders to government who enjoy a reputation for expertise.

quacy of assistance – and the traditional American preference for self-reliance, as found in private insurance plans emphasizing the *equity* acquired through financial contributions during employment.

This tentativeness concerning long-term goals was deliberate, and the policymakers' caution was prudent. Social security's architects gave themselves room to maneuver and time to sort out priorities. The program's early advocates were far from clear – in public or in private – whether or not the new legislation was to serve redistributive goals. Nor did they know precisely how the program should strike a balance between personal rights and collective responsibilities in order to reduce the risks of old-age poverty and dependency.

Thus, it is not surprising that the 1939 social security amendments constituted a major "re-vision" of the original "vision" – official assurances to the contrary notwithstanding. Even before the first old-age pension had been disbursed, the political and economic climate had changed dramatically. Without being fully explicit about what they were doing, officials shifted the balance between "equity" and "adequacy," seeking to protect a still larger segment of the population. This action did not please everybody, but it satisfied friendly critics and reduced trust reserves – a major item on the political agenda. In the process, lawmakers doubled the amount of American insurance by enacting seemingly minor changes that did not raise taxes. Artful rhetoric and technical adjustments soon led to a bolder vision of social insurance.

Amid postwar prosperity, social security grew in ways that some experts had anticipated long before, but important developments unfolded in a way no one could have predicted. Some growth, of course, resulted from the mere passage of time as the system itself matured. Other changes showed how effective "the politics of incrementalism" could be. It proceeded in a step-by-step manner and built support for the program by forging heterogeneous coalitions. When times were good, the economy booming, and public confidence in government high, people expressed little concern about the limits to social security's development. As long as the number of new and current contributors far exceeded the number of beneficiaries, legislators could liberalize existing provisions, expand coverage, and increase benefits – and still point to huge surpluses in the trust funds. It was considered self-evident that the sense of mutual responsibility could and should be enhanced by federal initiatives. Because few hard choices had to be made, there seemed to be no need to enunciate a straightforward, potentially divisive rationale for legislative priorities. Many consequences of social security policymaking were thus ironic, unintended, and unspoken.

In 1972, amendments were passed that finally completed virtually all of the original act's vision. Postwar priorities had been accommodated as well. Social security loyalists discovered after World War II that serving the interests of "Middle America" might create the means to wipe out poverty in a land of reputed affluence. Payments and services to those who would never earn enough to be self-sufficient established a nationwide "floor" for widows, the disabled, the blind, and the very old. Few bothered to learn how the system functioned – that never really seemed to matter, because it apparently abided by quintessential American values.

Social security has become a central feature of American life; more than 36 million people are eligible for old-age, survivors, and disability (OASDI) pensions as of 1985. More than a quarter of all households receive monthly Old-Age and Survivors Insurance (OASI) benefits. It is the most important source of income for people over the age of sixty-five, accounting on average for $42 of every $100 they receive. In addition, 9 percent of all households receive Medicaid benefits; 5 percent get Aid to Families with Dependent Children (AFDC) or other cash assistance. These figures do not include the millions of Americans who benefit from the "black-lung" program, food stamps, the low-income home energy assistance program, veterans' programs, or federal civil service and railroad retirement pensions – "entitlements" partly financed and operated by social security with other federal agencies.[1] Through 1,300 local offices, ten regional headquarters, and central offices in Baltimore and Washington, the Social Security Administration (SSA) issues more than 432 million checks each year and determines eligibility and benefits. By recording earnings from W-2 forms and posting those earnings for subsequent use, SSA handles another 380 million transactions. Less than 2 percent of its operating budget covers overhead costs; administrators make mistakes only 1 percent of the time. This is a remarkable achievement for any bureaucracy.[2]

Despite its past successes and present significance, however, a crisis mentality has plagued social security since the 1970s. The postwar economic boom made for enhanced expectations. But euphoria was misleading; bust invariably follows boom. The optimistic, expansionist philosophy that inspired social security planning since World War II has now changed to one of guarded hope. Ironically, troubles began when the system enjoyed its greatest support and appeared to be in good financial health. Politicians continually reaffirm their commitment to its ideals, but they do worry about OASDHI's fiscal problems and seemingly "uncontrollable" long-term costs. As social security comes of age in an uncertain climate, people are disturbed by media reports, econometric projections, and technical disputes they do not fully understand – but can ill afford to discount.

When fear of a shortfall in trust funds or some other problem arises, the palliative almost always involves a presidential or other bipartisan, high-level panel of experts. Some technocratic tinkering here, some actuarial juggling there, and the system is once more pronounced "sound." This strategy, so successful in the past, no longer is efficacious. Since 1972, there have been no more easy votes on social security. Leaders pronounced the system secure, but rampant inflation and loss of confidence among voters forced them to eat their words. Gerald Ford sensed that something had to be done, but he and his advisors were unable to disentangle short-term financing problems from long-term issues. Jimmy Carter was no more successful, largely because of the advent of "stagflation." Key members of Reagan's administration could not decide whether social security was a "sacred cow" or a "golden calf." The problem worsened.

The crisis mentality of the last decade makes it difficult to persuade a skeptical electorate and conservative critics that technical modifications in and of themselves are plausible substitutes for confronting the deeper policy issues brushed aside or finessed since social security's formative years. Short-term "solutions" enacted between 1977 and 1982, after all, proved highly ephemeral. Mounting frustration, associated with ineffectual ad hoc recalibrations, has demonstrated the importance of a broader focus on the hidden dimensions of America's social insurance program. Far from reversing the historical tide of recent years, the public philosophy underlying Reaganomics gives credence to the proposition that "affluence strains resources for enlightened compassion."[3]

To avert a "legitimation crisis" (in Jürgen Habermas's phrase), Congress and the president in 1983 endorsed a compromise package crafted by the National Commission on Social Security Reform (NCSSR). Changes long contemplated but politically unpalatable – mandatory coverage of new federal employees and workers in nonprofit organizations, a phased increase in the "normal" retirement age, and taxation of social security benefits paid to the wealthiest recipients – all those and more became law under the 1983 social security amendments. The changes were not enthusiastically adopted (one-fifth of the House and a quarter of the Senate did not vote on the final bill at all), and the reforms did not tackle some of the thorniest issues at stake. But they should provide a tactical margin of error *if* the economy performs at least as well as the underlying actuarial forecasts anticipate. This landmark legislation may well offer the last chance for a long-overdue reassessment of social security as a whole.

In tone and format, the 1983 amendments to the Social Security Act fit the pattern of incremental reform that has characterized social security policymaking for fifty years. The National Commission on Social Security Reform declared that "Congress, in its deliberations on financing proposals, should not alter the fundamental structure of the Social Security program or undermine its fundamental principles."[4] Raising the retirement age, taxing benefits for the wealthy, and delaying cost-of-living adjustments were all justified as ways to reaffirm social security's "traditional" functions. That the NCSSR package became law when many Reagan supporters were urging the division of OASDHI into strict annuity programs and welfare provisions underscores the depth of support for maintaining social security in its present form as far as practicable.

The 1983 amendments temporarily diffused the air of crisis besetting social security. OASDI trust funds are reportedly solvent for the next half century. Actuaries do not expect a shortfall in the HI trust funds for at least a decade. But key decisions on related matters of social policy remain to be made. Now is the time to ensure that the future costs of the baby-boom generation's retirement bill do not exceed revenues. Recurring charges that Federal Insurance Contributions Act (FICA) taxes are regressive and foster unemployment and inflation demand macroeconomic models adequate to explain the relationship between OASDHI and other facets of the economy. Nonetheless, social insurance's problems are not just actuarial or fiscal in nature. Economic concerns are assuredly relevant, but they do not constitute the crux of the matter.

The words of Thomas Jefferson, invoked by Senator Jennings Randolph (D–W.Va.) during the debate over the 1983 provisions, are illuminating: "As new discoveries are made, new truths disclosed, and manners and opinions change with the change of circumstances, institutions must advance also, and keep pace with the times."[5] Jefferson lived to see a younger generation reform and re-form institutions that he and the republic's other founding fathers had designed as the basis for "a new order of the ages." Today's situation is analogous. Because so many people have a stake in social security, it is politically tempting to treat the program (in Jefferson's exquisite phrase) as a "covenant, too sacred to be touched." Yet even those who share my view that the structure envisioned by the first generation of social security's policymakers should remain its cornerstone must acknowledge that major revisions are inevitable. Times change. Technical adjustments and implicit compromises that worked in OASDHI's formative years may not make sense under different circumstances.

Thus, if reforms are to succeed, they must bring a sophisticated historical sense to bear on the needs of the future. Social security has endured largely because of its resilience to short-term changes in the political economy. Issues raised in the Great Depression remain salient today even though the times bear little resemblance. Yet OASDHI's architects typically preferred not to engage in philosophical disputations concerning the meanings and functions of social insurance. They rarely have acknowledged all of the factors and constraints that influenced their tactical decisions, or admitted in retrospect that they wished that they had done things differently. To sustain and improve on the achievements of the program's first fifty years, a rising generation of policymakers perforce will need to probe beneath the "official" record and facts often taken for granted. Political leaders must reconsider how far to go in protecting Americans against the risks of contemporary life, in addition to reasserting what individual rights and mutual responsibility under social security should mean today.

The 1983 compromise affords an opportunity to move beyond mobilizing for the next crisis, and to take stock of the big picture. But few are ready to discuss social insurance in its totality. Reducing an unprecedented federal deficit (itself engendered by Reaganomics) provides an excuse to nibble away at social security: "Neoconservatives" like Peter Peterson, Martin Feldstein, and Michael Boskin advocate draconian measures to reduce OASDHI's scope, expecting the private sector to make up the difference. Social security's aging loyalists hardly underestimate the strength of critics on the right, but they have no desire to change things in any substantive way. "Neoliberals" have been distressingly silent about social security's future. Giddy about high-tech innovations, and banking on a new period of affluence, they seem to think that social security's continued existence is assured. But neither Gary Hart's *New Democracy* nor Paul Tsongas's *Road from Here* nor Robert Reich's *Next American Frontier* addresses social security's role in a world in which federal policy may be greatly restricted.[6]

The thesis of this book is that a fundamental reevaluation of social security is in order before time runs out, that previously expedient methods of piecemeal adjustments that rest on unspoken assumptions and highly technical recalibrations reached the limit of their usefulness with enactment of the 1983 amendments, and that social security's current problems can be fully understood only by recovering the real story of its origins and development, discarding the myths and misconceptions harbored by the public and policymakers alike. Confrontation with historical truth can free both from outdated assumptions and unexamined shibboleths. *Social Security: Visions and Revisions* aims to inform public policy debate and the lawmaking process with insights critical to re-forming social security for the challenges ahead.

Part I sketches the evolution of American social security. It is hoped that a clearer understanding of why the political process has failed to adopt a coherent approach to social insurance and social welfare throughout the last half century will foster honest talk and constructive change. Part II examines four aspects of social security urgently in need of revision: wasteful and counterproductive social and legislative arrangements regarding retirement, the consequences for women of putatively "gender-irrelevant" policies, the relationship between public and private insurance programs, and the problems generated by incorporating health care programs in an income-maintenance system dependent on intergenerational transfers. The final chapter sets forth specific policy recommendations based on the preceding historical, socioeconomic, and political analyses; it demonstrates how the proposed solutions are related to one another and how, taken as an aggregate, they might redefine and strengthen the enduring role of social security.

The only way to keep faith with the original vision of social security is to lift the veil that its creators themselves felt it necessary to spin in order to sustain the program for five decades. If social security is to remain at the heart of American society – to remain what Senator Bill Bradley (D–N.J.) calls the "best expression of community that we have in this country today"[7] –then its commitment to mutual responsibility must be perceived as no less important in our tradition than the ideal of self-reliance.

In making my policy proposals, I am under no illusion that they will be readily and overwhelmingly adopted. I do not pretend to have House and Senate majorities in my pocket, much less the nod of the president. The reader will find no misleadingly precise cost : benefit ratios in the concluding chapter, nor even short- and long-term cost projections for the reforms I advocate. Hegel's observation that Americans think of themselves as taxpayers first and as citizens last is perhaps truer today than ever. Enlightened self-interest, if nothing else, should give them pause, however. As this book will show, continuing along the same path of pragmatic incrementalism followed by social security during its first fifty years will lead policymakers into a cul-de-sac. But the contemporary fad for cutting back on all welfare programs will no longer yield substantial savings without serious loss to the nation's present and future well-being.

The "brutal truth" about social security's evolution and prospects shows that in fact Americans have been better than their Hegelian reputation – that in fact there is a strong Burkean component to the American ethos, one that affirms the vitality of a contract between the generations and regards the state as much more than a "partnership . . . in some . . . low concern" for individual enrichment.

Social security has served the nation well. As a vital symbol of the compact between present generations and those yet to come, it deserves the utmost intellectual and political effort to preserve it from obsolescence or even extinction. It is for this reason that I have ventured into the hotly contested debate over social security, past and present. I suggest major changes, but no reader will find me indifferent when it comes to the survival of social security itself. Quite simply, nothing can take its place.

PART I

Social security comes of age

1

Social security: the early years

It took the Great Depression to launch social security in the United States. Every major European country had already embraced the logic of social insurance.[1] But the rationale for a public income security program did not take root here until the Progressive period, when social insurance was promoted as a way to prevent and combat "the three fears" that plagued workers – unemployment, poverty in old age, and ill health.[2] Social insurance proponents also sought to promote "social efficiency" – to advance the well-being of some of the nation's more vulnerable citizens without infringing on middle-class ideals of self-reliance and prudence.[3]

Compulsory social insurance gained support among American Progressives, but it also met stiff opposition. Business associations worked tirelessly against old-age assistance and public retirement benefits, denouncing proposals for federal social insurance as "alien" to the American way of life.[4] Union leaders advanced their own reasons for opposing social insurance. Grassroots labor organizations lobbied for old-age relief at the state level, but Samuel Gompers argued that a federal program would threaten the viability of trade-union pensions and divert attention from the need to increase wages and improve working conditions.

The Depression, however, made it clear that economic misfortune was not always the consequence of individual irresponsibility or failure of character. The notion that economic insecurity was a *social* risk predates the 1930s. But there was insufficient popular and elite pressure for protection against the hazards of unemployment and old-age dependency until Franklin Roosevelt decided to act. Common sense – not an elaborate new theory about the role of the state – was the catalyst. America's leaders were convinced that the human and economic costs of doing nothing would rapidly mount, and would have to be paid for later.[5]

It was one thing to call for governmental action, but quite another to enact legislation mutually acceptable to business leaders, radicals, the aged, fiscal conservatives, states-rights advocates, union officials, constitutional experts, and a confused, anxious middle class. Social security legislation required an amalgam of familiar and innovative responses to a multifaceted problem. Was it Washington's responsibility to prevent as well as relieve destitution? Should there be a single federal system to provide cradle-to-grave coverage? Or should government's approach be more selective? How could current operating costs and long-term financial commitments be kept in bounds?

The program adopted was designed to defuse a political threat as quickly and sensibly as possible. But in the crisis of the Great Depression, federal policymakers created only the illusion of a coherent program. Four years after the Social Security Act was passed, its assumptions were dramatically changed to favor what some feared was a more "radical" approach.★ Even then, by leaving the direction of much social insurance to private industry and state officials, Roosevelt endorsed traditional American means to cope with the pressing need. His advisors and supporters in Congress increasingly used terms that obfuscated issues they neither fully understood nor could have anticipated. The decisions – as well as the nondecisions and confusions – that emerged during the Depression continue to influence the perception of social security in America profoundly.

The Depression makes action inescapable

Prior to the 1930s, working as long as possible and then relying on individual savings was the preferred way to financial independence in later years. Although the elderly's labor-force participation rate had been declining since the latter part of the nineteenth century, the 1930 census reported that 58.4 percent of all men and 8.1 percent of all women over sixty-five were gainfully employed.[6] Few older persons had acquired significant savings or property, but as late as 1936, 15 percent of the noninstitutionalized elderly relied on their assets to make ends meet; savings represented their largest single source of income.[7]

Yet old-age dependency had always been a problem in the United States. Americans dealt with it in time-tested ways. As in Europe, the family was the primary source of support. Ever since the colo-

★ More detail on the changes made in 1939 will be found in Chapter 4.

nial period, local communities had provided food and shelter for the old when there were no kin available or when family members defaulted on their responsibilities.[8] More recent times witnessed a growing number of alternatives to the almshouse. Private old-age homes and charitable relief programs supported about 5 percent of the population over sixty-five. Many elderly people qualified for veterans' benefits: The ever-expanding federal military pension program served as an indirect public means of relieving old-age dependency.[9] There were other ways to provide against disability and the vicissitudes of old age. In 1910, roughly a third of the labor force was insured against accidents and sickness: Private institutions – commercial companies, trade unions, and especially fraternal orders – underwrote most of the coverage.[10] After World War I, proponents of American "welfare capitalism" increasingly offered disability plans and life insurance discounts. Record amounts of disability insurance were sold during the 1920s. Older workers faced with imminent unemployment typically filed disability claims.[11]

Retirement pensions were available to a limited percentage of America's labor force, with the public sector as pacesetter. At the turn of the century, nearly every major American city provided pensions for firemen and police officers; by 1916, thirty-three states had enacted retirement provisions for elementary- and secondary-level teachers.[12] During the latter half of the nineteenth century, the federal government instituted "superannuation" policies for soldiers, sailors, naval revenue officials, and selected agents working in Alaska and in Indian territories. A federal Civil Service Retirement System was established in 1920.[13]

The development of private pension plans was initially quite slow. Less than 4 percent of the labor force was eligible for existing programs as late as 1915.[14] Changes in the federal tax code during the 1920s, however, induced large enterprises – mainly public utilities, railroads, iron and steel concerns, and firms manufacturing heavy machinery – to create pension funds for their employees.[15] As a result, the proportion of the labor force eligible for benefits rose to 15 percent by 1930. Few such plans required employees to contribute. The typical industrial plan permitted a worker to retire at sixty, sixty-two, sixty-five, or seventy, after completing twenty to thirty years of service. Pensions, generally graduated according to a worker's prior earnings, seldom provided for spouses and dependents.

Once old-age dependency was perceived as a "social problem," more and more state legislatures put helpless senior citizens on relief. By 1933, twenty-one states and Alaska and Hawaii operated such programs; seven other jurisdictions made coverage optional at the county level.[16] None of this was enough; the Depression proved that all existing methods of preventing and reducing old-age dependency were grossly inadequate.

The nation had endured severe economic downturns before. But this time the extent, intensity, and duration of the upheaval were unprecedented. Between October 1929 and June 1932, the common-stock price index dropped from 260 to 90. The nation's real GNP, which had risen 22 percent between 1923 and 1929, fell 30.4 percent over the next four years. Nearly 5,000 banks, with deposits exceeding $3.2 billion, became insolvent; 90,000 businesses failed. Aggregate wages and salaries in 1933 totaled only 57.5 percent of their 1929 value. The gross income realized by farmers was cut nearly in half; the farm-product index took a dive from 105 to 51 between 1928 and 1932. More than a thousand local governments defaulted on their bonds; the rest managed to stay afloat only by firing staff and slashing social services.[17]

Insecurity pervaded the land. The Depression called into question perennial notions of self-reliance. A sizable proportion of middle-class Americans discovered that they were less self-sufficient than they had presumed. Unemployment rose from 3 percent to 25 percent – the highest it has ever been. More than a million adults took to the road. Eighteen million sought public relief in order to subsist.[18] Breadlines formed; shanties were erected on vacant lots. "The sense of the big- and out-of-handedness of our contemporary world is neither illusion nor merely another expression of this recurrent restlessness of man in civilization," sociologist Robert S. Lynd observed. "We feel ultimately coerced by larger forces not controllable within our immediate area of personal concentration."[19]

Because misery was not just the lot of the shiftless and improvident, but a threat to everyone, the public became more responsive to the problems of those growing older. The Depression, declared economist (later Senator) Paul H. Douglas in 1936, "increasingly convinced the majority of the American people that individuals could not themselves provide adequately for their old age and that some sort of greater security should be provided by society."[20] The Depression deprived millions of older workers of jobs; it seemed unlikely that they would ever reenter the labor force.[21]

Hard times rent asunder the elderly's "safety net." Bankrupt firms obviously could not honor their pension obligations to superannuated workers: Forty-five plans covering 100,000 employees were discontinued between 1929 and 1932 alone. Indeed, only 10 percent of the programs established before the economic downturn legally obligated employers to honor their promises to employees. Thus, many companies simply decided not to pay retirement benefits; instead, they tapped those pension funds to meet other financial obligations. Managers lacking adequate reserve funds announced that they would curtail benefits until the economy recovered. Trade-union pensions fared no better.[22]

More traditional means of support also proved insufficient. Savings were lost when banks collapsed.[23] Intergenerational tensions mounted: Relatives and friends often found it impossible to care for the aged while providing for their more immediate families. Private charities were overwhelmed by the increased demand for assistance. Local relief agencies imposed stringent eligibility criteria, but even then could not help all who qualified.[24] State legislatures, faced with imminent bankruptcy, had reached the limit of what they could do.

Desperate, the elderly wrote to Washington pleading for aid. "Dear Mrs. Roosevelt," a woman from Petersburg, North Dakota, began, "It's hard to be old and not have anything." A Georgian senior citizen appealed directly to the president:

> I am a old Citizen of West Point and I am about 75 or 6 years old and Have Labored Hard all My Days until depression Came on and I Had No Job in three years and I have a Little Home I Bought when times were good and I managed to Pay my state and County tax But they claim I owe about 15 fifteen dol City tax and going to sell my Little Home for that and will you Please sir Help me out the government Can Have a Lean on the Little House until I Get some way to Pay Back Please Sir do what you Can for me I am to old to be turned out of doors.[25]

Some older applicants stressed that they could not feed, clothe, and shelter their jobless adult children. Middle-aged citizens sometimes wrote on behalf of their parents and the older generation: "Well whither my mother ever gets anything or not, I hope all the other old people that is intilted to it gets it soon, because there is nothing sadder than old people who have struggled hard all there lives to give there family a start in life, then to be forgotten, when they them self need it most."[26]

In this context, millions of Americans seized on utopian schemes promising the aged far greater assistance than was available from the states or private charity. Upton Sinclair ran for governor on a pledge to grant $50 pensions to all who had resided in California for at least three years. Senator Huey P. Long's "Share Our Wealth" Society wanted to give $30 per month to every American over sixty with an annual income of less than $1,000 and property valued at not more than $10,000; Long's program would be financed by federal taxes on income, on inheritance, and on property exchanges. Dr. Francis E. Townsend rallied support for his proposal that all persons over sixty be given $200 monthly on the condition that they not be gainfully employed and that they spend their pensions within thirty days; this program was to be financed from the proceeds of a new nationwide tax on transactions.[27] Critics quickly noted serious economic flaws in these radical ideas, but they attracted national attention and gained support in Congress. If these panaceas were not to be enacted, then something else had to be done.

For example, there was new and renewed interest in social insurance. Abraham Epstein's American Association for Old Age Security (founded in 1927) changed its name to the American Association for Social Security in 1933, thus broadening its efforts to protect citizens of all ages.[28] In 1932, the American Federation of Labor reversed its previous stand, endorsed state-funded unemployment insurance, and called for federal old-age relief and insurance. Many business officials also became more supportive of the drive for social security.[29]

During Herbert Hoover's presidency and the initial two years of Roosevelt's first term, Congress considered several prototypes of social security legislation. Roosevelt signed the Railroad Retirement Act in 1934.[30] Some in Washington hoped that a broader program of contributory old-age annuities could be enacted in its wake. But the administration chose neither to initiate nor to support any social insurance measure before the seventy-third Congress. Only after other foundations for a "New Deal" had been laid did the president decide to move ahead in this area.

The birth of social security

On June 8, 1934, Franklin Delano Roosevelt admonished Congress that

If, as our Constitution tells us, our Federal Government was established among other things, "to promote the general welfare," it is our plain duty to provide for that security upon which welfare depends. . . . Hence I am looking for a sound means which I can recommend to provide at once security against several of the great disturbing factors in life – especially those which relate to unemployment and old age. I believe that there should be a maximum of cooperation between States and the Federal Government . . . These three objectives – the security of the home, the security of livelihood, and the security of social insurance – are, it seems to me, a minimum of the promise that we can offer to the American people. They constitute a right which belongs to every individual and every family willing to work. They are the essential fulfillment of measures already taken toward relief, recovery, and reconstruction.[31]

FDR's declaration signaled Washington's first sustained effort to alleviate the hazards associated with a modern economy. If using the power of the federal government to enact an economic security measure bolstered the New Deal's "three R's" – recovery, relief, and reform – so much the better.[32]

But because this *was* relatively uncharted territory, the president emphasized that such intervention merely reinforced long-standing American commitments to self-reliance and mutual responsibility. FDR acted because of the immediate crisis and his commitment to Progressive principles. But he did not intend to displace American self-reliance and capitalist principles with a federal Leviathan. All of the president's decisions, and those of executive and legislative experts supporting him, were shaped by this fundamental ambivalence. There was no clear-cut strategy behind the policymaking process; lawmakers were learning what they could and could not do as they went. Policymakers moved to control disturbing economic factors only in ways consonant with traditional values and administrative methods. Hence, the original social security bill sought to improve existing systems, taking new initiatives only when absolutely necessary. As a result, even seemingly daring innovations had avowedly conservative overtones.[33]

The president's cabinet-level Committee on Economic Security (CES) heard vigorous debate among experts over what should be included in the legislation to be drafted. Today one tends to think of social security as an institution to assist the elderly. In 1934, however, dealing with the long-term costs of retirement was not the top priority. Early in the drafting process, in fact, the president and Congress seemed likely to table consideration of old-age insurance. Edwin E. Witte, CES's staff director, was primarily interested in designing a program of unemployment compensation; his efforts attracted the most attention and generated the most controversy. J. Douglas Brown, a Princeton economist, and Barbara Nachtreib Armstrong, a Berkeley law professor who had studied European social insurance schemes, were assigned to develop ideas on old-age security, but they and their small staff worked on the sidelines. Indeed, in a speech prepared by Witte and delivered by FDR before the National Conference on Economic Security, the president noted that "I do not know whether this is the time for any federal legislation on old age security."[34] Media reaction to this remark was swift – and sharply critical. He and his advisors thereafter made old-age security a matter of higher priority.

It is thus ironic that when Roosevelt submitted his legislative proposals to Congress on January 17, 1935, the problem of old-age dependency was given top billing. For strategic reasons, the old-age assistance proposal – the item certain to gain strongest support in both the Senate and the House – was listed as Title I. The Committee on Economic Security proposed a three-step approach to the problem of old-age dependency: Besides partly underwriting old-age relief, the government would establish a compulsory old-age insurance system for every manual and non-manual worker (with certain exceptions) who earned less than $250 per month and would administer a program of voluntary annuities so that Americans could build nest eggs for their later years. On the day before he was supposed to submit his legislative proposal, Roosevelt learned that a large deficit would probably arise in the old-age insurance system after 1965. Alarmed by the size of the projected shortfall, FDR had the disturbing figures deleted from the official report. Thus, even at the beginning, the amount of money involved in social insurance was sufficiently large to cause political problems. Rather than deal candidly with the relationship between this new legislative measure and larger political, social, and economic concerns, the president found it expedient to hide the figures. FDR's successors have too often acted in a similar manner.

Congress modified the CES plan to make its programs politically more palatable and fiscally responsible. The proposal to offer government-administered voluntary annuities was dropped. Initial coverage and benefits under the old-age security schemes were changed. By mid-July, the differences in the various versions were ironed out, and a social security bill made its way through both houses of Congress.[35]

The speed with which the whole program was developed, debated, and approved was remarkable, to say the least. Some scholars have attributed this to such factors as "demand-side" (i.e., popular) pressures, the all-or-nothing way in which key aspects of the proposal were offered to Congress, the less than fair balance in the pro-and-con "expert testimony" provided to legislators, and the heavily pro-social-insurance composition of the CES itself. Insofar as the president was personally responsible for manipulating the process of formulating and then getting congressional approval for social security, one must admit that FDR's performance was adroit and formidable indeed. However, there are several facts that critics and supporters of the program alike have failed to remark on: Roosevelt was careful to exclude outspoken critics of the program from the CES (and, to a lesser extent, from testimony before House and Senate). And congenitally more comfortable as a fox than as a lion (to use James MacGregor Burns's metaphor), FDR also saw to it that the CES did not contain overzealous proponents of the social insurance idea itself. After all, men like Abraham Epstein and I. M. Rubinow had vociferously advocated social insurance long before Roosevelt became a figure of national political importance; presumably they would have been too much of a good thing. They were of European (Russian-Jewish) immigrant background, and their ideas about the nation's responsibility to care for all its downtrodden and disadvantaged – regardless of the contributions these people had made to the commonweal – did not seem to fit the American grain. Epstein and Rubinow were too wedded to their visions of social insurance – some said too obstinate, cantankerous, or zealous – to bend principles to practical politics. Eschewing the role of lion, then, Roosevelt and his advisors avoided a direct confrontation over the normative foundation of social security in America. This made for smoother political sailing. Exactly where the ship of state's domestic compass was pointed, however, was a matter of some obscurity. Doubts grew more pronounced as social security became an ever more integral part of American life.

The 1935 Social Security Act mounted a two-pronged attack on the problem of old-age dependency. "An effective old-age security program for this country involves not a choice between assistance and insurance but a combination of the two," the Committee on Economic Security declared. "Regular benefits are unquestionably to be preferred to assistance grants . . . Assistance, moreover, in fairness to the legitimate demands of other needy groups, must limit all grants to a minimum standard. Insurance benefits, on the other hand, can be ample for a comfortable existence, bearing some relation to customary wage standards."[36] Given the magnitude of the funds committed in this initiative, federal officials assumed ultimate responsibility for the program's direction. The demands and needs of many different interest groups and constituencies had to be considered in this legislation. It is instructive, therefore, to highlight some of the assumptions, compromises, and hopes embedded in Titles I and II.

Under Title I, Congress initially appropriated $49,750,000 "for the purpose of enabling each State to furnish financial assistance, as far as practicable under the conditions in such States, to aged needy individuals."[37] By establishing formal appeal procedures at the state and federal levels, Washington indicated that public relief in old age was no longer considered a gratuity. As long as an applicant could meet the age, residency, and needs requirements established by a state and approved by the federal board, that person had a right to the corresponding benefits.

Yet the wording of Title I precluded minimal national standards for old-age assistance. The bill drafted by the Committee on Economic Security had stipulated that states provide a "subsistence compatible with decency and health." During congressional hearings, however, corporate executives and the president of the U.S. Chamber of Commerce complained about the difficulties in defining and implementing "decency"; southern lawmakers denounced it as the harbinger of an infringement on states' rights.[38] As a result, this CES proposal was dropped; states were permitted to establish their own eligibility criteria and benefit levels. Furthermore, the ceiling of $15 per month on federal contributions to state programs meant that the elderly poor could expect only a meager level of support. And because almshouse residents were deliberately excluded from Title I benefits, the long-term health care needs of some elderly people were unlikely to be met.

Plans for old-age insurance (Title II) called for an Old-Age Reserve Account funded by a 1 percent tax on an employee's wage (up to $3,000) and the same amount from the employer.[39] Such taxes, the president believed, had a value that transcended economic considerations: "We put those payroll contributions there so as to give the contributors a legal, moral, and political right to collect their pensions and unemployment benefits. With those taxes in there, no damn politician can ever scrap my social security program."[40] Once the public had a stake in social security, it would naturally want to protect existing benefits and even press for more.

Title II nonetheless raised thorny questions about its immediate objectives and long-term goals. Policymakers expected that all workers would someday participate in the old-age insurance plan, but practical administrative and constitutional considerations persuaded them to limit coverage at first. Roughly 9.4 million workers (including farmers, domestic servants, and government employees) were excluded from the new program. The law did not require employers to make contributions for their own later years, and so it was not certain how many would be involved; economists estimated that 7 or 8 million workers were intermittently or simultaneously employers and employees. Furthermore, employees had to have worked at least a specified length of time in occupations subject to the social security payroll tax before they could lay claim to a monthly old-age pension.[41] Thus, not all workers could reduce the likelihood of old-age dependency through the new system. That most of the poorest workers – such as Southern blacks – were excluded from coverage suggests that policymakers were willing to make politically expedient compromises. As a result, the goal of "universal coverage" under social security was not to be attained until the program was more than fifty years old.

Not only did the architects of the 1935 act retreat on the question of coverage, they also tried to avoid charges of "welfarism" leveled against European-style social insurance. They made their system as "American" as possible, for they shared the belief that individuals should take primary responsibility for their own welfare. As far as possible, they preferred not to interfere with the free play of market forces. Hence, benefits were fairly well graduated according to a recipient's work history and earnings record: Those who contributed more got more back. But social security did not entirely adhere to the principle of "equity" found in private-sector insurance programs. Instead, the benefit formula favored those retiring with comparatively low "total covered wages."[42] An element of progressivity was thus characteristic of the benefit structure from the outset. A minimum Title II benefit of $10 per month was introduced, for example, but the figure was chosen for administrative convenience, not eleemosynary considerations. The legislative draftsmen thus showed a keen sense of the need to limit redistributionist aspirations (although, as the following chapters show, once a "minimum monthly benefit" was accepted as a permanent feature of the program, successive increases in its amount became virtually inevitable). Policymakers also rejected the idea of giving all older workers a fixed sum of money each month, although this strategy had an impressive pedigree.[43] More than cost considerations weighed against flat-rate retirement pensions. Benefits were related to a considerable extent to the contribution rates on total taxed wages in order to reassure all those covered that the concept of self-help was not being abandoned. Recognizing workers' differential statuses, achieved through lifelong effort, "would reinforce rather than counter the normal incentives in our economic system."[44]

Thus, it is as important to consider what the 1935 legislation did *not* attempt as what it did. Sometimes, maintaining a particular aspect of the status quo can buttress proposed innovations. To illustrate: Policymakers might have designed the old-age insurance program to regulate older people's employment behavior.[45] There was widespread support for the notion that older workers should make room for the young; it was often stated that employment opportunities for those past forty-five would improve if they did not have to compete with their elders for jobs.[46] The Committee on Economic Security and President Roosevelt considered including a mandatory retirement provision in the old-age insurance program, but did not propose it to Congress.[47] Under the 1935 provisions, aged employees who wanted to keep working could simply choose not to accept a social security check when they turned sixty-five. Regardless of their personal opinion about the worth of older workers, legislators wanted no Gadarene exodus of such employees from the marketplace. They enunciated no explicit *requirement* for those over sixty-five to retire, nor did they take the gentler (but much costlier) step of sweetening the inducement to retire by, in effect, *paying* older workers to leave their jobs in return for substantial pensions.

Thus far I have discussed Title I and Title II as if they were designed exclusively to benefit older persons in the Great Depression. Such a perspective is inadequate by itself, for it downplays the extent to which policymakers sought to transcend the immediate economic crisis and to provide a measure of security for all citizens. Through social insurance, Washington had committed itself to a vision of income transfers that would benefit every age group. The elderly would receive relief and future protection; the middle-aged would be free to devote more of their resources to their own children. By coordinating the old-age insurance program with a system of old-age assistance, the federal government adopted a plan that "amounts to having each generation pay for the support of the people then living who are old."[48] Titles I and II were thus inspired by a genuine (and imaginative) concern for addressing the vicissitudes of old age in the context of the family and the passage of generations.

Yet here, too, policymakers had made a choice with profound implications for the development of social security. Had they been fully committed to the idea of social insurance, they could have offered *transgenerational* protection, from birth to death; the claim that they were protecting individuals by reinforcing family values would then have had more substance. Instead, they established programs using "age" as a surrogate for categories to identify people vulnerable to various social risks. This age-specific strategy saved money and imposed what were considered to be necessary limits on social insurance initiatives. But these decisions later assumed a significance of their own. Among other things, adoption of an incremental, category-by-category approach to "social need" and "individual rights" forced defenders of social security to advance an ideological rationale that often masked and diverged from the objectives originally set forth in CES and congressional debate.

Still, several titles of the 1935 legislation did address the needs of citizens who were not "old." Under Titles III and IX, Congress appropriated $4 million the first year and guaranteed at least $49 million annually thereafter for a new unemployment compensation scheme that forged a partnership between the public and private sectors. Washington gave the states considerable latitude in determining benefits, which were largely paid for by taxes on employers. Nearly $25 million was earmarked for the states to provide "aid to dependent children" under Title IV; another $3 million was to be spent on relief to the blind (Title X).[49] And just as Title II addressed contemporary workers' future needs, so, too, the architects of social security took steps to promote the "general welfare" of generations to come. Under Title V, "Grants to States for Maternal and Child Welfare," Congress initially appropriated more than $9 million for crippled children, rural public health services, and vocational rehabilitation; another $10 million was given to the Public Health Service for training new personnel and investigating diseases.[50] These titles were intended to reduce future relief and health maintenance costs, thereby relieving some of the tax-payers' burden. Proponents argued that preventive measures to benefit selected groups of children would indirectly benefit the middle-aged.

To placate critics, federal officials emphasized the limitations of their legislation. On signing social security into law on August 14, 1935, President Roosevelt reminded the public that "We can never insure one hundred percent of the population against one hundred percent of the hazards and vicissitudes of life."[51] The president was not oblivious to the risks of timidity. He appreciated the dangers in basing decisions on tactical compromise. He did not want to discredit such "a sound idea – a sound ideal" by attempting to do too much too fast: "The place of such a fundamental in our future civilization is too precious to be jeopardized now by extravagant action."[52] He had no doubt that history would vindicate his program, but a thorough study of social insurance in foreign countries had demonstrated that actuarial and financial forecasts were often erroneous because so much depended on the state of the economy.[53] Social security did not try to get at the underlying causes of structural unemployment or old-age pauperism. It neither relieved individuals of primary responsibility for their own well-being nor diminished the importance of family duty. The law was hardly a get-rich-quick scheme; it certainly did not "soak the rich." Rather, it sought to give Americans a *floor* of protection. Actually, it was more a foundation than a floor; living exclusively on social security grants and benefits would not provide an acceptable standard of living. The Social Security Act, therefore, constituted a cautious and open-ended attempt to deal with major hazards of modern America. There would be plenty of room for bolder initiatives once the implications of what had already been done became clearer.

The vision revised

Although FDR and his advisors hoped for a step-by-step expansion in social insurance programs in the United States, it was not clear at first that this was going to happen. The Supreme Court was expected to test the constitutionality of the measure, and the outcome was uncertain. Conservative opposition by no means went away; it actually increased during the 1936 election campaign. Radicals denounced social security, and even friendly critics discovered flaws in it. The public seemed to support the idea of old-age pensions, but it obviously did not understand how the system worked. Thus, the Roosevelt administration responded to the recession of 1937 and mounting concern over social security's effect on the economy by revising the program in 1939. The arguments advanced and the steps taken reveal the uncertainty even its advocates harbored concerning the fledgling system.

One of the most important facts to remember about the early years of social security is that it got off to a slow start. Without a large staff, or even the money that had been appropriated to hire administrators, the Social Security Board's three members and their assistants had to establish procedures for a maze of new programs.[54] Meanwhile, in anticipation of federal aid, many states passed new laws or amended existing legislation in 1935 and 1936 to make their old-age assistance programs conform to the criteria set forth in Title I. New York, for instance, substituted "assistance" for each reference to "relief" in its law and lowered the eligibility requirement from age seventy to sixty-five.[55]

The enactment of social security led to more uniformity in the ways states administered assistance to their aged poor. Yet many inequities remained – and new ones emerged. As late as 1937, citizens in Arizona, Georgia, Kansas, North and South Carolina, Tennessee, and Virginia received no help from Washington because their state legislatures had not yet established relief programs. Elderly Americans who were equally poor were not treated equally – despite social security's attempt to induce all states to provide "adequate" support. The average Mississippian receiving old-age assistance was given $3.92 per month in 1936; the average "pension" in California (note the variation in terms to designate the same thing) was $31.36. Even taking into account differences in living costs and prevailing wages, such wide variance was disturbing. Finally, the wording of the 1935 legislation accelerated the decline of the almshouse and the rise of the nursing home. Some residents of the poor farm moved to proprietary "rest homes" because the federal law banned assistance to "an inmate of a public institution." Contrary to lawmakers' expectations, however, many states did not close their poorhouses, because most of the older residents "require institutional care and hence cannot be removed."[56] In their effort to provide immediate relief to the elderly poor, policymakers had largely overlooked that segment of the aged population needing long-term health care.

The fact that retirement benefits did not begin for several years had a significant impact on Title II. Workers participating in the new retirement program began paying taxes after December 31, 1936, but under the original legislation they could not draw Title II benefits until January 1, 1942, at the earliest. In posters, press releases, speeches, and newsreels prepared by social security officials, American workers were assured that the taxes they were paying were like insurance premiums. Having a social security card meant that one had opened "an insurance account" with the government. By making contributions to the new system, employees were "earning a right" to future benefits – not qualifying for a "dole." Benefits, in turn, would bear a relationship to the amount deducted from wages over the years.[57] In the interim, however, workers paid money to the government without knowing, for the most part, precisely what return they could expect in the future.[58]

As advocates of social security played on the murky distinction between insurance and welfare, they were less concerned about the confusion they were arousing between private insurance and social insurance than they were about the constitutional tests that the Social Security Act faced. At issue was the federal government's right to use its taxing and spending powers to underwrite a compulsory national "insurance" program. Opponents of Title II could not very well challenge Congress's right to impose a payroll tax, but they did claim that using that tax to finance old-age benefits violated states' rights as defined by the Tenth Amendment.[59] In 1935 and early 1936 the Supreme Court had invalidated seven major New Deal initiatives, suggesting that the justices might rule against the use of payroll taxes to finance retirement pensions. Legal counsel consequently advised the Social Security Board's informational services to play down terms such as "insurance" and to avoid coupling tax titles with benefits titles in official reports and publicity materials. Lest the Court take judicial notice of the way officials were trying to "sell" the program, administrators believed it was imperative to keep the language "sufficiently opaque."[60]

Well before the Court had rendered its decision, however, those who were disappointed with the initial legislation began to criticize it. And those most vehemently opposed to social security sought an opportunity to sabotage the program before it really got off the ground. Older people's movements pressed for broader programs. About eighty different old-age welfare schemes were presented to the public in California alone between 1936 and 1938.

With more than 3.4 million members and a million dollars in their war chest, Townsendites mobilized sufficient support in Congress and across the nation to make it seem possible that a Townsend plan might yet replace social security. Officials feared that if Title I's old-age assistance program was greatly expanded to mollify the public, Congress might be reluctant to broaden the contributory pension program.[61] On the other hand, conservative groups, such as the National Association of Manufacturers, attacked the payroll tax on employers; many small-town shopkeepers remained hostile to any type of old-age pension.[62]

The most dramatic assault on social security occurred during the 1936 presidential campaign. In a speech on September 26, Governor Alfred Landon, the Republican candidate, attempted to capitalize on American fear of the growing scope and power of the federal government by attacking the new social insurance program. Landon's assault was part of a larger strategy – implicit in that year's Republican campaign platform – to persuade the American electorate that such New Deal initiatives posed a threat to prevailing consumption patterns and jeopardized future capital formation. He hoped thereby to rally support for more familiar ways of handling economic problems.

Landon condemned the Social Security Act as "unjust, unworkable, stupidly drafted and wastefully financed . . . If the present compulsory insurance plan remains in force, our old people are only too apt to find the cupboard bare."[63] Landon later claimed to have based his attack on an unpublished report on old-age security sponsored by the Twentieth Century Fund, a report that emphasized the danger of accumulating large reserves to underwrite Title II. Yet whereas Landon denounced the insurance program as a "cruel hoax" and favored the expansion of old-age assistance under administration of the states, the Twentieth Century Fund study recommended *expanding* Title II, altering its financing provisions by refining the contributory principle, and ensuring that benefits under Title I were indeed adequate to care for aged dependents. "Suggestions that the act may be improved in certain directions," concluded the study, "involve no criticism of its fundamental purposes and principles."[64] Had Landon assumed a more temperate position (or had he used the Fund's report more judiciously), he might have forced Roosevelt's supporters to address his objections according to the merits of the case. Instead, the GOP standard-bearer delivered himself and his party up to partisan attack. Their defeat at the polls was a spectacular vindication of the New Deal.

With the election past, social security's future was becoming more secure. Liberals took comfort when the Supreme Court validated the program's most controversial features in May 1937.[65] Naturally, the Court did not rule on the wisdom of Title II, but it clearly certified its constitutionality. Furthermore, in the public mind, social security soon became an important way of dealing with the problems of old age. Already in December 1935 a Gallup poll found that 89 percent of those interviewed endorsed the idea of providing old-age assistance for "needy" senior citizens; six years later a remarkable 91 percent were "in favor of Government old-age pensions." Survey data indicated that the public supported a contributory retirement program. In 1937, some 73 percent of those asked approved of the current social security tax on their wages; 85 percent rejected the idea that employers should pay the whole cost of the program.[66]

Nevertheless, serious reservations were expressed about the size of the retirement program's reserve fund and Title II's narrow coverage, limited benefits, and complicated administrative procedures. In January 1937, Senator Arthur Vandenberg (R–Mich.) introduced a resolution calling on the Social Security Board to develop plans "to abandon the full reserve system," and to extend coverage to domestic workers and farmers. The senator also wanted the board to recommend whether, under a new financing arrangement, it was better to liberalize benefits or freeze contributory rates for ten years.[67] Even experts who had long supported social insurance had their qualms. Criticisms found in Eveline Burns's *Toward Social Security* and Paul Douglas's *Social Security in the United States,* both published in 1936, received wide coverage.[68] "The situation cries for a bold national policy," warned Abraham Epstein. "Unless the American old-age security system is made free from politics as those of other countries, everything we have gained for the aged in a generation may be destroyed."[69]

Had officials wanted to ignore such pointed advice, new political and economic developments prevented them from doing so. A sharp recession began in June, causing a decline in productivity and a rise in unemployment. During the following year, much of the previous four years' economic gain was erased. Many attributed the downturn in the economy to sudden cuts in government spending and the collection of $2 billion in social security taxes.[70] Its supporters could not allow critics to blame social security for the recession.

Meanwhile, the Social Security Board published figures showing that the economic plight of old people still constituted a major social problem and probably would do so for the indeterminate future. The board reported that 34.7 percent of all elderly men and women were able to maintain their financial independence through earnings, savings, annuities, and pensions; another 19.8 percent were currently recipients of public or private assistance. The status of the rest of the aged population (45.5 percent) was not known. This meant, in the board's view, that this group was *potentially* dependent on federal assistance or charity.[71] Public assistance was not enough, the board stressed, but Title II offered a "reasonable solution."

In September 1937, Arthur J. Altmeyer, chairman of the Social Security Board, urged President Roosevelt to convene "a detached advisory council of experts" to defuse mounting attacks on social security:

> While, of course, we should not be stampeded into taking unwise action, I think that it is most necessary to consider at this time the general character of the Administration's policy regarding amendment of the Social Security Act. As a matter of fact, I think it possible not only to offset these attacks on the Social Security Act, but really to utilize them to advance a socially desirable program, fully in accord with present fundamental principles underlying the Social Security Act and within our financial capacity.[72]

FDR agreed with Altmeyer's assessment; the Advisory Council on Social Security met for the first time on November 5.

On December 10, 1938, the Advisory Council issued its *Final Report,* which recommended sweeping changes in addressing "the basic needs of our people, now and in the future . . . through the existing old-age insurance program."[73] The council reported that 35 percent of all those collecting old-age assistance in 1938 received less than $15 per month; over 40 percent of all married persons accepting relief had spouses receiving separate grants. More than half the senior citizens of Oklahoma were receiving Title I benefits, but only 7.2 percent of their peers in New Hampshire could do so. The council considered the situation deplorable:

> It is highly desirable in preserving American institutions to remove from as many individuals as possible, in the years to come, the necessity for dependency relief and to substitute instead protection afforded as a matter of right, related to past participation in the productive processes of the country . . .
> It is only through the encouragement of individual incentive, through the principle of paying benefits in relation to past

wages and employment that a sound and lasting basis for security can be afforded.[74]

Experts reasoned that older people could be better protected against old-age dependency by expanding the umbrella of "social insurance." The nation as a whole would benefit from the intergenerational transfers involved. Heartily supported by the president and the Social Security Board, this report became the basis for critical amendments to the original act that altered the target population, the actuarial basis, and the philosophical underpinning of Title II even before the first benefit was paid.

The 1939 amendments

To get social security started, the Roosevelt administration and a Democratic Congress had invoked familiar insurance themes in 1935. Four years later, lawmakers continued to use this language as they sought to raise the minimum standard of protection afforded by social security. In the process, the direction of social insurance in America was subtly changed.

The 1939 amendments to the Social Security Act placed greater emphasis on "social adequacy" than had the 1935 law. The old-age insurance program was extended to cover seamen and bank and loan-association employees. The first Title II benefits became payable in January 1940, two years earlier than originally scheduled. The benefit formula was changed to reflect *average* rather than total covered earnings – which had the effect of increasing the sizes of pensions for all recipients in the early years of operation. Furthermore, following recommendations made by the Social Security Board, Congress chose to modify rather than eliminate the "retirement test": Beneficiaries could receive old-age insurance benefits as long as their earnings in covered employment were less than $15.00 per month.[75]

Probably the most significant change was the establishment of monthly payments for the survivors of both active and retired employees and dependents of retired workers. Washington redistributed benefits without raising taxes. Thus, for the first time, federal policymakers provided life insurance coverage comparable in extent to that existing in the private sector. By introducing a whole new set of eligibility criteria and payment schedules for elderly wives, aged widows, widows with children, dependent children, surviving children, and, under certain circumstances, the needy parents of workers who had died, Congress underscored the importance of maintaining the family's integrity. "Safeguarding the family against economic hazards is one of the major purposes of modern social legislation," observed John McCormack (D–Mass.) in the House debate. "Old-age legislation, contributory and noncontributory, unemployment compensation, mothers' aid, and general relief by several States and then political subdivision, aid to the blind and incapacitated, all have an important bearing on preserving the family life."[76]

McCormack's statement suggests that lawmakers devoted as much attention to Titles III, IV, and X (provisions affecting the unemployed, dependent children, and the blind) as they did to Titles I and II. The historical record shows otherwise. Congressional debate emphasized the problems of old age in addressing familial and intergenerational concerns. Legislators chose not to take many bold steps to make American social insurance a more effective way to deal directly with the hazards of life's earlier stages.[77] Because this decision greatly affected the subsequent evolution of social security, let us spell out its consequences in some detail.

The principle of mutual responsibility was the intellectual key that justified expanding rights to help Americans deal with the financial problems of old age. Old-age dependency was not the only risk or even the most important hazard of modern life, but public officials hoped that providing more security in this area would not only bolster public morale but also increase citizens' concern to protect themselves and their children.[78] Social security was more than ever envisioned as a system of intergenerational income transfers; payroll taxes and benefit levels were to be determined in light of competing national priorities and existing economic resources. Such a procedure made economic, political, and moral sense only insofar as younger age groups as well as the elderly benefited from the exchange. If payroll taxes were insufficient to cover benefit costs, the implicit assumption was that the federal government would make up the difference. Policymakers were willing to underwrite additional protection for more people within a certain age bracket because they believed that it would benefit an aging society in the long run.[79]

An age-specific approach to the problem of societal risk had profound policy consequences. After all, the 1939 amendments might appear to increase the long-term cost of the old-age insurance program. (In point of fact, the long-term cost of the 1939 act was less than that projected under the original act, though the current cost was about the same.) Thus, advocates of the 1939 changes made a special effort to reassure fiscal conservatives that overall expenditures would not grow dramatically. The ultimate monthly retirement benefits for single wage earners were significantly reduced, and the increasingly large lump-sum death payments were eliminated. The Advisory Council proposed setting the minimum age for wives' supplementary allowances at age sixty-five – both to save money and to prevent "anomalies and inequities" between wives of annuitants and women with wage credits in their own right.[80] Giving an additional 50 percent to support an annuitant's wife was characterized as a "reasonable provision," because 63.8 percent of all men over sixty-five in 1930 were married, and because increasing *all* pensions (regardless of marital status) would have involved "unwarranted costs." Nor was it perceived as unfair to give additional benefits to married men, because a single worker would receive "potentially" the advantages of the protection of the family unit. But in any case, "widowers, bachelors, and women workers . . . should receive in all cases insurance protection at least equal in value to their individual direct contributions invested at interest."[81] In cases of dual entitlement, moreover, a woman at age sixty-five would receive either 50 percent of her husband's pension or an annuity based on her own covered wages, which-ever was larger. This provision, lawmakers assumed, would be relatively inexpensive: "Because most wives in the long run will build up wage credits on their own account as a result of their own employment these supplementary allowances will add but little to the ultimate cost of the system. They will, on the other hand, greatly increase the adequacy . . . of the system by recognizing that the probable need of a married couple is greater than of a single individual."[82]

The amended Title II sought a greater measure of "adequacy" by guaranteeing a minimal level of support for workers and their families. Yet the 1939 amendments did not disavow the concept of "equity." The new emphasis on adequacy was couched in the language associated with private insurance plans. Benefit protec-tion was still related to the amount a wage earner had contributed into the system. Nor had federally supervised old-age insurance become a universal right; the new pensions would be paid only to dependents and survivors with specific relationships to workers who satisfied the system's eligibility criteria.

Any dispassionate analysis of the 1939 debate over social secu-rity must recognize that there was a gap between what policymakers were doing and what they said. Recognizing that many Americans feared the creation of a welfare state, social security's "insurance" features were emphasized. People eligible for Title II benefits, President Roosevelt claimed, more than a little disingenuously, could be "likened to the policy holders of a private insurance company." The Old-Age Reserve Account established under Title VIII in 1935 was renamed the Old-Age and Survivors Insurance (OASI) Trust Fund. The original employer and employee taxes were repealed; instead, "insurance contributions" were now imposed under the Federal Insurance Contributions Act (FICA) as part of the Internal Revenue Code.[83] The president and his advisors knew that it would be easier to expand social security if Americans believed that they had earned the right to draw benefits from a system untainted by the stigma of "welfare."

Many of social security's critics see the seeds of the welfare state in the mildly redistributionst features introduced into Title II by the 1939 amendments. Defenders of the change claim that this measure was intended to impart a special dynamic to the system, tempering "insurance" principles by expanding "welfare" concerns and vice versa. Neither interpretation is quite right. In my view, both liberals and conservatives underplay the pragmatic shrewdness – and genuine uncertainty about policy consequences – that permeated discussions at the time. Policymakers in the late 1930s wanted to improve the benefits afforded by social insurance, but *not* because they hoped to import European practices and concepts. Far more parochial, short-term issues were at stake: Above all, they wanted to protect their program from demagogues like Huey Long or the Townsendites, as well as critics on the right – all of whom wanted to abolish social security before it fully began operations. Social security loyalists were also concerned about the economic downturn threatening the recovery promised by the New Deal; they worried that the size of the reserve fund might be exacerbating hard times. But they did not acknowledge the risks implicit in their policy initiatives. Rather than put choices between "welfare" and "private insurance" bluntly, they employed euphemisms like "equity" and "adequacy." And rather than wait for the public to appreciate the necessity of "social insurance" for preserving basic institutions, they decided to protect those in the greatest need with a program they characterized as essential to mitigate basic modern "social risks." Insofar as Americans ever accepted programs that were welfare-oriented, social security officials believed that they would do so because of the demonstrated success of worker participation in a "social insurance" scheme. All this helps explain why the system subsequently developed as it did, as well as why social insurance's purposes have so often seemed unclear at best.

The decision to deal with both "equity" issues and "adequacy" concerns in Title II set into motion what has become a familiar relationship between statutory entitlements and popular expectations. As benefits expanded, so did the pressure for more and more growth. This is exactly what the president intended. "We shall make the most orderly progress," FDR stressed, "if we look upon social security as a development toward a goal rather than a finished product."[84] Speaking before the Teamsters Convention in September 1940, he suggested the next steps:

> It is my hope that soon the United States will have a national system under which no needy man or woman within our borders will lack a minimum old-age pension that will provide adequate food, adequate clothing and adequate lodging to the end of the road and without having to go to the poorhouse to get it. I look forward to a system coupled with that, a system which, in addition to this bare minimum, will enable those who have faithfully toiled in any occupation to build up additional security for their old age which will allow them to live in comfort and happiness.[85]

Nevertheless, as social security's advocates sought to underwrite additional protection for a greater proportion of the population, they acknowledged clear limits to the system's expansion. J. Douglas Brown, chairman of the Advisory Council, put it this way: "The pattern cannot be larger than the cloth; the degree of security afforded must be limited by the national income and the proportion of that income properly available for any specific purpose . . . The protection of the aged must not be at the expense of adequate protection of dependent children, the sick, the disabled, or the unemployed."[86]

Old-age assistance and insurance were only two parts of the patchwork social welfare program pieced together in the 1930s. But in the years ahead they became the foundation of social security itself. Subsequent changes in the program reveal much about both "the pattern" and "the cloth" of American life during the last half century. I shall argue that by emphasizing the societal risks associated with the end of the life cycle, the burden of costs on younger people have been downplayed; worse, factors that wreak havoc on the family and intergenerational harmony have been lost from sight. By adopting the language of private insurance and sharply increasing the role of the federal government in matters traditionally left to individuals, private enterprise, charitable organizations, and state and local agencies, the architects of the original social security laws may have inadvertently hampered later attempts to preserve a sense of national community.

2

Social security matures, 1940–1972

Even without the legislative changes of 1939 the social security system would have grown. Simply because of the passage of time, more and more workers paid enough into the program to claim retirement benefits. When the 1939 amendments were enacted, 43.6 percent of the civilian labor force contributed to the system. Ten years later the figure had risen to 56.7 percent; 48.3 million wage and salary workers reported taxable earnings in 1950. The number of beneficiaries also increased, of course, but the number of contributors grew far more rapidly. Because start-up costs were low and tax rates remained modest, the system actually operated with a surplus during the period.[1]

Although social security was growing as anticipated, those who were committed to social insurance knew the system was still quite vulnerable. In internal memoranda and speeches to social welfare groups, members of the Social Security Board acknowledged that the program's slow but steady growth would not be enough to protect it from attack. Political and economic changes, moreover, often upset policymakers' plans for social security. In the midst of World War II, for instance, the formula for old-age insurance benefits was frozen; proposals to liberalize the program were rejected. Because most analysts expected the United States to lapse into the same kind of economic slowdown that had followed World War I, conservative politicians were able to reject the passage of costly new provisions; a Republican-dominated Congress, supported by Southern Democrats, not only made Title II eligibility criteria for employee coverage more stringent but also defeated bills to enact national health insurance.[2] Thus, the first decade of social security's actual operation was one of natural growth within the parameters laid down in 1939. Surprisingly consistent economic prosperity in the postwar era, however, provided more room for political initiative in expanding the system during its second decade.

Not that such expansion took place suddenly or was all of a

piece; conservative influence and widespread fear of "welfare-state" measures were too strong for bold innovations. Instead, the program's administrative and legislative supporters embraced "the politics of incrementalism" – the strategy of working toward broad policy goals in a gradual, step-by-step manner. Social security's chief architects, people like Arthur J. Altmeyer, Robert M. Ball, J. Douglas Brown, Wilbur J. Cohen, and Robert J. Myers, were deeply committed to assuring its financial integrity and popular appeal. These insiders were "loyalists" with generally compatible values and goals; they had formidable technical expertise regarding social security's operations and were politically astute enough to know what could or could not be recommended at any given time.[3] Their proposals typically were first endorsed by some public agency or private organization, matured in the policy arena, and – after fine tuning by the House Ways and Means Committee and Senate Finance Committee – incorporated into the social security system.

An important victory for extending coverage was scored with the 1950 amendments. They required regularly employed farm and domestic laborers, workers in Puerto Rico and the Virgin Islands, and federal civilian employees not covered by the Civil Service Retirement System to join the social security program; state and local government workers without formal old-age protection and employees (other than ministers) of nonprofit organizations could elect to be covered.[4] Amendments in 1954 and 1956 extended compulsory coverage to self-employed farmers, most self-employed professionals, and all military personnel. Ministers, members of religious orders not bound by a vow of poverty, and state and local public employees under a retirement system (including firemen and police officers in designated jurisdictions) could now also choose to join the system. Meanwhile, average monthly benefits rose. In part this reflected the higher wage histories on which benefits were based, but successive amendments boosted social security checks beyond that level. In September 1950, for instance, Harry S Truman signed into law a 77 percent average increase to the benefit levels established in 1939. Subsequent rises were frequent and substantial – if not as dramatic.[5]

Perhaps the most remarkable thing about this incremental expansion was the lack of conflict about broadening coverage and increasing benefits. Between 1950 and 1972, Congress tended to approve amendments by overwhelming margins; no president vetoed a social security bill. Regardless of party affiliation, appointees to the Department of Health, Education, and Welfare generally agreed on the next legislative and administrative steps. Conservative opposition in Congress was largely ineffective. Special-interest groups, such as the American Medical Association and the U.S. Chamber of Commerce, were able to prevent radical changes, but this did not preclude eventual enactment of a modified version of the rejected proposals.

The success of incremental politics, however, was not just the result of shrewd calculations and lobbying by a policy elite. Unanticipated prosperity in postwar America made this incrementalism possible: Social security was able to take in larger and larger revenues without making a noticeable dent in individuals' take-home pay or reducing consumption and productivity. Social security's future became more secure because so many different groups had a stake in it. More and more older people counted on benefits, and younger citizens recognized that the system reduced the degree to which their parents would depend on them in later years. Democrats and Republicans alike saw obvious advantages in supporting a program that appeared sound and enhanced the quality of voters' lives. Business and labor organizations disagreed now and then about specific legislative initiatives, but their respective constituencies viewed social security itself as inviolable. Tough choices could be avoided in affluent times, and so consensus prevailed over dissent. However, easy choices are not necessarily good choices.

Social security developed in unexpected ways as a result of the auspicious demographic conditions, economic climate, and political circumstances favoring its growth after a cautious start. To understand its development since 1939 requires an examination of socioeconomic trends, politics, and cultural history. It is essential to appreciate the dynamics of incremental policymaking under conditions of economic boom and, more particularly, to grasp the limitations of such an approach during social security's troubled recent history.

Building on the past and planning for the future

World War II's impact on social security policymaking

The Depression provided sobering lessons to those shaping social security in the 1940s. Economic stability and the preservation of traditional political institutions were the foremost goals of western nations. The rise of totalitarian regimes amid profound economic dislocations posed a genuine threat to democracy. To bolster the legitimacy of the state, leaders developed programs to foster economic growth while alleviating the plight of the unfortunate. The advent of World War II made such efforts all the more urgent. Thus, Roosevelt established a National Resources Planning Board (NRPB) to devise a blueprint for citizens' future security. The NRPB, like Britain's 1942 Beveridge Report, stressed that government should guarantee "minimum economic security" for all citizens in order to make the nation itself more stable and productive. Officials on both sides of the Atlantic perceived social insurance as a cushion against the dislocations anticipated after the fighting stopped.[6]

Accordingly, many influential members of the legislative and executive branches pressed for greater social security coverage and benefits. They rallied around the Wagner-Murray-Dingell bill (1943), which proposed a purely federal old-age assistance program to replace the federal-state arrangements of Title I, recommended extending coverage to farmers and domestic workers under Title II, and called for a federal health insurance system. Arthur Altmeyer, chairman of the Social Security Board, argued that "it is through social insurance that great masses of the citizens of our countries can be assured decent food, clothing, and shelter and essential health services necessary to make them able and willing defenders of their country and their way of life."[7] Protecting wage earners through social security, it was hoped, would reduce the appalling extent of unemployment and old-age dependency. During the war, older people stayed on the job longer, and the disabled were rehabilitated to boost production. Still, the National Resources Planning Board indicated that even in the best of times, at least one of seven households fell short of a subsistence standard of living. To demonstrate popular support for their position, lobbyists cited a Gallup poll conducted in early August 1943; 64 percent of those interviewed favored extending coverage to "farmers, domestic servants, Government employees, and professional persons."[8]

All the same, Congress chose not to enact any new programs during World War II. Indeed, even though increases in contribution rates had been mandated in the 1935 law and 1939 amendments, existing schedules remained in effect throughout the conflict; winning the war took precedence over social welfare.[9] Though many social security advocates were discouraged, Roosevelt looked forward to a new era once peace returned. In his 1944 state-of-the-union address, FDR declared that "We have accepted, so to speak, a second Bill of Rights under which a new basis of security and prosperity can be established for all – regardless of station or race or creed. All of these rights spell security . . . to new goals of happiness and well-being." Roosevelt was prescient indeed in limning this vision of a second bill of rights. Breaking the lockstep of insurance terminology, he had sketched the outlines of a nation-wide system of care that was not again fully addressed until the advent of Lyndon Johnson's "Great Society" initiatives.[10]

Adjusting for postwar realities

The federal government increasingly functioned as a broker, mediator, and senior partner in all spheres of economic life after 1945. Besides the Servicemen's Readjustment Act, which assisted veterans and their dependents with mortgages, job training, and college tuition, Congress approved other ambitious measures, among them the Employment Act of 1946, which made full employment a national goal.[11] In the social welfare field, federal officials envisaged a program that "would provide 'cradle-to-grave' security, but in amounts not so large as to discourage industry and initiative, providing only a floor below which Americans would not fall whatever catastrophe might strike them."[12] There were, however, mighty obstacles to making a reality of this vision. Congress resisted new liberal reforms, and the insecure middle class was anxious to protect its interests. Convincing these groups of the need to broaden social insurance programs was the most dif-ficult task for social security's champions.

These supporters worried that if Congress did not soon expand the Title II program, it would languish or become moribund. Twice as many people were receiving old-age assistance (OAA) as OASI benefits in 1949; the average OAA benefit was $42 per month, compared to the average Title II retirement check of $25 – a figure only 10 percent greater than it had been in 1939. Largely because of depressed wage levels, most OASI beneficiaries in the South depended on OAA as well. Such statistics were disturbing to those who felt that "from the standpoint of freedom, democratic values, and economic incentives," social insurance was preferable to relief: "It [should] be made clear that public assistance is not a rival to the insurance method but a supplement to it, performing the residual task that will always exist for a last-resort program that takes responsibility for meeting total need," wrote Robert Ball in 1947. "The goal of a progressive social security program should be to reduce the need for assistance to the smallest extent possible."[13] People like Ball knew that in the early stages of social security's development, OAA would serve proportionately more older Americans and that many recipients would qualify for higher Title I benefits than they had earned under Title II. However, social security's leaders presumed that the stigma associated with means-tested relief would limit popular support for the old-age assistance program. They believed that the public would eventually recognize the advantages of *preventing* dependency through old-age insurance.

Liberals decried conservative tightening of coverage rules as an attempt to shackle the growth of social security and devalue its current worth. Truman, in fact, made the "reforms" passed by the Republican-dominated Eightieth Congress a campaign issue in the 1948 election. But whereas almost all British politicians embraced the Beveridge plan and the National Health Act (1946), Truman was rebuffed in his effort to enact national health insurance in America.[14] By the late 1940s, American social insurance was at a critical juncture. Public officials who wanted more direct federal engagement in financing insurance and health care programs had to settle for an incrementalist approach. They gave highest priority to extending coverage and increasing benefits under the old-age insurance program. They hoped to establish a wedge for broader objectives by serving the elderly's needs effectively. This entailed an even more definitely age-specific strategy than had previously been the case.

Sometimes officials pressed for small technical changes in Title II because they knew that "blanketing in" various categories of potential recipients would serve as a precedent for subsequent action.[15] At other times lawmakers were persuaded to enact legislation that had been under consideration for years. After eighteen months of congressional deliberation, President Truman signed the result – thirty major changes in the Social Security Act – into law on August 28, 1950.[16] Similarly, the struggle for disability insurance had begun with the debates on the 1935 Social Security Act. The idea that these benefits were basically payments to unfortunate individuals who had to "retire early" because of mental or physical impairment eventually won (grudging) executive and legislative approval under Eisenhower. In 1954, his administration backed a "disability-freeze" proposal; this provided for calculation of a worker's retirement benefits as if contributions had been paid for a period of time and at a level that would have obtained had that worker gone on working until age sixty-five. The 1956 amendments to the Social Security Act authorized a permanent disability insurance program with benefits first payable to disabled workers at age fifty; at age sixty-five, recipients of disability insurance automatically became eligible for old-age insurance benefits.[17] Once again a measure with condition-oriented goals was tied to preexisting age-specific programs and criteria.

That old-age insurance continued to expand in the Eisenhower years does not mean that social insurance no longer aroused conservative opposition. On the contrary: Between 1952 and 1954 the U.S. Chamber of Commerce advocated a universal flat-pension system; it would have assured every American over sixty-five a minimum retirement benefit of $25 per month, underwritten on a pay-as-you-go basis. This was indeed a mean-spirited parody of the various Townsend plans. Social security officials saw it as a direct assault on the wage-related contributory scheme, an attempt by business interests to turn back the clock by reducing to a minimum federal commitments to those no longer deemed productive members of society. Somewhat surprisingly, insurance companies (who found that social security had made Americans more sensitive to the need for private as well as public insurance) were tepid at best about the Chamber of Commerce proposal; their recalcitrance, joined with the aloof posture of the president's strategists and vigorous opposition from organized labor, ensured that the Chamber of Commerce initiative got nowhere.[18] Had it succeeded, social security would have been undermined from within. Nearly two decades would pass before conservatives again launched so serious an assault.

The public and private spheres of social security

Social security had gained legitimacy during its first quarter century of operation; more and more Americans perceived it as essential to their welfare.[19] Furthermore, a reciprocal relationship between old-age assistance and insurance seemed to be emerging – just as many social security advocates had predicted. Thanks to maturation of the system and liberalization of its eligibility requirements, the proportion of superannuated workers depending on Title I declined, while the proportion of employees (and their dependents) eligible for Title II benefits rose. As a result of the 1950 amendments alone, nearly 100,000 men and women receiving old-age assistance became eligible for old-age insurance pensions. In February 1951, the number of those receiving old-age insurance pensions surpassed the number of those receiving Title I benefits; just six months later, more money was distributed to Americans through Title II than through Title I. Officials used such evidence to argue that welfare assistance for the aged would continue to diminish in the years ahead.[20] In addition, Title II beneficiaries were receiving a good return on their investment; in most instances they were actually getting back far more than they had contributed, even with interest added. In J. Douglas Brown's words,

> Social insurance in the United States has evolved as an extension of the differential wage system. To the extent that benefits are related to wages, the motivation to increase the rate and regularity of earnings is carried over into the social insurance system . . . The problem of the planner of social insurance is to so relate benefits to normal earnings as to afford reasonable protection without reducing motivation in any serious degree. This becomes a problem in which psychology, economics, and public administration must be joined in seeking a solution.[21]

Finding a solution was made easier because of the way social security was financed. A long-term "surplus" existed in the system, in part because Robert Myers, who served as the Social Security Administration's chief actuary between 1947 and 1970, had prudently assumed that real wages would not rise. This assumption was of vital importance in calculating the financial status of the trust funds. There were shrewd political reasons (as well as actuarial caution) behind the adoption of Myers's "level-earnings assumption" for determining benefits – and thus for raising taxes during social security's formative decades.[22] Because revenues were accumulating at a faster rate than benefits were paid out, those who wanted to keep benefit levels up to date could always point to "surpluses" in the system to justify at least part of the increases they requested. As long as liberals continued to play by the unstated rule of the game – making no demands on general tax revenues – their more conservative colleagues were willing to go along, because they knew that substantial increases in the FICA tax would be a strong medicine – one even their rivals would hesitate to prescribe. Once again confrontation over the real nature of social security was avoided by recourse to a technical feature of the maturing system. Lawmakers could mandate larger payments for lower-income beneficiaries while upholding the principle that past contributions should be positively related to the size of individual disbursements. In the process, an unacknowledged further tilt in favor of the "adequacy" criterion took place.

The age-specific eligibility criterion was used in the same way. As a result, age sixty-five was increasingly perceived as the beginning of old age. The framers of the 1935 act began the process by designating sixty-five as the benchmark for Title I and Title II eligibility. Another number could just as reasonably have been chosen. (At least six other ages were used as criteria in relief programs and retirement plans in the United States during the 1920s and 1930s.[23]) Congress later instituted other age-based eligibility criteria. The disability program, for example, reinforced the significance of age sixty-five.[24] Efforts to adapt social security to the changing roles of women, men, and children had a similar effect.[25]

For policymakers, defining coverage on the basis of age had important advantages. Administratively straightforward, it avoided the stigma of "welfare" associated with means-testing formulas. Those who favored age-specific benchmarks realized that they could not cover all situations at once. But because they were adjusting the rules to accommodate the needs and desires of "most" people, they felt justified in viewing age as a reliable measure of "normal" risk. In so doing, they helped to make modern America more bureaucratically age-conscious than ever before.[26]

A new middle-class vision of social insurance emerged during the 1950s. Americans seemed to prefer that government officials reduce the risk of dependency rather than broaden efforts to relieve poverty. Public and private institutions were to assume complementary, not adversary, positions; they were to be partners in promoting continued economic growth. It was necessary to care for those in need, but that should not jeopardize the preeminence accorded a fair return (or, ideally, a handsome profit) on investments.[27]

As social security became a more essential feature of American life, both business and labor discovered that it served their purposes. The private sector took every advantage of public-sector benefits. In every single group insurance contract for permanent disability, for example, private benefits were offset against public benefits. If a policy promised $125 and a disabled worker was eligible for a monthly benefit of $75 under social security's disability insurance program, then the private payment was reduced to $50. Increasingly, private insurers required a person to be receiving social security benefits as a condition for the receipt of a private pension; those who were rejected for social security disability insurance were expected to appeal the decision.

Corporations as well as small businesses designed their retirement programs to mesh with federal old-age insurance eligibility criteria. Very often the value of employees' private pensions would be pegged to the anticipated worth of their monthly retirement checks. Corporate planners found that social security enabled employers to arrange for an orderly succession of responsibilities, while giving workers increasingly well established guidelines for predicting promotions and departures. Mandatory retirement schemes keyed to social security guidelines gave managers a convenient way to dismiss older workers without damaging those older employees' self-respect.[28] Unions also quickly gained a stake in the system. During the late 1940s, the United Mine Workers and United Auto Workers made pensions a part of contract talks. This set a crucial precedent for future negotiations on wages and benefits. Mandatory retirement ages in contracts, claimed union leaders, created job opportunities for younger and middle-aged workers. Thus, union officials could plausibly claim to serve the best interests of older workers at the same time.[29] Nor were there serious rifts between Republicans and Democrats over the meaning of "retirement" under social security.[30] The executive and legislative branches agreed, moreover, that an "earnings test" was necessary to keep the cost of old-age insurance within reasonable bounds.[31] Social security officials and congressional lawmakers collaborated each time the retirement test was altered.[32]

Business executives and labor leaders, Republicans and Democrats, middle-aged taxpayers and retired workers – all valued social security, emphasized experts like Edwin E. Witte, because its stability and efficiency contributed to the well-being of American society at large without undermining traditional norms:

> With all the increases in government, industry, and labor and management programs, it is a fundamental part of the American way of life that primary responsibility in preparations for meeting the economic consequences of the many great personal hazards of life rests upon the individual and his family. Social security and private institutions for economic security have not rendered unnecessary or valueless individual initiative, enterprise, and thrift . . . Social insurance not only is

consistent with free enterprise, but is a bulwark for its contin-
uance.[33]

Echoing Witte's reassurance, but with strongly Keynesian overtones of concern for capital formation and the maintenance of purchasing power, John Kenneth Galbraith remarked in *The Affluent
Society* that "a high level of economic security is essential for maximum production."[34] Social security fostered prosperity by alleviating many fears associated with unemployment, disability, and
old age. More important, according to its supporters, social security bolstered individual self-reliance while promoting a sense of
mutual responsibility. Because "Social Security was a social mechanism for the preservation of individual dignity,"[35] it was viewed
as a conservative institution that strengthened individualistic values.

Although the increasing availability and generosity of social
security benefits had reduced the incidence of poverty among older
Americans, a sizable proportion of them were still in desperate
straits. The Social Security Administration reported that 35.2 percent of all men and women over sixty-five had inadequate incomes
in 1959. James Morgan and his associates at the University of
Michigan, using data collected in the same year, estimated that
whereas 28 percent of all American families were potential welfare
recipients, 48 percent of all households headed by an aged person
risked becoming dependent.[36] Such findings prompted little
immediate response, but they did renew policymakers' conviction
that market forces and private institutions alone could not solve
the problem of old-age destitution.

Thus, in the late 1950s, the paradox of poverty amid prosperity
disposed the nation's leaders to remedial action. Election year politics triggered consideration of ideas that had been germinating for
years. With both Richard M. Nixon and John F. Kennedy calling
for enactment of a new "medical assistance program for the aged,"
Congress in 1960 increased federal grants-in-aid to states offering
medical payments to old-age assistance recipients. Lawmakers also
approved the Kerr-Mills bill, which allocated funds for those not
on public relief yet unable to pay for necessary medical treatment.[37] Had the 1960s been a period of social tranquillity, economic stagnation, and political passivity, then conservative legislators might have more effectively restrained the growth of social
security.[38] But in an era of rising expectations and seemingly
boundless prosperity, Congress worked instead to achieve goals
first set forth by FDR. The unfinished agenda was a full one.

The rediscovery of poverty

Liberals of the 1960s were more successful than the New Dealers had been in promoting the social welfare features of programs like social security. This was partly because the economic and political climate had changed so much; those who advised Presidents Kennedy and Johnson were convinced that the prosperity blessing America for more than a decade would continue indefinitely. If an expanding economy and rising productivity continued to sustain growth, all Americans could look forward to a better standard of living. In addition, federal officials were prepared to do things that FDR had suggested only in vague terms. After two decades of gradually increasing federal intervention, people had come to accept Washington's efforts on behalf of the poor through social security as consistent with American traditions. In any case, few analysts thought that a radical shift in income distribution would be necessary to deal with the nation's poor. In its 1964 report, the Council of Economic Advisers estimated that approximately $11 billion would guarantee *all* poor families at least $3,000 per year. That figure represented less than one-fifth of the defense budget at that time and less than 2 percent of GNP.[39] Money and commitment, it was confidently presumed, would make all good things possible.

Poor people required many things that money per se could not satisfy, but policymakers thought that they could calculate the income needed to maintain individuals or households at "minimum" levels of "comfort," "adequacy," or "sufficiency."[40] Federal officials adopted the "poverty index" developed by Mollie Orshansky, an economist in the Social Security Administration's Division of Research and Statistics. Orshansky's formula attempted to measure how much money people needed to pay for a minimally balanced diet and still afford the other essentials of life.[41] Her calculations assumed that an average family of four could spend a third of its budget on food and would need only $1.40 for all other vital items each week; she did not adjust for long-term economic changes. "The standard itself is admittedly arbitrary, but not unreasonable," Orshansky contended.[42]

Orshansky's statistics corroborated the arguments set forth in Michael Harrington's 1962 best-seller, *The Other America,* and in Dwight Macdonald's influential review essay on "the invisible poor" in a January 1963 issue of the *New Yorker.* Almost half of all Americans who lived alone or with nonrelatives were "poor." So were

14 percent of all the nation's families; the incidence of poverty among households headed by women and blacks far exceeded the national average. Furthermore, 40 percent of all men and nearly 67 percent of all women over sixty-five who lived alone in 1963 had incomes below Orshansky's "economy level." She found that 30 percent of the aged poor lived in the inner city and another 14 percent lived on farms. A much larger proportion of the white poor (23 percent) than of the nonwhite poor (8 percent) were aged. True, in the population at large, minorities were disproportionately represented among the poor; however, their death rate was also much higher than that for whites, so that the pool of those sixty-five and older was correspondingly smaller. Whereas poverty tended to be a lifelong problem for minorities, lower-income whites typically managed to avoid financial hardship until they lost their jobs because of disability or old age.

Great Society initiatives

Mounting public pressure and acts of civil disobedience by the disenfranchised and poor, combined with an activist Supreme Court, a sympathetic Congress, an energetic executive branch, and a popular mandate from voters as well as rising prosperity – all these factors inspired the federal government to launch a "War on Poverty." Public officials boldly began building a "Great Society" that would satisfy the housing, health, employment, educational, and psychological needs of all. "An age attuned to the idea that a government has vast responsibilities for the material welfare and human rights of citizens can hardly share the founders' fear of strong national government."[43] The Great Society was not simply the New Deal reshuffled. The times both demanded and facilitated bolder steps than ever before to protect and advance individual rights. Federal intervention in favor of civil rights, education, and social welfare underscored a genuine commitment to disadvantaged groups.

By and large, the problems of older Americans received less attention in the 1960s than did the problems of blacks, the Appalachian poor, unemployed heads of households, high school dropouts, and children. This was because the government sought to create opportunities for people to lift themselves out of poverty through education, job training, and hard work. "Let us deny no one the chance to develop and use his native talents to the full," declared the Council of Economic Advisers in 1964. "Let us, above

all, open wide *the exits of poverty* to the children of the poor."[44]
Policymakers typically defined and dealt with the elderly's needs
in a manner different than they dealt with the needs of younger
people. For instance, public-sector employment and training programs were seldom designed to help older people. The 1962 Manpower Development and Training Act was amended six times
between 1963 and 1968 to improve the employment prospects of
disadvantaged minorities, but *not* to assist the elderly who wanted
to work. Duke University economist Juanita M. Kreps argued
that Great Society legislation was ensuring the creation of a large
class of aged poor in the future – those who would have to survive on meager resources because, to escape the menace of job loss
or expiration of unemployment benefits, they took early retirement.[45] In fact, the new laws were doubly counterproductive, for
they implicitly regarded aging workers as a universal class of the
useless – regardless of individual desires and abilities.

Enhancing *opportunities* for various disadvantaged groups was
one thing; at the same time, however, Washington promised to
do more to advance the *rights* of the elderly than any other age
group. In enacting the Older Americans Act (1965), Congress made
Roosevelt's vision of postwar America a matter of public law for
senior citizens: "The older people of our Nation are entitled to . . .
an adequate income in retirement in accordance with the American standard of living; the best possible physical and mental health
which science can make available and without regard to economic
status . . . pursuit of meaningful activity within the widest range
of civic, cultural, and recreational opportunities . . . freedom,
independence, and the free exercise of individual initiative in planning and managing their own lives."[46] Note that the Older Americans Act dealt with much more than the financial and health hazards of late life. It presumed that *every* aspect of life for the elderly
might require government intervention if they were to live in
"health, honor, and dignity."[47]

On July 30, 1965, President Johnson demonstrated his concern
for the elderly by signing into law important new provisions under
social security. More affordable and accessible health care for older
Americans had been a goal of federal officials since at least the
1930s; it became a major priority during the Kennedy administration. "Fear of illness and lack of sufficient money are uppermost
in the long list of worries that plague most of the nearly 18 million
old Americans," asserted HEW Secretary Anthony J. Celebrezze in
the first annual report of the President's Council on Aging (1963).[48]

Gallup polls taken in 1962 and 1965 indicated, moreover, that the public approved of increasing social security taxes to meet the hospital costs of beneficiaries.[49]

Medicare (Title XVIII of the Social Security Act) was the keystone of the new legislation. Its provisions reflected the politics involved in accommodating the health and insurance industries, labor unions, key legislators and influential bureaucrats, the elderly, and the families of the aged.[50] Part A was a hospital insurance plan for social security beneficiaries, people eligible for Title II benefits but not on the roll (because of the earnings test), and those covered by the federal railroad retirement program. Part B was a voluntary, supplementary insurance plan that initially cost participants only $36 per year; it was intended to cover payments for physicians and surgeons, as well as diagnostic tests, ambulance service, prosthetic devices, and the rental of some medical equipment. A variation of an American Medical Association substitute proposal for Medicare was concurrently enacted as Medicaid (Title XIX). This was a federal-state program that financed medical services for welfare recipients of all ages and those who were deemed "medically indigent." Designed to mesh with Title I provisions, Medicaid greatly expanded the scope of the Kerr-Mills program of medical assistance for the aged.

Lyndon B. Johnson was mindful of this legislation's historical significance; he flew to Independence, Missouri, so that he could sign Medicare into law in the presence of Harry Truman. The symbolic gesture was apt. Truman had pressed for hospital insurance in the late 1940s and early 1950s, and the aging former president personified the very target population Medicare was designed to assist. But as Johnson reminded Truman, the philosophical basis for Titles XVIII and XIX had even deeper roots: "In 1935 when the man that both of us loved so much, Franklin Delano Roosevelt, signed the Social Security Act, he said it was, and I quote him, 'a cornerstone in a structure which is being built but . . . is by no means complete' . . . Those who share this day will also be remembered for making the most important addition to that structure."[51]

Social security's growing significance

In addition to extending the scope of social security to promote the health of needy groups, Congress broadened other social insurance measures in response to changing longevity and social patterns. Three OASDI benefit increases were authorized between 1965 and 1970. Provisions concerning eligibility for Aid to Families with Dependent Children (AFDC) were liberalized. Policymakers also expanded social security to reach economically vulnerable women.[52] Officials stressed that all age groups benefited from better protection against age-specific risks, invoking the transgenerational theme first enunciated in the 1930s to sell the ever-expanding OASDHI program to taxpayers.

For instance, to demonstrate the advantages of social insurance throughout an average person's life, Ida C. Merriam, an assistant commissioner of social security, traced the benefits that the 2.27 million Americans born in 1935 had enjoyed during their first thirty-three years. Some 140,000 members of the social security cohort had received or were receiving payments; most of them were the children of retired or deceased workers insured under the program, though 8,000 received benefits because of their own childhood disabilities. Merriam also calculated the number of people deriving support from social security who were potentially or actually dependent on the 1935 age cohort. She noted that 750,000 parents of those under consideration were receiving Title II benefits in 1968, which relieved those children of much of the financial responsibility for their parents. And because 13,000 workers in the social security generation had become fully insured under OASDHI at the time of their deaths or disabilities, 57,000 of their survivors or dependents were receiving pensions. Indeed, 16,000 women born in 1935 were entitled to widows' benefits, and another 7,000 got benefits because their husbands were disabled.[53] Even at this stage in their lives, Merriam concluded, young adults had benefited greatly from the institutionalization and liberalization of social security; they had gained a measure of financial security against hazards that might arise long before they attained old age.

Yet there was no doubt that social security had the greatest impact on people during retirement. Whereas at least 50 percent of the elderly population was presumed to be "poor" in the depths of the Depression, the proportion fell from 35.2 percent to 24.6 percent between 1959 and 1970. According to a survey conducted in 1968, 49 percent of all elderly couples, 71 percent of all single men, and 75 percent of all unmarried women over sixty-five did not derive any income from employment; they relied primarily on retirement benefits. "Had it not been for OASDHI benefits," Social Security Administration researchers found, "two to three times as many beneficiary couples would have been classified as poor in

1967 – more than half of all the beneficiary couples – instead of one-fifth."[54] Independent experts confirmed that benefit increases since 1958 had made social security important in reducing financial insufficiency. Using 1966 data, Marilyn Moon found that in absolute dollars, social security provided larger transfers to the elderly poor than did unemployment insurance, public assistance, public housing, veterans' benefits, or the government's health programs.[55] As long as the American economy prospered, there was no reason that social security recipients should not continue to get more out of this system of intergenerational transfers than they ever contributed. "Social insurance makes sense," remarked the eminent economist Paul Samuelson, "because we're all in the same boat." He assured his readers in a 1967 *Newsweek* column that social security was undoubtedly the "most successful" program developed by any modern welfare state, adding that "Social Security is squarely based on what has been called the eighth wonder of the world – compound interest. A growing nation is the greatest Ponzi game ever contrived. And that is a fact, not a paradox."[56]

Changing social security to fulfill Great Society promises

In the mid-1960s it seemed economically feasible and politically advantageous for Washington to exploit social security's success at reducing poverty in order to justify still more generous provisions. Robert Ball, then commissioner of social security, put the matter this way:

> The easy part of poverty to get rid of in a prosperous and successful economy is that which can be prevented by insurance – social insurance . . . Perhaps a third to a half of the poverty that exists in the United States could be prevented by the improvement and broader application of the social insurance program . . . [Social insurance's] objective is not solely the abolition of poverty, but in its operation it does prevent poverty. It can be used much more effectively for this purpose . . . The fact that today we have the capacity to abolish poverty means that we must.[57]

Ball's statement, I believe, signaled another important, though subtle, new direction in official views on the relationship between social security's "welfare" and "insurance" objectives. Some phrases sound quite consistent with themes he and others (such as J. Douglas Brown and Edwin Witte) had enunciated in the 1940s and 1950s: He reaffirmed that "protection is earned by work and contributions" and, as such, conforms to Americans' preference for self-reliance and economic incentive. Three decades of experience had shown, however, that social insurance could reduce or prevent poverty through income redistribution. Now that more than 90 percent of the work force was covered under the program, and nearly every older person was entitled to some benefits, Commissioner Ball and liberals in the Social Security Administration thought it humanitarian to provide benefits that would ensure a "socially adequate" standard of living.

Such a restatement of goals echoed broader intellectual and political currents influencing national policy after 1960, even though social security was not conspicuous in the front ranks of the battle to extirpate poverty. New policy initiatives such as the Job Corps, VISTA, and community action programs operated by the Office of Economic Opportunity attracted far greater attention. Furthermore, officials in competing bureaucracies often espoused views that made social security administrators appear staid by comparison. The Bureau of Labor Statistics, for example, had devised a poverty index that counted greater numbers of needy Americans than did Orshansky's measure.[58]

And yet, as the nation's commitment to building a Great Society began to falter after 1966, daring experiments and innovations were rejected – especially if they required new bureaucratic structures and large amounts of revenue. In this changed climate, social security's incremental approach to the problem of inequality made it appear the most appropriate vehicle for social reform. Wilbur Cohen, who became secretary of HEW in 1968, proposed six changes in social security intended to ensure that the program was *the* basic system of income security in America.[59] Yet even as Cohen set ambitious goals for OASDHI, social security was having a dramatic (if unanticipated) impact on welfare expenditures.

Perhaps most surprising was the extraordinary growth in the Aid to Families with Dependent Children program. AFDC began modestly as Title IV of the 1935 Social Security Act. By 1960, roughly 3 million people were receiving monthly benefits totaling about a billion dollars. Then the public welfare amendments of 1962 made funds available to states for intensive social casework to help the poor. Eligibility rules for social services under AFDC became even more elastic under the 1967 amendments. In 1969 there were more than 6.7 million AFDC recipients, whose support cost about $3.5 billion; three years later the support for nearly 11 million cost Washington $6.9 billion.[60] Analysts attribute this explosion in welfare rolls largely to a marked rise in the proportion of eligible families receiving assistance. By the end of the 1960s, nearly 90 percent of the poor who qualified were drawing on AFDC; the demand was fueled by a growing awareness among blacks regarding their rights, as well as by recent court rulings, simpler bureaucratic procedures, and higher benefits.[61]

A growing number of experts, however, contended that more ominous forces were at work. Conservatives seized on incidents of fraud and carped about the "malingerers" and "cheaters" who were abusing the system. "There is no humanity or charity in destroying self-reliance, dignity, and self-respect," California's new Governor Ronald Reagan proclaimed in 1967.[62] Liberals worried that increased federal support might be the reason behind the rising number of black families headed by women; worse, it might actually foster the "tangle of pathology" and violence among poor people. Public opinion polls revealed middle-class respondents' growing frustration with the system. Because officials had other priorities, including reorganization of welfare administration, and were careless about fiscal considerations, no effort was made to contain costs until 1972. The American way of welfare, in short, was increasingly portrayed as a "mess."[63]

Having campaigned against the excesses, mistakes, and broken promises of the Kennedy-Johnson era, President Richard Nixon made welfare reform a major priority. He assigned Daniel Patrick Moynihan to design a new agenda consonant with the conservative temper of the new administration.[64] One result was Nixon's proposal in August 1969 of a Family Assistance Plan (FAP) that would provide a federally determined minimum income for all who complied with its guidelines. Benefits were coupled with an elaborate system of penalties and incentives designed to force able-bodied recipients (including women with children older than three) to work.[65] Four months later, the President's Commission on Income Maintenance Programs asserted that some Americans were poor, and would remain poor, because they were disabled, superannuated, or untrainable. Although such people might never be able to work their way out of poverty, their need for a "minimum stable income" was no less real for all that.[66] By the end of 1969, therefore, policymakers could choose between two alternatives designed to give the needy enough income to maintain a minimal, but seemingly tolerable, standard of living. Both plans provoked immediate controversy, in part because it was not altogether clear which of them deserved support from liberals, which from conservatives.[67]

Nixon's welfare reform was ultimately defeated. Various income-maintenance proposals, including the negative income tax, were ignored. Why this happened is no mystery. Short-term political considerations outweighed the merits of taking the long view, so that shifting constellations of legislators routinely defeated programs that either put too much emphasis on work or relied too heavily on "handouts." Congress, moreover, was increasingly responsive to a growing number of lobbies like the National Welfare Rights Organization. Such groups succeeded in their opposition to any significant alterations in existing categorical assistance measures or in other parts of the nation's social insurance program.

In the midst of this ideological confusion and legislative maneuvering – and perhaps because of it – a political drive began that culminated in the 1972 social security amendments. The Republicans, who had proposed expanding the social security system in their 1968 platform, endorsed recommendations made by the Nixon administration in 1969–70 and seized on the final report of the 1971 Advisory Council on Social Security. That document called for an automatic adjustment in benefits to keep pace with price increases, recommended a liberalization in the retirement test, set forth a new formula for determining widows' and dependent widowers' benefits, and specified ways to improve disability protection.[68] Politicians took special note of a recommendation that estimates of what social security could afford to pay be based on the assumption that earnings would indeed rise. Adopting the Advisory Council's suggestion would give Congress a plausible way to raise benefits substantially: They could pay the increased costs in part by tapping the "surplus" dollars that existed in trust reserve funds.[69] By adjusting technical devices in the program's operation, legislators were again able to shift social security's objectives toward the "welfare" end of the spectrum without explicitly admitting that this had been done.

Political considerations in a presidential-election year, moreover, tempted both parties to vie for the old-age vote. The December 1971 White House Conference on Aging had focused on older people's inadequate income; it called for an increase in social security benefits and services. "In this age of self-liberators," observed a *New York Times* editorial, "the aging should certainly not let themselves be forgotten."[70] Because by then the elderly constituted roughly 10 percent of the population and 15 percent of the electorate, few lawmakers discounted the growing power of the "gray lobby."

Consequently, 1972 was an extraordinary year in the history of social security. On June 30, Congress authorized a 20 percent increase in pension benefits for 27.8 million Americans. Amid shouts of "Vote! Vote!" the House approved the measure by a margin of 302 to 35; the Senate concurred 82 to 4.[71] This increase in real dollars was the largest in social security's history. It meant that the average check a retired single worker could expect in October – a month before the national election – would rise from $133 to $166; the average retired couple's monthly payment would go from $223 to $270. Maximum benefits for single retired persons and married retired persons would be $259 and $389, respectively. Beginning in 1975, moreover, a "cost-of-living adjustment" (COLA) would be made annually whenever the Consumer Price Index rose by at least 3 percent.[72]

The 20 percent benefit increase was not the only big news about American concern for the aged in 1972. Congress enacted another key piece of legislation: On October 30, Nixon signed a $5 billion social security bill (H.R. 1) that greatly expanded and liberalized the entire OASDHI program. Among other things, it extended Medicare benefits to 1.7 million Americans under sixty-five eligible for disability benefits for at least two years, as well as to 10,000 who suffered from acute kidney disease. The new law augmented the minimum monthly benefit for those who had been employed for at least thirty years in low-income positions, raised the pension benefits for 3.8 million widows and dependent widowers, and liberalized skilled nursing home coverage. It authorized the government to re-form public assistance schemes for the adult poor, aged, blind, and disabled who were unable to work. Finally, it dramatically changed the 1935 OAA formula (Title I of the Social Security Act): Effective January 1, 1974, Washington would provide Supplemental Security Income (SSI) guaranteeing at least $130 per month to eligible individuals and $195 for couples. These amendments set a crucial precedent for universal income-maintenance programs that might come in the future. Nixon expressed his "very great pleasure" in approving H.R. 1: The measure was "landmark legislation that will end many old inequities and will provide a new uniform system of well-earned benefits for older Americans, the blind and the disabled."[73]

By the end of 1972, every major idea that the 1935 Committee on Economic Security had considered for social security had been enacted. As its creators had hoped, coverage under social security was nearly universal. The proportion of Americans eligible for Title II benefits had risen from 20 percent to 93 percent between 1941 and 1974; those over seventy-five had been entitled to government benefits for more than a decade. Furthermore, periodic increases in average monthly social security checks after 1950, passage of the SSI program, and the indexing of Title II benefits can all be interpreted as attempts to reduce the vulnerability of the elderly to inflation, thereby advancing their economic "freedom." Average monthly benefits for retired workers rose to $207 by the end of 1975. This increase was significant in terms of purchasing power; mid-1970s beneficiaries got roughly 40 percent more than their counterparts a decade earlier.[74] Supporters claimed that disability insurance, Medicare, and Medicaid were the first victories in a thirty-year struggle to enact some sort of national health plan under the aegis of social insurance. The adoption of a wide range of community services and outreach programs was clearly consonant with principles that can be traced back to the New Deal.

And yet, while the social security program had grown as part of FDR's legacy, it was a unique combination of affluence and consensus politics that made New Deal promises a reality. Insofar as the War on Poverty went beyond New Deal hopes, a distinctively American way of addressing the problems of economic insecurity matured during the 1960s. Adaptation of social insurance programs to Great Society objectives manifestly advanced the rights of older people as individuals and as citizens. Unlike legislation specifically designed for the poor, social security also sought to bolster the resources of aging middle-class workers and their dependents. As a result, older Americans (and, in many instances, their families) became "entitled" to basic social services and income support. Indeed, increasing use of the term "entitlement" to describe social security benefits was characteristic of a shift in public perception and official definition of claims to social insurance protection.[75]

Furthermore, the 1972 amendments altered current and anticipated entitlements in profound ways. Beginning in 1975, whenever the Consumer Price Index rose 3 percent or more in a year, benefits would rise correspondingly. This change enjoyed bipartisan support. To pay for the increases, the employer and employee tax rates were to rise from 5.50 percent to 5.85 percent between 1973 and 1978; the OASI and DI trust funds, which then had about $42.8 billion in reserves, were thought to be large enough to cushion against short-term fluctuations in contributions. Conservatives hoped to save money by indexing benefits; their rate of increase, legislated on an ad hoc basis since 1950, had actually exceeded the rise in consumer prices during that period. Liberals cited impressive precedents for adopting the idea.[76] This change meant that the economic well-being of millions of older Americans was increasingly insulated from day-to-day politics. Although no one in 1939 could have foreseen the hybrid way social security would evolve by 1972, few doubted that the politics of incrementalism could succeed for decades to come.

3

The mid-life crisis of American social security

Most commentators were convinced that the social security changes enacted in 1972 made sense. Edwin Dale, writing for the *New York Times,* was

> persuaded that Social Security at the worst is not a bad deal, and is safe, even for the young worker with 40 years of paycheck deductions ahead of him. It is not a bad deal, either, for the doctors and salesmen and other self-employed who tend to do the most squawking. Unless the world blows up, or the country goes bankrupt, it is highly likely that current workers will get back from Social Security more than they paid in if they live only a few years past their retirement age, and a great deal more if they live a long life.[1]

Because it was unlikely that the world would blow up or that the government would ever stop writing checks, social security looked like a good bet.

In one form or another, social insurance had become central to the political economy by 1972. It absorbed an increasing share of workers' earnings and constituted an ever larger percentage of federal expenditures. As long as prosperity lasted, social security's scope expanded. Policymakers justified new programs and increased benefits by citing precedents in the private sector and in other branches of government. Critics later charged that this was a shortsighted policy, one that neglected the inherent limits of what could be done. "Far from strengthening the welfare state, the politically cheap expansion of programs actually tended to devalue the commitment to social policy and transform it into a predicate of economic growthmanship and mass consumerism."[2] The truth of the matter is a bit more complex.

A burgeoning U.S. economy had made social security's recent expansion seem reasonable. When the economy went sour, social security itself became vulnerable to attack. Policymakers of the 1970s finally had to make tough choices about the program's future.

Because social security had grown so large, its financial problems had a disproportionate effect on the national economy; a decade of "stagflation" drained the trust funds at an alarming rate. Conservatives warned that social security was near collapse. Those who once pronounced social security "safe" for the rest of the century now worried about how to save it before 1984. Edwin Dale, for instance, was acutely aware of the changes since his *New York Times* article. As chief public affairs officer in the Reagan administration's Office of Management and Budget, Dale played a role in seeking the answer to social security's financial problems. "This system is going to land on the rocks," predicted Budget Director David A. Stockman late in 1981, "and by '83, you will have solvency problems coming out of your ears. You know, sometimes sheer reality has a sobering effect."[3]

Neither inexorable demographic realities nor technical snafus nor the volatility of public opinion nor the flowering of a neoconservative public philosophy can account for the "crisis" outlook on social security that emerged during the 1970s. Basically, the new mood arose because few could differentiate between unexpected developments in social security's own dynamics and new problems besetting society at large. Thus, even federal officials who were deeply committed to the program found themselves unable to define central issues clearly or to effect necessary changes.

Social security had come of age. When the system began, few Americans were entitled to benefits; four decades later, nearly every senior citizen received some support. The ratio of beneficiaries to workers fell from 1 : 40 in 1940 to 1 : 16.5 in 1950 and to 1 : 3.3 in 1980. Such demographic trends had long been anticipated, but financing social security depends as much on accurate economic forecasts as it does on long-term demographic projections. Any sudden and unanticipated changes in wages and prices wreak havoc on the pay-as-you-go system. During the 1970s, inflation reduced consumers' purchasing power, while productivity fell; meanwhile, rising unemployment reduced the flow of FICA taxes into social security trust funds; the formula for cost-of-living adjustments overindexed for inflation. The impact of these adverse conditions was staggering. Congress hoped that the 1977 amendments would strengthen the program's financial base. But lawmakers increased employee and employer payroll taxes and made the assumption that the economy would grow. Because the economy did not grow, contributions did not cover benefit payments, which proved to be higher than anticipated because they were automatically keyed to soaring prices. The system continued to suffer huge deficits, thereby fueling new doubts about its soundness.

Lawmakers attempted to "fix" social security by making technical changes in existing provisions. But this in no way confronted the grave policy issues that had long shadowed its development. These adjustments did not prove sufficient amid prolonged stagflation. Those who called for major changes in existing operations and a reordering of program objectives were stymied by opposition from those loyal to the program as it was and by critics more interested in interment or dismemberment than in regeneration through genuine revision. Largely because there had never really been an explicit consensus on the goals of social insurance in America – much less on its relationship to other key institutions – social security became the center of political controversy in a way it had avoided for roughly twenty-five years.

Moving beyond the 1972 amendments

The next steps in expanding the social security program

Lawmakers continued the search for ways to improve America's social insurance system after 1972. Because inflation rose faster than anticipated, Congress in 1973 approved a two-step, 11 percent increase in social security benefits during the coming year.[4] After more than fifteen years of study and deliberation, the government provided for the creation and regulation of retirement income sources to supplement OASI. In 1974, President Ford signed the Employee Retirement Income Security Act (ERISA), which established vesting and funding standards for pension plans managed by private firms. Those not covered by such a pension plan were encouraged to establish individual retirement accounts (IRAs). A Pension Benefit Guaranty Corporation was created within the Department of Labor to insure workers whose employers were unable to make good on their pension liabilities.[5]

Concurrently, the Social Security Administration investigated how to make basic health care and social service delivery systems more effective and how to reach groups without the same level of access as white adult males. Special congressional hearings were held on ways to improve the disability and Medicare programs.

In addition, the impact of the new Supplemental Security Income program (Title XX) was carefully monitored. Because those who had participated in the federal-state old-age assistance, aid to the blind, and aid to the permanently and totally disabled programs were automatically transferred to SSI in 1974, some of the country's neediest citizens benefited most from the switchover.[6] Furthermore, the administrative guidelines for SSI enabled nearly 3 million more Americans to qualify for federal aid than under state-administered programs.[7] Most SSI recipients felt that they were treated courteously by agency administrators. Among those who had received OAA payments before switching to SSI, the proportion who felt "bothered by the fact that [they] had to accept aid" was cut in half.[8] Nevertheless, many social security officials were disappointed that fewer older people made claims for SSI than they had anticipated. Analysts initially attributed this to the target population's ignorance about the program and its eligibility criteria. They also hypothesized that those who perceived themselves to be getting by adequately were less inclined to apply for benefits than the "most needy."[9]

Finally, the status of minorities and women under social security received careful scrutiny, in part because these groups represented a more vocal constituency than ever before. Blacks and Hispanics complained that their benefits were inadequate because they had usually been employed at lower pay scales, had fewer employment opportunities, and had shorter life expectancies. Lobbyists for women objected to "gender biases." They noted, for example, that women, who usually live longer than men, received smaller average monthly benefits. Most women received pensions based on their relationships to male wage earners, not on the basis of their direct financial contributions to the system; such "dependent" status, feminists charged, was especially misguided when family circumstances and women's positions in American life were rapidly changing.[10]

The 1975 Quadrennial Advisory Council on Social Security endorsed many proposals for broadening social insurance. "Future changes in OASDI should conform to the fundamental principles of the program: universal compulsory coverage, earnings-related benefits paid without a test of need, and contributions toward the cost of the program from covered workers and employers," the panel recommended.[11] The expansion recommended conformed to the politics of incrementalism that had prevailed since the 1950s.

Those telltale signs of middle age

Not all of the 1975 report was devoted to ways to liberalize regulations, extend coverage, and improve benefits. Financing received considerable attention. The panel reported that although social security's trust funds had reserves exceeding $50 billion, payments under the cash benefits programs would soon begin to surpass tax receipts; in addition, the system was headed for serious deficits several decades hence as the baby-boom generation began to retire – at a time when there would be relatively fewer workers paying into the system.[12] The Advisory Council was not the only body in 1975 expressing concern about short- and long-term deficits. The Senate Finance Committee announced that FICA taxes would have to be increased roughly 20 percent between 1975 and 2010, and an additional 40 percent by 2050 in order to keep the system solvent. In its annual report, social security's board of trustees predicted that "without legislation to provide additional financing, the assets of both [the retirement and disability] trust funds will be exhausted soon after 1979."[13] To allay public concern, a bipartisan "white paper" signed by five former HEW secretaries and three former social security commissioners stressed that "the size of the problem over the next 25 years is easily manageable and certainly does not constitute a financial crisis."[14]

President Ford suggested in his 1975 state-of-the-union speech that a 5 percent ceiling be imposed on social security benefit increases but his proposal went nowhere. A year later, Ford declared, "I am concerned about the integrity of our Social Security Trust Fund."[15] The Ninety-fourth Congress implemented some minor changes in the Medicare program in 1976, but election-year prudence dictated that serious deliberation be postponed. Policymakers *sensed* that the expansionary trend could not continue much longer. But until there were compelling grounds for reform, politicians chose to avoid measures that might alienate their constituencies.

National economic and political crises reduced the likelihood that federal officials *could* devote much time to the financial problems of social security. Inflation had accelerated: Between 1965 and 1968, it rose from 2.2 percent to 4.5 percent; for the next eight years it fluctuated between 5.5 percent and 11 percent. The hidden costs of Vietnam, the skyrocketing price of previously cheap and plentiful gas and oil, the relentless upward surge of the wage-price spiral, shifts in monetary and fiscal policies occasioned partly by sudden alterations in international trade balances and currency values, and disappointing harvests – all these helped sustain the high inflation rate. They also contributed to a decline in productivity growth (which fell to 1.1 percent per year between 1972 and 1978) and a rise in unemployment to 9 percent – the highest it had been since World War II.[16] At the same time, disillusionment with various Great Society initiatives, disgust over the Vietnam and Watergate debacles, and the steady decline of public confidence in government diminished its ability to reform existing federal programs, much less to further redress economic conflicts between various groups. Presidents tried to inspire unity and maintain the semblance of "normalcy," but too often their actions merely added to the pervasive malaise.[17] Given the circumstances, it was difficult to address *any* issue as tricky as social security's immediate shortfalls – or as remote as its possible long-term financing difficulties – with any hope of success.

Some experts emphasized that the program itself was at a critical juncture. As social security entered middle age, they claimed, policymakers could take pride in its accomplishments, but would also face some hard choices. Adjustments were inevitable, according to Juanita Kreps, an economist widely respected for her studies on labor and social insurance, because the worker–beneficiary ratio, which had so well served the program in its early decades, could not sustain current operations much longer:

> In its maturity, the program will face other questions of similar magnitude – questions that were not of such pressing importance in its youth. Can the social security system assume the obligation of having benefits keep pace with growth as well as cost of living? How high a replacement ratio should be maintained?* Should the benefit vary with the age at which one retires, either beyond or before age sixty-five? Will it be necessary to establish a later age of eligibility for benefits to offset the increasing number of elderly persons relative to middle-age and younger workers? Most troublesome of all, perhaps, is the question of whether imposition of the additional payroll taxes needed to pay for benefits will be acceptable to workers or whether some significant portion of the funds will be collected via other taxes.[18]

Unexpectedly high cost-of-living adjustments (COLAs) initially caused the most concern. As explained in Chapter 2, Congress had decided in 1972 to increase OASDHI benefits automat-

---

*A "replacement ratio" refers to the proportion of a worker's prior earnings replaced by a pension.

ically whenever the annual increase in the CPI rose 3 percent or more, in order to protect the elderly from inflation and to help retain the value of recipients' benefits. But the economic rationale lying behind "indexing" quickly proved invalid. When new benefit and tax schedules were established under the 1972 amendments, future social security revenues and outlays were projected on the assumption that wages would continue to rise about 2.25 percent faster than prices. Between 1973 and 1977, however, that differential averaged −0.5 percent, which caused the program to run sharp, wholly unanticipated, annual deficits. Worse, the formula compensating for inflation was faulty. Critics charged that young disabled workers and middle-aged survivors of deceased contributors were getting "windfall" benefits. Low-income workers could retire with benefits exceeding their most recent wages. Replacement ratios for both low- and middle-income workers would be far higher than prior to 1972.[19]

Americans, to be sure, were not the only ones worried about the future of their social welfare programs.[20] But an acknowledgment that social insurance programs in nearly all advanced industrial countries had entered a transitional phase did not make it much easier to identify problems and advance solutions in the United States. Precisely because its supporters had long prided themselves on the distinctive features of America's system, ideas discussed elsewhere could not always be readily introduced here. Hence, a detailed analysis of action and debate at the federal level is the key to understanding efforts to reform social security in the United States.

Washington exercises restraint as social security enters its fifth decade

Carter's attempt to reform social security

To their credit, key members of Jimmy Carter's administration recognized that social security had entered a transitional phase and that corrective steps were needed to sustain the program's health into the future. President Carter relied on Democrats in Congress to secure passage of the 1977 social security amendments, which raised FICA taxes and the wage base to which they were applicable, increased the taxes paid by self-employed workers, shifted revenues from the social security retirement trust fund to the dis-

ability fund, and made a technical adjustment to correct the indexing formula. Carter held that these reforms should banish doubt
about the program's financial integrity: "From 1980 through 2030,
the Social Security system will be sound."[21]

Unhappily, even after the elimination of double-indexing and
the imposition of new tax formulas, macroeconomic problems still
beset social security. COLAs were still pegged to changes in prices
rather than changes in wages, because wage indexes had historically outstripped rising prices. This pattern was reversed in the
1970s, however. At decade's end, inflation still hovered in the
double-digit range and seemed out of control. Most workers' pay
did not keep pace with inflation; real wages actually declined about
0.6 percent during the period. Increases in FICA taxes consequently did not keep pace with rising benefit levels. And even
though the percentage of Americans in the labor force was greater
than ever before, unemployment rose steadily, reducing the relative number of contributors. Trust fund reserves thus provided
less and less of a cushion for social security's pay-as-you-go
financing.

Political storm warnings went out over the rising cost of social
security. Juanita Kreps, who served as Carter's secretary of commerce, warned that the scheduled increase in social security taxes
would "impede consumer spending" unless other tax cuts offset
it; other economists shared her fear about a "fiscal drag" as wages
became subject to ever stiffer tax rates.[22] Even though a national
survey revealed that 56 percent of the public approved (only 35
percent opposed) the higher taxes "in order to improve the financial health of the Social Security system," middle-class voters,
conservatives, and business groups pressured Congress to roll back
some of the increases and to prevent further rises. Amid growing
Democratic disarray, Republicans renewed their attack on the tax
hikes.[23] In April, House Ways and Means Committee Chairman
Al Ullman (D–Ore.) suggested that revenues generated by a new
excise on crude oil be earmarked to pay for a cut in social security
taxes. Ullman's effort was to no avail; by mid-May, all efforts to
rescind the tax increases had failed.[24]

Seizing the initiative in late 1978, HEW Secretary Joseph A.
Califano proposed social security cuts totaling $600 million. Cali-
fano wanted to eliminate the $255 lump-sum burial benefit, tighten
disability insurance eligibility criteria, and repeal the automatically
indexed "minimum benefit" guaranteed to all social security
recipients.[25] Reaction to these proposals was as swift as it was neg-

ative. "This is not the year to pass a Social Security bill," Representative Ullman declared, because it would "open up a Pandora's box."[26] AFL–CIO President George Meany criticized the White House for failing to consult with organized labor. Wilbur Cohen organized "Save Our Security" (SOS), a coalition of more than two dozen nationally based welfare and labor organizations to lobby against the proposed changes. Nelson Cruikshank, the president's counselor on aging, threatened to resign unless he could speak against Califano's policy. Testifying before the House Select Committee on Aging in February 1979, Cruikshank argued that "reducing benefits on a budgetary consideration represents a breach of faith between the government and millions of Social Security contributors and could go a long way toward eroding the confidence people have in their government."[27]

Despite such criticisms, the Carter administration defended its stand. "The optimistic expansionist philosophy that underlay Social Security planning since World War II has now changed to one of guarded hope that the best of the past can be preserved while the considerable needs of the future are addressed," claimed Social Security Commissioner Stanford G. Ross. The coming decade, he added, would witness "painful adjustments in which finances and benefits will have to be closely scrutinized and balanced."[28]

Carter eventually secured some of the benefit changes he had requested, but during the rest of his term the White House was reluctant to wrestle with the issue in any substantive way.[29] "To confront the graying of America," observed Califano, "may demand more political courage than any other domestic issue of the 1980s."[30] Lack of such political courage is not the only reason for the Carter administration's failure to develop a workable policy. The replacement of Califano by Patricia Roberts Harris in 1979 illustrates the contrary tendencies of Jimmy Carter's presidency in this area. Unlike Califano, Harris hesitated to recommend major changes in social security, thereby undercutting support for initiatives from within the administration itself without bolstering loyalty among the Democrats' traditional constituencies. In the end, the Carter administration emerged with only a comprehensive reform of disability insurance.

Changes in the budgetary process, moreover, introduced a new element to policymaking. Amendment of social security was now tied to the complex annual budgetary process. The OASDHI program began as a self-supporting, self-sustaining system. Since 1969, however, it had been a line item in federal budgets. This meant that it was not enough to justify amendments to social security in terms of the system's own financial situation. In addition, the case had to be made that social security changes fitted in somehow with the budgetary priorities under debate by legislators. The Budget Reform Act of 1974, moreover, made it harder to resolve differences over line items – even though this measure was designed to balance federal spending against anticipated revenues. As more of the budget became "uncontrollable" – either because of indexing for inflation or because specific programs were treated as sacrosanct – Congress was increasingly straightjacketed.[31] A policy conundrum ensued. The Carter administration wanted to reduce the size of social security in order to deal with the program's immediate and projected long-term difficulties, yet it had to defend its recommendations primarily in terms of the coming year's fiscal budget. However important long-term savings might be, they were largely irrelevant to lawmakers for whom the political future depended on short-run advantages. Al Ullman spoke with real prescience when he observed that "There are not going to be any more easy votes on social security."[32]

The administration not only was unable to get serious talks under way on social security problems to be expected once the baby-boom generation began to retire but also was surprised to find that its proposed cuts were so distressing to longtime supporters of the OASDHI program. The changes recommended by the executive branch hardly represented a major shift in social security operations, but they were still viewed as assaults on hallowed "rights." "You are cutting benefits," the president's counselor on aging told the HEW secretary. "These benefits are earned rights that people have paid for and are entitled to."[33] Secretary Califano thought that Cruikshank and his colleagues Wilbur Cohen and Robert Ball were out of touch with the times. He failed to understand their fear that if *any* existing entitlement were abolished to satisfy other government priorities, then *all* benefits under social security were vulnerable.[34] These veteran social insurance experts worried lest a precedent be set for more draconian measures against the system they had helped forge. Yet they would not admit that the program's "welfare" and "insurance" features did not mesh as effectively as official rhetoric claimed.

Social security experts have traditionally characterized the problem of ensuring fair treatment to all while helping those most in need as a tension between the demands of fiscal *equity* and social *adequacy*. "The structure of benefits under contributory social insurance is a closely integrated and interrelated element of the system, universal in application and based upon a reasonable pre-determination of *imputed,* not *actual* need in many diverse situations," observed J. Douglas Brown, one of the program's original architects and faithful supporters, in 1977. "It involves a balanced judgment of adequacy of protection relative to funds available. In the United States, this judgment should be made by the Congress as the body most responsive to the people in respect to both the taxes to be levied and priorities in the coverage and level of benefits among various categories of persons to be protected."[35]

As I have shown in Chapter 2, social security's hybrid ability to ensure middle-class Americans a fair return on their FICA taxes while reducing the threat of poverty among lower-income workers in their later years accounts for much of its popularity. Throughout the first three decades of the program's history, however, there was genuine disagreement and uncertainty about how much a bureaucracy like the Social Security Administration should be allowed to offset market forces by shifting income from one socioeconomic group to another. Even during the Great Society period, social security's welfare ("adequacy") aims were intentionally hidden by insurance ("equity") terminology. The 1972 amendments patently tipped the scales toward welfare. Ironically, amidst hard times, inadequate funds made it harder to fulfill such redistributionist aims. For this reason, more than one critic blasted social security as "an inherent contradiction."

Strains between adequacy and equity

The twofold domestic challenge of the 1970s was how to improve the lot of the poor while keeping the costs of doing so at an acceptable level. Its advocates had expected the SSI program to reduce differences in "basic" levels of support nationwide, but it was not easy to agree on what constituted a "minimal standard of adequacy." SSI levels were set well below official poverty criteria; in 1974, the first year of this program's operation, the average benefit for all ages was only 70 percent of the government's own poverty level for an individual (80 percent for a couple).[36]

Federal officials had a hard time ensuring the "adequacy" of benefits. Although the federal SSI benefit automatically increased with rises in the CPI, the states did not have to index their component. Thus, unless a state's legislature made voluntary adjustments, its elderly poor found their economic situation worsening because of rising prices. Furthermore, SSI earnings limits imposed extremely high tax margins on those who found employment.[37] Given these policy defects and seemingly uncontrollable inflation, it is not surprising that the steady decline in old-age poverty in the 1960s was not sustained in the 1970s. Government statistics showed that inflation eroded the buying power of SSI benefits; the U.S. Senate Special Committee on Aging concluded that official statistics tended to underestimate the number of older people in "genuine economic distress."[38] Ironically, while policymakers tried to deal with continued poverty among senior citizens, critics became more concerned than ever that social security's "minimal" benefits had grown so large that it could no longer guarantee fairness as compared with what would be "actuarially purchaseable" from FICA payments.

The "social adequacy" case made by the Social Security Administration for various old-age entitlements *has* become less convincing recently. This is due in part to the substantial overlap between the SSI and Title II programs. Less than 8 percent of all OASDI beneficiaries were eligible for SSI checks in December 1981, but some 70 percent of SSI recipients were also receiving social security benefits at an average $219 per month. At that time, the *minimum* Title II benefit for a disabled worker or one retiring at age sixty-five was $170.31.[39] The "minimum benefit" – originally set at $10 – had gradually increased in the interest of both "social adequacy" and price changes; those who had worked intermittently in low-paying jobs, officials claimed, relied most on social security's mildly redistributive benefit structure. SSI should have eliminated exclusive reliance on Title II to ensure the elderly poor a "basic" income floor. But under the 1972 amendments, Congress also raised – and indexed – the minimum benefit. Defenders of the increases rightly characterized the minimum benefit as vital for very old women who otherwise would have to rely exclusively on inadequate SSI benefits. Critics, however, were also right when they decried the Title II changes as an expensive windfall for workers (such as civil servants with other means of support) who received the same "minimum" benefits after contributing to the system for a short time.

Failure to think through the overlap between a national old-age *welfare* program and a social *insurance* system created a difficult public policy issue. Controversy raged over the rising costs of minimum benefits, because their relative values differed among groups who happened to have paid minimal FICA taxes during their careers. To save money and to promote better integration between SSI and other social security income-transfer titles, the 1975 Social Security Advisory Council urged that the escalator provision of Title II be phased out. In 1977, J. Douglas Brown recommended freezing Title II benefits. Another respected analyst, Alicia Munnell, argued that ensuring the "adequacy" of benefits for those with minimal covered earnings could be handled more efficiently through SSI.[40] When President Carter proposed to eliminate the minimum benefit, he was denounced by members of his own administration. As will be shown later in this chapter, when Ronald Reagan tried to emulate Carter, he, too, faced a storm of protest. Experts, officials, and the public alike found it hard to grasp that the overlap between SSI and social security made the minimum benefit's welfare function less important than it would have been without Title II.

Debate over the minimum benefit pales, however, in comparison with the controversy among experts and politicians about the "adequacy" and "equity" of Title II benefits for middle-class Americans. The 1977 amendments had corrected a serious technical error in the adjustment for inflation in the computation of the initial benefit amount, but conservatives were distressed by the benefit formula itself. They noted with dismay that the replacement ratio had risen sharply. The replacement ratio for workers retiring at age sixty-five with "average" covered earnings increased from 31 percent to 44 percent between 1952 and 1981. During the same period, the replacement ratio for low-income workers grew from 46 percent to 62 percent; for workers with the highest level of covered earnings it varied between 29 and 32 percent, though it reached 36 percent and 35 percent immediately after enactment of the 1972 and 1977 amendments, respectively.[41] These critics feared that such levels of support jeopardized the system's solvency.

Examining the new strains between "equity" and "adequacy" under social security reveals that rhetorical obfuscation and tinkering with various components of the system delayed difficult albeit inevitable choices. Was social security's major objective to reduce the risk of old-age dependency? Or was it to guarantee middle-class wage earners a fair return on their prior contributions when they retired? How much longer would it be possible *not* to choose between these objectives? An honest restatement of policy goals, careful planning, and bold political initiatives would be necessary if social security were to meet the human-resource needs of a "graying society."

Two ways not to resolve social security's mid-life crisis

Suggest policy options with little bearing on the situation at hand

Carter had four blue-ribbon panels study specific aspects of social security and recommend reforms.[42] There was new interest in the system among scholars, policy analysts affiliated with think tanks, and various interest groups.[43] Policymakers gained something important from both official and independent publications. Citing expert opinion made it easier to support controversial ideas. Above all, it was imperative to the legislative process that any proposed changes affecting large segments of the population be discussed by the public at large.

Good ideas and research were vital for creative reform; by themselves, however, they were not enough. The timing and conditions under which reforms were proposed clearly affected the likelihood that they would be translated into law. Carter's Commission on Pension Policy and the National Commission on Social Security, for instance, did not issue their final reports until Reagan had become president. Furthermore, debates among experts confused public and policymakers alike. Economists sharply disagreed about social security's effect on private savings and capital accumulation.[44] There were similarly esoteric disputes over the program's impact on labor supply, the "real" economic status of older Americans, and the way in which retirement options affected individual behavior and family decisions. In the meantime, critics renewed their assault, sometimes posing as "friends" bearing radical plans for reform.[45]

Some scholars went even further, arguing that social security's problems were both symptoms and products of a more deeply rooted "crisis of legitimacy" in western societies. Conservatives and neoconservatives asserted that rising expectations and increased entitlements had resulted in "governmental overload," threatening a breakdown of democracy itself.[46] Others elaborated a neo-Marxist theory about the "structural contradictions of capitalism," claiming that American and European leaders had erected an "old-age welfare state" to maintain and increase their own power. Undermining confidence in social insurance programs was one way to attack the redistributive aspects of the welfare state.[47] In *Social Limits to Growth,* Fred Hirsch argued that to increase social spending beyond a certain point results in greater unhappiness for its recipients: Greater spending temporarily increases political legitimacy, but ultimately is disruptive to economic performance; it thus heightens political discord.[48] Critics on both the left and right rejected "welfare capitalism" and shared certain pessimistic views about the future of advanced industrial societies. Yet neither side was able to discriminate precisely between social security's difficulties and the "disarticulation" manifest in western political economies. Nor did they prove that this convergence of ills was more than temporary.[49]

Meanwhile, unforeseen economic problems significantly altered the debate over social security. Carter's 1977 assurances that the program was on a sound footing were based on forecasts that quickly proved erroneous. Government economists had predicted that inflation would be only 4.7 percent in 1980; independent forecasters had estimated that it would not exceed 7.5 percent. The inflation rate that year was actually 13.5 percent. Because social security checks rose directly according to increases in the CPI, overall payments rose by 14.3 percent in 1980 – nearly three times what the administration had projected.[50] Rising unemployment reduced the tax income needed to operate the pay-as-you-go system, threatening to exhaust trust fund reserves. "Serious issues of public policy – the shift of resources from the private to the public sector, the impact of government budgets on the economy, a large proportion of the population dependent on government for some or all of its income, and the removal of most of the budget from annual review or control – are tied to current spending levels," observed political scientist Dennis Ippolito. "And *spending* is the key; virtually everyone agrees that it is too high, but there is sharp disagreement on how to reduce or control it."[51]

Government appropriations between 1969 and 1980 for all types of income maintenance and health care (not just those under the Older Americans Act) had risen from 20 percent to more than 40 percent of the total domestic budget. In light of "the graying of the federal budget," liberals and conservatives alike urged greater scrutiny of cost–benefit ratios. Public sympathy for the aged was undermined; experts feared intergenerational conflicts. "Established interest groups and governmental factions alike, unaccustomed to strong partisanship on social security issues since the earliest years of the system, may have to come to grips with divisions that are unusual in American politics and an atmosphere unusual in its intractability."[52]

The short-term problems besetting social security were far worse than anyone had anticipated, and rising public anxiety about its financial health introduced a new element into the policy making process. Consider the results of seven public opinion surveys between 1978 and 1982.[53] People were asked about their confidence in social security financing. Each poll indicated that younger people were less sure than their elders that the system would still be solvent when they reached retirement age. This pattern was all the more disturbing because it paralleled a longer-term disenchantment with governmental effectiveness.[54] Thus, in a marked switch from the overwhelming support that social security had previously enjoyed, Americans were suddenly worried about its soundness.

"Every time the press writes that Social Security has money problems," complained one congressman, "we get a ton of letters and phone calls from people who want to be reassured."[55] Newspaper articles and television specials conveyed the impression that social security was nearly bankrupt. For example, charts comparing current numbers and future numbers of people over sixty-five, or the decline in the worker–beneficiary ratio between 1940 and 2030, were used to show why the system had become so vulnerable. The data presented were usually accurate, but the accompanying interpretation tended to sensationalize the facts. Erroneous ideas about social security were perpetuated, and stereotypic images of older people were reinforced. Those who wanted to show the elderly as relatively blissful interviewed healthy residents in "Sun City." Those who saw old people as a drain on productivity and economic growth viewed "dependency" and the leisure-time activities of the elderly from the perspective of Ebenezer Scrooge. In short, the mass media eschewed subtlety, ignored ambiguity, seized on cliché, and illustrated their points with worst-case scenarios. Americans continued to support social security, but what they read, heard, and saw reinforced its sharp decline in popular confidence during the 1970s.

By the time Carter left office, social security's financial problems had become increasingly difficult amid academic disagreement over their causes and the media's misleading interpretation of the situation, coupled with an unexpected economic downturn and flagging confidence in the federal government. Policymakers who had trouble coping with budgets on a year-to-year basis found it still harder to deal with fiscal issues that spanned decades – or even generations. Yet quick action was clearly necessary.

Formulate policies without testing the political waters

Congressional leaders decided that 1981 was a propitious year to deal with social security's problems. In April, a House Ways and Means Subcommittee approved a measure presented to its chairman, J. J. Pickle (D–Tex.), that would have increased the retirement age to sixty-eight by the turn of the century, while eliminating the benefit penalty for outside earnings after that age. Meanwhile, the Senate Finance Committee under Robert Dole (R–Kan.) voted to institute a new formula for adjusting cost-of-living increases.[56] The White House, which was busy establishing its foreign policy and domestic agendas and preparing budget and tax-reform proposals, gave only a few hints concerning its views on the OASDHI program early in 1981.[57] However, the executive branch knew the day of reckoning was nigh. "President Reagan's delay on Social Security has been understandable so far," noted a *New York Times* editorial. "But his own Administration estimates that the cost of Social Security is now rising by $45,000 a *minute*. These days, time for reflection does not come cheap."[58]

On May 12, Secretary of Health and Human Services Richard Schweiker advocated "Social Security reforms which will keep the system from going broke, protect the basic benefit structure and reduce the tax burden of American workers . . . Our package consists of major changes to restore equity to Social Security benefits and to restrain the growth of nonretirement portions of the program which are out of control."[59] The administration proposed a 25-percent point reduction in early retirement benefits (effective for those first eligible in January 1982) and a three-month delay in the cost-of-adjustment scheduled for July 1982; subsequent adjustments would be made on October 1. The White House also wanted to tighten eligibility rules for disability and eliminate "windfall" benefits to retirees with minimal covered earnings.[60] Schweiker and other officials emphasized the proposal's attractive features. Unlike schemes then being considered in Congress, this measure would not raise the retirement age or reduce the benefits of current recipients. The administration predicted that the contemplated savings would eliminate immediate financial worries and keep future FICA hikes to a minimum.[61]

Though Schweiker acknowledged that "some of the changes will be difficult," the electoral firestorm that ensued stunned Reagan's administration. Leaders of the gray lobby were outraged. "The President's safety net is under water," claimed the head of the National Council on the Aging, "and old people are being thrown to the sharks." The president of the National Council of Senior Citizens condemned the plan as "the biggest frontal attack on Social Security ever launched." Wilbur Cohen charged that the package was "a calamity, a tragedy and a catastrophe."[62] Senator Daniel Patrick Moynihan (D–N.Y.) stressed that cutting early retirement benefits would make it "financially impossible to retire at 62." Lane Kirkland, the new AFL-CIO president, assailed the plan as one that would punish those whose poor health or disability forced them to leave the labor force prematurely.[63] The proposed benefit reductions "will compound the existing inequities against women in Social Security," contended Representative Patricia Schroeder (D–Colo.), and "worsen the already precarious financial situation of women nearing their retirement years."[64] House Speaker O'Neill (D–Mass.) even called the proposals "despicable" and "a rotten thing to do . . . that robs the system of its most important feature: the confidence of the American public."[65] Reagan's social security package, in the words of a conservative, Senator William Armstrong (R–Colo.), was a "masterpiece of bad timing."[66]

What had gone wrong? Senator Edward Kennedy (D–Mass.) suggested that the proposals were "hasty, ill-advised and devastatingly punitive."[67] Changing the reduction factors for early retirement on just seven months' notice did seem precipitous, because few older workers could change their own plans so quickly.[68] Because amendments in 1980 had already tightened the disability program's eligibility rules, Reagan's efforts to eliminate remaining loopholes were excessive. But other elements were not so controversial; many were based on campaign pledges, and some had already gained support from political moderates. The Reagan administration made two serious miscalculations:

1. Too many of its legislative particulars were freighted with ideological assumptions and purely budgetary considerations. "Reaganomics," after all, supposed that economic recovery

depended in part on correcting abuses and superfluities in existing federal programs. If, at the same time, government deficits were decreased and taxes were reduced, Americans would have more freedom in spending their hard-earned dollars.[69] Accordingly, social security's immediate impact on the economy and its short-term financing problems took precedence over long-range issues. As OMB Director David Stockman told a reporter, "I'm not going to spend a lot of political capital solving some other guy's problem in 2010."[70] The result was that many administration proposals were made without thinking through their human consequences. "The budget office," as Robert Myers later complained, "develops policy without regard to the social and economic aspects of the Social Security program and even the political aspects."[71]

2. The administration was eager to accomplish as much during its first hundred days in office as FDR had. By late spring, officials were increasingly confident that Reagan's tax-reform legislation and his 1982 budget would get through Congress largely intact. If additional "savings" could be realized through social security reforms, victory would be that much sweeter. But the executive branch did not check with key congressional leaders about its plans for reforming social security, even though it was assiduously monitoring public opinion and counting votes on other major initiatives. No administration official consulted Robert Dole, chairman of the powerful Senate Finance Committee. Nor did the executive branch consult J. J. Pickle or Barber Conable (R–N.Y.), pivotal conservative members of the House Ways and Means Committee. Senator John Heinz (R–Pa.), who chaired the Senate Special Committee on Aging, was also neglected.[72]

The new administration had failed to do its political homework. Negotiations would have to start anew, but these missteps would not be quickly forgotten.

Picking up the pieces

Policymakers handled social security delicately for the rest of 1981.[73] The difficulties involved in putting together a successful reform package were underscored at the 1981 White House Conference on Aging in early December. Delegates to the 1961 and 1971 conferences had set future legislative agendas by reaching consensus on specific recommendations.[74] In 1981, however, the atmosphere was highly partisan. There were charges that the administration had changed program guidelines, delegate selection criteria, and voting procedures to protect the president. No consistent position emerged from the proceedings: Representative Claude Pepper (D–Fla.), the eighty-one-year-old chairman of the House Select Committee on Aging, called for a federal health insurance program that would include home health care for the elderly; President Reagan, who turned seventy shortly after entering the White House, pledged to "put Social Security on a sound financial basis," but gave no details pending further study. Major recommendations and "supplemental statements" in the conference's final report differed markedly on several issues, including whether or not to use general revenues to fund the nation's retirement program.[75]

Another independent panel, the National Commission on Social Security Reform (NCSSR), was established to break the impasse. The NCSSR's mandate was to review the current and long-term financial condition of social security's trust funds, identify problems that might jeopardize the program's solvency, "analyze potential solutions" that would assure the system's integrity and simultaneously guarantee recipients' benefits – and report its recommendations by December 31, 1982. "Saving social security will require the best efforts of both parties and of both the executive and legislative branches of government," Reagan noted. "I'm confident this can be done and that in its deliberations this commission will put aside partisan considerations and seek a solution the American people will find fiscally sound and fully equitable."[76]

No one doubted the difficulties that lay ahead. National commissions play a curious role in American politics. Established in times of crisis, they are expected to clarify issues and propose judicious remedies. But what makes sense in theory rarely occurs in reality. The reports of the National Advisory Council on Civil Disorders (1967) offended Lyndon Johnson, who simply ignored the evidence gathered by his experts. Likewise, President Nixon and members of Congress denounced the findings of the Commission on Obscenity and Pornography (1970). "Such commissions seem to come and go in the nation's capital with the frequency of tourist buses, and with about as much political effect."[77] Given the failure of recent social security panels, there was little reason to expect that the NCSSR would be any more successful.

4

Social security gets a new lease on life

Social security's deteriorating short-term financial situation (the latest available Social Security Trustees' report indicated that by July 1983 there would not be adequate funds to pay old-age benefits) provided a powerful incentive for constructive action by the National Commission on Social Security Reform. The panel's composition, moreover, increased chances that Congress would take its recommendations seriously. The chairman, Alan Greenspan, and four others were appointed directly by the president; the Senate and House leaders designated five members each. The resulting balance – eight Republicans and seven Democrats – qualified as bipartisan, especially in view of the power lineup in Washington at the time. Seven of the fifteen (Representatives Bill Archer, Barber Conable, and Claude Pepper; Senators William Armstrong, Robert Dole, John Heinz, and Daniel Moynihan) were ranking members of congressional committees that dealt with social security matters or policies on aging. Former Representatives Martha Keys and Joe Waggoner still had influence on the Hill. Robert Ball and Robert Myers (the NCSSR executive director), of course, had been high-level social security officials for decades. Mary Falvey Fuller had served on the 1979 Social Security Advisory Council and had been a member of the Reagan transition team. Robert Beck, president of Prudential Life Insurance, and Lane Kirkland, president of the AFL-CIO, were the best-known experts for big business and labor on the subject. The only two commissioners who had not dealt intimately with the program before (Alexander Trowbridge of the National Association of Manufacturers and Alan Greenspan) were nonetheless undeniably well versed in economic matters.

Yet the commission's chief assets could be viewed as liabilities. Because most members understood how the system operated, many had been outspoken about its shortcomings and how to remedy them. Unfortunately, their views were too diverse to make agreement easy. Furthermore, as veterans of politics, they knew that their social security recommendations could later be held against them; their roles as disinterested commissioners and as actors in the policy arena would be difficult to separate. It might seem more prudent to do as little as possible rather than take risks they would later regret.

The NCSSR's deliberations could hardly be insulated from current issues. Throughout the spring, Republicans and Democrats wrangled over the 1983 budget. On May 5, for instance, President Reagan and the Republican majority on the Senate Budget Committee called for $40 billion in social security "savings" – by reduced payments, tightened eligibility criteria, increased FICA revenues, or some combination thereof – over the next three years.[1] Representative Pepper charged that "this Commission has been compromised." Senator Moynihan excoriated the administration for actions that "terrorized older people into thinking that they won't get their Social Security."[2] Senator Heinz feared that "the budget process itself is coming very close to wrecking this bi-partisan effort. As long as there is something in the budget resolution dealing with Social Security, the public perception will be that we are trying to use the Social Security program to slash budget deficits."[3] The Senate Budget Committee concurred, precluding consideration of social security issues from its deliberations.

The budget crisis moved both NCSSR Republicans and Democrats to evaluate their immediate political risks. The Republicans' predicament was manifest. If Democrats could convince the electorate that the GOP was "slashing benefits" to preserve its administration's economic experiment, the Republicans would be an endangered species after the November elections. Democrats, on the other hand, were expected by liberals, organized labor, and the elderly to defend the existing system; failure to do so – and vigorously at that – would surely cost them many votes. Public opinion polls revealed, moreover, that most Americans disapproved of *any* reduction in social security benefits.[4] Assuming that Democrats like Pepper and Moynihan were being "emotional" in order to placate their constituencies, Republicans felt that it was better to have them do this in May rather than later on, when such public gestures might well prevent a compromise.[5]

The commission's public meetings from June through September featured presentations of data by outside experts on death rates, health, and capacity for work among those over sixty.[6] During this period, the NCSSR staff, under Executive Director Myers, produced more than sixty memoranda and other background material. "Having Bob Myers on board has saved the Commission a great deal of money," quipped Alan Greenspan, "because we don't need a library."[7] All summer long the commissioners discussed various options privately. Myers, with the chairman's encouragement, circulated his idea for operating social security on a "self-adjusting, self-stabilizing" basis.[8] The five Democratic-appointed commissioners met before each meeting, and Robert Ball served as de facto minority staff director at the private meetings that followed the plenary sessions.[9]

Even though the NCSSR kept a low profile, social security became a major campaign issue in 1982. The Republican National Committee spent $1 million for a television commercial featuring a winsome postman delivering social security checks. "This year's 7.4 percent cost-of-living increase [in benefits]," said the mail carrier, "was promised and delivered by the President."[10] The advertisement, declared an outraged Claude Pepper, "lowers the art of deception to depths not explored since the Nixon administration."[11] The Democrats quickly prepared a counterattack: "Save Social Security – Vote Democratic" appeared in brochures and on bumper stickers, while commercials warned that "a vote for the Republicans is a vote against social security."[12] The rhetoric and charges became nastier as the campaign drew to a close. The president, repeatedly insisting that he would protect social security, called the Democratic attacks "sheer demagoguery." Nevertheless, a *New York Times*/CBS exit poll revealed that concern over social security was a key factor in the Democrats' success.[13]

The National Commission on Social Security Reform was then reminded of the need to reach a fairly quick and thoughtful political settlement by two unrelated developments. On November 5, social security's old-age insurance trust fund borrowed $581,252,000 from the disability insurance trust fund to meet current expenses. Such interfund borrowing had been authorized only through the calendar year. Congress could extend this provision, but this temporizing measure obviously was not a "solution."[14] Furthermore, because leaders of both parties had decided not to convene a lame-duck session to grapple with social security's financing problem, the new Congress would have to take it up as one of the first orders of business. Unfortunately, the new Congress did not fully recognize the difficulties facing it. At least two-thirds of the reelected and newly elected members of Congress were opposed to both higher taxes and reduced levels of COLA increases.[15] Clearly, the commission's task was to guide legislators to compromises in these areas.

On November 11, the NCSSR voted unanimously to accept Robert Myers's analysis, which showed that OASDHI faced a $150–200 billion deficit between 1983 and 1989 and that over the next seventy-five years projected benefits would outstrip payroll-tax income by the aggregate sum of $1.6 trillion (expressed in 1982 dollars).[16] Using these figures, the commission estimated that the long-range problem represented 1.8 percent of taxable payroll over the period in question. Having "adopted a yardstick against which people can measure the adequacy of steps to be taken by Congress,"[17] it then looked into how to eliminate the potential deficits. Myers distributed actuarial cost estimates for every option that the commission had considered, as well as for some ideas introduced by the Reagan administration and by the House Ways and Means Subcommittee on Social Security.[18]

The next day, Robert Ball outlined to Chairman Greenspan and Senator Dole what he, Keys, Kirkland, Moynihan, and Pepper proposed as the basis of a bipartisan agreement. The Democrats had included features (such as a three-month delay in providing new COLAs under Title II) they knew their Republican colleagues would find attractive. The other side's reaction was restrained, however. Dole considered Ball's proposal a "serious effort" to negotiate, but thought that it relied "too much on increased" taxes for him to endorse it at that point. Within an hour after White House Chief of Staff James A. Baker III learned the details, Reagan concluded that the concessions did not go far enough.[19] However, Republicans on the commission did not have a counterproposal of their own. Robert Beck devised a list of items generally favored by conservatives, but he could not win over the liberals and moderates. John Heinz then suggested making a "core package" of those items that both Democrats and Republicans could support. He also introduced a set of options to complete the package – Democrats would choose the most palatable benefit reductions and Republicans the least offensive tax increases.[20] The Democrats rejected this scheme outright; the Republicans were divided about their next step. "It would be foolish for us to forge ahead now," observed William Armstrong, "without finding out what is acceptable to the president and the Speaker."[21]

The commissioners were stymied. The Republicans feared to offer a proposal that the Democrats would reject out of hand. They were also worried that the White House might not back them.

The Democrats were in a similar quandary. Did Reagan and O'Neill want to use the commission as a cloak for their own negotiations? (Implicit in this question was the assumption that *nothing* would be recommended unless it were agreeable to these two major figures.) What, in fact, *did* the White House want to do – negotiate within the commission, or fight matters out in Congress? The Democrats also had to determine whether they stood a better chance of getting what they wanted within the NCSSR or in the House of Representatives. At that point the commission asked for a thirty-day extension; the White House granted an extra fifteen days. "Like so many issues in a democratic society," Alexander Trowbridge declared with rare wisdom, "you almost have to be up to the precipice before you get a decision."[22] Indeed, domestic brinkmanship had become the name of the game, but the rules were to undergo some changes.

In *Artful Work,* Paul Light argues that the NCSSR was effectively defunct by Christmas, although its continued pro forma existence served as a useful smokescreen behind which White House and congressional leaders could return to the good old/bad old days of closed-door negotiations. This interpretation does not do full justice to the complexity of what happened next. Certainly, those charged with redrafting the social security compact – including Reagan advisors who were not NCSSR members – formed an inner circle removed from the glare of publicity, more determined than ever to share the pain equally. Yet this group could scarcely bargain without an acute awareness that it was not enough to placate the president and the Speaker. It was at least as important that virtually all of the bipartisan panel endorse any deal if it were to clear both White House and congressional barriers.

Robert Dole sought to break the impasse with an op-ed article in the *New York Times* of January 3, 1983. Social security, he wrote, "overwhelms every other domestic priority. [But] through a combination of relatively modest steps . . . the system can be saved."[23] Senator Moynihan read the piece with interest, taking note of Dole's intimation that the president was ready to act. Moynihan suggested that he and Dole confer; they invited Ball to join them. During that meeting, Dole proposed that Greenspan return to Washington for "one more try" at bridging differences between the president and the House's Democratic leaders. Moynihan suggested that Conable join in the talks.[24] This so-called gang of five became the commission's team for intensive negotiations with the president's men, who included White House Chief of Staff James Baker, aides Richard Darman and Kenneth Duberstein, and Budget Director David Stockman.[25]

The White House people dominated the proceedings, clearly trying to develop proposals that Baker could get the president to accept. Reagan, however, would not endorse a set of recommendations unless Speaker O'Neill agreed to back them as well. In addition, the GOP negotiators had to satisfy the demands of at least some of the six Republican commissioners not directly involved in these talks. Should only one of the "outsiders" (Heinz seemed the most likely) agree to a compromise, it would have the approval of five Democrats and four Republicans. Reagan could not sanction such an outcome.[26] The Democrats also had to rally support in key places. Ball did not think he could present an agreement to Speaker O'Neill without knowing that Keys, Kirkland, and Pepper would go along with it. Hence, Ball's tactic throughout the negotiations was to tell the Republicans that he needed such-and-such a concession if he were to persuade his three colleagues to accept another part of the compromise.[27]

The negotiators created a new "middle ground" out of their differences. Robert Ball (a mainstream liberal in his late sixties) and David Stockman (a neoconservative in his thirties) gradually emerged as the chief advocates on either side. Whatever deal they struck would have a bipartisan, intergenerational patina. By dint of much maneuvering, a compromise package was agreed to on January 15. The final vote was 12 to 3, thus giving the president and congressional leaders the overwhelming majority they had insisted on.[28] The National Commission on Social Security Reform achieved its goal by satisfying the most pressing concerns of policymakers and the public. "Social Security is the most universal and most valued expression of our nation's conscience. It is also good business for the nation," wrote Claude Pepper eloquently. "And the agreement . . . represents a fair exchange of concessions by all of us in return for a restoration of national faith that this nearly half-century-old institution will be alive and well as far into the future as we reasonably can see."[29]

From commission report to public law

Because the NCSSR *Final Report* underlay the 1983 social security amendments, the specific steps agreed on and the pivotal issues left unresolved must be outlined. The commission's recommendations generated $168 billion during the 1980s – an amount deemed sufficient to keep the OASDHI program solvent during that period – and eliminated slightly more than two-thirds of its long-range deficit. Nearly half of the short-term savings were realized by delaying the COLA on social security benefits for six months and by revising the tax-rate schedule for 1984–90. It was not by chance that both of these measures "saved" the system $40 billion. This symmetry was vital, because those who negotiated the compromise knew it would be carefully scrutinized for any imbalance between benefit cuts and tax hikes.[30]

Other provisions also underscored the ingeniousness with which the commissioners sought to solve OASDHI's financing problem. Taxing the benefits of higher-income persons generated the third largest source of revenues in the short run.[31] Depending on one's economic perspective and political philosophy, this measure could be interpreted as either a benefit cut or a new tax; it surely was a bit of both. The rest of the short-term savings were realized by imposing more uniformity in social security coverage and financing.[32] Many provisions that ameliorated the short-term financial situation also helped reduce the long-range deficit. Taxing benefits to the wealthiest segment of the beneficiaries alone cut the projected deficit by one-third. Almost the same amount was to be realized over the next seventy-five years by extending coverage and shifting COLAs to a calendar-year basis. Overall savings from the other recommendations were fairly small in comparison. The only measures that "cost" the system anything came from four changes in the way benefits were calculated, changes that affected mainly disabled widows and aged, divorced spouses. To eliminate the remaining shortfall, eight members of the NCSSR called for a gradual raising of the retirement age in the twenty-first century; five others suggested another increase in tax rates, if necessary, in 2010.[33] Because it failed to settle this issue, the commission set the stage for a major congressional debate.

With a final report in hand, Congress speedily drafted revisions to the Social Security Act. House and Senate leaders emphasized that there were two reasons for keeping to the commission's final set of recommendations.[34] First, it was doubtful that 435 representatives and 100 senators could develop a better set of proposals than those already endorsed by the president, the Speaker, and powerful members of Congress. Second, the social security system could not meet its expenses by midsummer without prompt legislative action. And if Congress were to impose a six-month delay in COLAs (as the commission had recommended), then this had to be done by May, because otherwise computer programs would have to be reworked to reflect the change in July's social security checks.

Critics had ample opportunity to express their views. The American Association of Retired Persons spent thousands of dollars on a mail campaign protesting the COLA delay and taxation of social security benefits; the National Alliance of Senior Citizens, which claimed to be the nation's second largest old-age interest group of individual members, rejected the compromise; Maggie Kuhn of the Gray Panthers praised some items but declared the package as a whole unacceptable.[35] The U.S. Chamber of Commerce and the National Federation of Independent Business denounced the new taxes imposed on older people and self-employed workers. The National Association of Wholesale Distributors and the National Association of Realtors gave their grudging approval – *if* Congress made certain changes they favored. Several public employee unions protested the mandatory coverage of new federal workers.[36]

Those who lobbied against the compromise package, however, were no match for the forces lined up to ensure its quick passage. The commissioners themselves worked to win support among legislators.[37] Fuller, for instance, made her substantive objections to the package quite clear. Nevertheless, she subordinated her reservations to the interests of social security beneficiaries and the need to avert financial emergency.[38] The case for enacting the compromise was further strengthened by influential witnesses, perhaps the most important of whom was Arthur Flemming, who had been HEW secretary under President Eisenhower and U.S. Commissioner on Aging under Nixon, Ford, and Carter, and who currently served as president of the National Council on the Aging and co-chairman of the Save Our Security (SOS) organization. Because politicians are likely to have second thoughts when senior citizens denounce a social security bill, it was reassuring to see Flemming, Representative Claude Pepper, and former HEW secretary Wilbur Cohen all testify on behalf of this one. Efforts by Robert Beck and Alexander Trowbridge proved equally valuable; endorsements by the Committee on Economic Development, the Business Roundtable, and the National Association of Manufacturers kept major business interests in line. And although Lane Kirkland and other AFL-CIO leaders tried to protect the interests of federal workers in their ranks by opposing mandatory social security coverage of new civil servants, they gave strong support to the other provisions.[39]

Once it was clear that the social security hearings would not produce any damning evidence or counterproposal likely to jeopardize acceptance of the commission's recommendations, both House and Senate concentrated on correcting technical deficiencies and strengthening some provisions of the compromise package.[40] The biggest stumbling block was how best to eliminate the long-range deficit of OASDI. The House Ways and Means Committee proposed that initial benefits be reduced 5 percent (beginning in 2000) and payroll taxes on employers and employees be raised from 7.65 percent to 7.89 percent (beginning in 2015). J. J. Pickle, who chaired the Ways and Means Subcommittee on Social Security, wanted to raise the retirement age so that by 2027 one would have to be at least sixty-seven to receive full benefits. Claude Pepper, who opposed changing the retirement age, supported the NCSSR Democrats' proposal to increase taxes instead – if necessary. Debate over these three options was sharp. Representative William Thomas (D–Calif.) tried to ease the tension with this humorous analysis:

> The [Ways and Means] committee proposal is not worthy of being in the garden. The two remaining alternatives are garden variety, one a "pepper," and the other a "pickle" . . . Hot peppers bring tears to your eyes. Sweet peppers are hollow and need to be filled to give them substance. Make no mistake – the Pepper amendment's stuffing will be more and more taxes. The pickle, on the other hand, is derived from the cucumber, a solid, fleshy vegetable which is set aside to age and develop more character . . . So as the air fills with numbers during the debate, if things get a bit confusing, relish this thought: make mine pickles.[41]

By a narrow margin the House voted to raise the retirement age. The Senate also wanted to increase it, but only to sixty-six. In conference, the House plan was adopted with slight modifications. The two versions of the amendments were reconciled on March 24, the last working day before Easter recess. "The conference report may not be a work of art," observed Representative Barber Conable, "but it is artful work . . . It will do what it is supposed to do. It will save the nation's basic social insurance system from imminent disaster."[42] The legislation passed both houses, though 190 representatives and 43 senators either voted "nay" or abstained. No consistent patterns or particularly strong correlations are revealed by a roll-call analysis of these final votes.[43] For better or for worse, Congress was willing to trust its leaders – who in turn relied on the collective wisdom of the NCSSR.

When Reagan signed the amendments into law on April 20, he aptly summarized what had taken place:

> Just a few months ago there was a legitimate alarm and worry that Social Security would run out of money . . . On both sides of the political aisle there were dark suspicions that opponents from the other party were more interested in playing politics than in solving the problem. But in the 11th hour, a distinguished bipartisan commission, appointed by House Speaker O'Neill, by Senate leader Baker and by me began to find a solution that could be enacted into law . . . None of us here today would pretend that this bill is perfect . . . but the essence of bipartisanship is to give up a little to get a lot. My fellow Americans, I think we've got a great deal.[44]

The significance of the 1983 amendments

How does the sequence of events just narrated fit into the larger history of policymaking for social security? Will the crisis now abate? Or do the developments between 1972 and 1983 signal a new phase in the program's evolution, in which partisan fights will escalate? The only other moment that engendered so much nervousness and uncertainty about social security occurred at the very beginning of its history. Is debate over first principles again the order of the day?

At first it may seem odd to seek parallels between those two periods. Policymakers in the 1930s had to establish a bureaucracy and invent procedures for an institution with a nonexistent past, an unknown constitutionality and constituency, and an ill-defined future. For all the novelty of the 1983 amendments, policymakers were not starting afresh: They stressed their allegiance to established tenets and always sought to preserve as much of the existing framework as possible. The dynamics of change in these two periods, moreover, contrast sharply. Although a variety of constraints dictated caution in 1935, Congress enacted bold amendments four years later that altered the original policy objectives and reoriented the program's development. By contrast, in recent years experts have been obsessed with restoring confidence in the beleaguered system; they have struggled to "save" billions amid mounting deficits at home and rising concerns abroad about the future of "the welfare state."

Are there nevertheless concerns and similarities in policymaking then and now that might prove instructive to those who must deal with social security in the future? History has not come full circle, but neither are present circumstances altogether novel.[45] I think that three lessons regarding social security policymaking emerge from this study so far.

1. *Because it is so difficult to talk sensibly about the complex, long-range issues that surround social security, policymakers typically seize on an immediate "big problem" that they think they can solve.* The catalyst for reform in both the late 1930s and the early 1980s was the size of social security's reserve funds and their presumed impact on the economy. Many experts in the first period believed that the creators of social security had erred in their decision to accumulate large sums of money in order to provide old-age pensions for workers under Title II. The existence of such funds, they feared, might tempt federal officials to spend money "foolishly"; some economists claimed that taxing workers for benefits that had not yet been disbursed was reducing consumption and causing a drag on the economy, thereby prolonging hard times. In the 1980s, fiscal conservatives were alarmed that there was too little money in the OASDHI trust funds and that deficits would balloon out of control in the twenty-first century. Many liberals believed that general revenues would have to make up the difference if no corrective action was taken, because the social security system could not be allowed to go "bankrupt." Yet this remedy was hardly an attractive one in view of prevailing economic conditions and the growing number of old people who would be dependent on social insurance.

In both situations the money involved was staggering. The $47 billion social security reserve fund projected in the 1930s represented more than eight times the amount of money then in circulation and roughly five times the amount deposited in savings banks. By early 1983, in contrast, the OASDI trust funds had only eight weeks' worth of reserves. Over the next seventy-five years the system annually would need about $25 billion (in 1983 dollars) over and above anticipated revenues; this meant that the discounted present value of the deficit would be at least $1.6 trillion by 2058.[46] Such figures frightened thoughtful citizens because they seemed to provide "hard evidence" that something needed to be done. It did not appear to matter greatly that such exorbitant estimates ignored key facts about the current situation. After all, far less than $47 billion had yet been collected in 1939. The architects of the 1983 amendments, moreover, knew that the OASDI trust funds were expected to run a surplus in the 1990s because of already-scheduled tax increases and the comparatively modest growth in costs necessary to take care of those born in the Depression. Nonetheless, to address immediate financing problems, policy-makers in both periods had to work with figures that justified taking actions unthinkable except in an emergency.

Particularly in social security's most recent crisis, arriving at a set of figures that could serve as a basis of negotiation depended a great deal on accommodating the commissioners' ultimate politi-cal and economic objectives. For example, Greenspan and other conservatives preferred to address long-range issues before dealing with short-term deficits.[47] Commissioners Ball, Pepper, and Moynihan, among others, carved out a liberal position; they thought it made more sense to deal with the temporary imbalance in trust funds than to allow long-term fears undue influence.[48]

Given such differences, it is interesting to note how each side reacted to Robert Myers's assessment of social security's financial problems at the November NCSSR meeting. The Republicans were surprised when the Democrats accepted their pessimistic assump-tions about the magnitude of the problem. Actually, the Demo-crats were playing their hand cleverly. "On the grounds of pru-dence," observed Lane Kirkland, "the decision was that we should vote our fears and not our hopes."[49] A major concern was that the economy would continue to stagnate. In such a case the liberals had to protect themselves from the charge that they prevented the conservatives from dealing with the full scope of the problem. On the other hand, should favorable economic conditions return, act-ing cautiously would reduce the likelihood of future benefit cuts.

No genuine agreement about the scope of the current social security problem ever really emerged. Considerable differences of opinion about the sizes of immediate and long-term problems were also evident during congressional deliberations.[50] Nor did inde-pendent witnesses always bolster confidence in the projections. A. Haeworth Robertson and Dwight K. Bartlett, former chief actu-aries of the Social Security Administration, expressed misgivings about the NCSSR's long-range estimate and criticized the panel's failure to go beyond its mandate and tackle Medicare financing issues. The U.S. General Accounting Office warned that continuing economic problems could undermine proposed solutions, as had been the case in 1977.[51]

In the end, Congress was willing to accept the numbers that the commission had adopted, but only after the Social Security Administration vouched for them. Once this step was taken, experts and legislators could devise remedies for generating revenues and reducing outlays. Because the social security problem was defined in monetary terms, every option had to be assigned a price (or certified as a noncost item) if it was to "count" in the debate. Policy issues that demanded serious consideration – such as the role of minorities under social security – were left to one side.

2. *Debates over social security shy away from considering major structural changes and gloss over ideological differences. Instead, they focus on technical adjustments.* Radical proposals to restructure social security often have impressive advocates and sometimes muster considerable popular support. For this reason they frequently affect the tone of policy debate. But they rarely become the basis for reform, because social security is seen as a major federal institution; politicians generally prefer to appeal to the country's "vital center." When no obvious middle ground can be found, lawmakers typically prefer to tinker with existing operational procedures rather than spark a debate over unresolved philosophical issues. Comparing the passage of the 1939 and 1983 amendments shows that at a certain point, room for free-wheeling discussion and bold legislative action is intentionally constrained.

In the 1980s, many well-known conservatives appealed to Reagan to take bold steps. They offered impressive critiques showing that social security's woes jeopardized the nation's economic health. They recommended that the nation's social insurance program be reduced as much as possible and that greater emphasis be given to private retirement plans.[52] Although these appeals did not culminate in any specific title in the 1983 amendments, the assault on social security did influence the policymaking process. Liberals accepted more pessimistic assumptions about social security's solvency than they would have preferred; conservatives worried that their own solutions did not go far enough. The threat to popular confidence in the program, moreover, made it all the more necessary for policymakers to reaffirm their loyalty to its fundamental principles.

Similarly, in the late 1930s, social security's defenders faced a dual attack: Those on the left demanded a program that would transfer income from rich to poor. Those who opposed establishment of any "welfare" program wanted the federal government to do as little as possible lest the canons of a democratic, capitalist polity be violated. Extremist attacks thus forced policymakers to decide what they would *not* do to amend the original old-age insurance program. Unfortunately, the actions lawmakers took to defuse radical attack confounded efforts to clarify both the current and ultimate purposes of social insurance. Policymakers relied on technical jargon – terms such as "equity" and "adequacy" – to mask the full intentions and likely consequences of their initiatives.

Many legislators and commentators, both in 1939 and in 1983, found it difficult to assess the merits of any option designed to bolster the overall system if it departed from traditional practices. Some had trouble distinguishing "necessary modifications" from "big changes." Others became so sensitive to charges of sabotaging social security that they were overwhelmed by details. Hence, in an increasingly fractious political environment, a crisis of legitimacy loomed: Government officials could afford neither inaction nor demagoguery, but no obvious middle course seemed acceptable.

Federal officials accordingly sought assistance in 1982, as in 1938, from bipartisan groups of distinguished citizens. No appointees were thought to be hostile to the program per se, but many had quite incompatible opinions about social security. Both panels depended heavily on technical advice and recommendations from "outside" experts or social security administrators instrumental in shaping earlier developments.[53] They found themselves weighing the merits of various policy options that had already been fully discussed in the political arena. Furthermore, just as the NCSSR had to deal with election-year politics and a budget crisis, so, too, the first Social Security Advisory Council found its proceedings influenced by congressional opponents and grassroots pressures beyond its control.[54]

Because the 1937–8 Advisory Council and the NCSSR embodied a broad range of moderate and partisan positions, it was impossible to predict what proposals might emerge as part of a consensus. In the final analysis, "solutions" were found not because real differences of opinion were settled but because members knew how and when to voice their reservations in ways that could be resolved by compromise.[55] Particularly in the recent crisis, constructive reform was possible only because policymakers eschewed intellectual debate to seek agreement on technical changes in the existing program.

Prior to the NCSSR's November meeting, for instance, Lane Kirkland and Claude Pepper never believed that the commission could reach a satisfactory agreement. Both thought that the Democrats could get a better deal by making their case in Congress after the commission had expired.[56] After the November meetings failed to produce a compromise, other commissioners increasingly doubted that the problems could ever be "solved." But Alexander Trowbridge and his staff at the National Association of Manufacturers went ahead and crafted seven different sets of options based on Senator Heinz's compromise strategy and Robert Myers's cost estimates.[57] Robert Ball, meanwhile, believed that the commission needed a fresh option that would keep benefits and tax increases to manageable size. The initial reaction to Ball's proposal to tax the benefits of higher-income retirees, however, was as lukewarm as had been the reaction to the Trowbridge memoranda.[58]

Still, in spite of formidable resistance, administration and commission negotiators were able to achieve a compromise. By early January, the major remaining difficulty was how to satisfy the Democrats' desire to increase social security tax revenues while assuring conservatives that no new taxes would be imposed.[59] Ball proposed moving the previously mandated 1985 tax hike to 1984 (providing a one-time refundable tax credit for employees) and switching some of the 1990 tax hike to 1989 and 1988. In the delicate eleventh-hour negotiations, therefore, it appeared that the stalemate could be broken only if the principals accepted highly technical procedural changes. As Ball and White House officials worked to convince Kirkland and Pepper, a rebellion broke out on the Republican side. The White House realized that whatever it did would cost it some support. Alienating a significant bloc of conservatives on the commission might lose the administration votes in the House later on. Given Republican alarm over the size of the federal deficit, however, it seemed far safer to reduce the size of the budget deficit than to ignore politics entirely by placating ideological conservatives.[60]

The dynamics of social security policymaking required loyalty to the compromise once it had been agreed on. I do not mean that Congress had no opportunity to make significant changes. (After all, the commission had not proposed specific measures to shore up the Hospital Insurance Trust Fund, because that task had not been part of its original charter. Nonetheless, Congress made

Medicare reform a major feature of the 1983 amendments. Something of the same sort happened in 1939, when Congress had reworked the benefit structure and tax schedule proposed by the Advisory Council and the Social Security Board.[61]) Nevertheless, in both major crises, once the major figures in government committed themselves to a set of recommendations – or at least accepted them as the best option available – then serious criticism could have jeopardized the legislative outcome.

During debate over the 1939 amendments, critics complained that "the American people should know that we are now changing rulings in the middle of the game."[62] But supporters hammered away at persuasive themes: The federal government had a responsibility to care for the aged; more than ever before, American families were being guaranteed a measure of protection.[63] Furthermore, in 1939, lawmakers who wavered were reassured about the provisions before them by the fact that many paralleled ideas endorsed by the nonpartisan Social Security Commission (underwritten by the Hearst newspaper chain) and by the Brookings Institution; supporters pointed out that experts of different political and economic orientations supported this package.[64] Similarly, both sides tried to limit debate on the 1983 amendments. A House resolution in essence permitted no further discussion except on whether to raise the retirement age or increase the tax rate in 2010. As a result, the House finished its work on H.R. 1900 on schedule.[65] In a mere forty-one hours of debate during six days the Senate considered seventy-two amendments and approved forty-nine changes.[66]

Haggling over technical matters increasingly took precedence over thoughtful discussions of the issues. Floor managers, whose job it was to get a complex bill enacted, appreciated such restrictions. Deliberations proceeded faster. It was easier to deflect unwelcome proposals. Shrewd politicians could "demonstrate" that the alternative they favored most clearly built on existing principles and procedures. Unfortunately, this strategy had a stiff price: It meant that the moment for thoughtful consideration of broader issues had passed. "Cutting the best deal" became an end in itself.

3. *In planning for the future, social security policymakers try to satisfy current concerns by reaffirming principles they expect to endure – without fully appreciating the limitations of this approach.* Policy options result from the historical interplay of numerous economic, political, legal, social, and cultural factors. Thus, to understand why social security provisions were designed as they were, why they operate as

they do, and how these rules and regulations may influence the future requires a sense of how past policies developed.

There never has been a genuine consensus in this country over what constitutes a "credible and sound" social security program. Americans do count on receiving something when they become disabled, widowed, or retired, but there is no empirical basis for asserting that they plan their lives around current rules. Furthermore, precisely because the structure of American life will continue to change in the future, policymakers must act as if they can anticipate later developments, knowing full well how little they can do so. In presenting its views on the long-term financial status of the social insurance program, the 1938 Advisory Council solemnly affirmed that "we should not commit future generations to a burden larger than we would want to bear ourselves."[67] Similarly, as he signed the 1983 amendments, President Reagan declared that "the changes in this legislation will allow Social Security to age as gracefully as all of us hope to do ourselves, without becoming an overwhelming burden on generations still to come."[68] To court future generations is politically expedient, but claiming to know the burden they have been spared borders on hubris.

The 1939 amendments represented a major turning point in the evolution of social security: They changed key provisions of the original measure before they ever took effect. The 1983 amendments may perform a similar historic function. Enacted after it became painfully clear that social security had entered a new phase of development, reforms were needed if the program was to age "gracefully." Policymakers in both crises were aware that their actions would have profound and long-lasting consequences, but they could not have known what they were to be. Indeed, given the way they defined the problems they sought to solve, and given the Byzantine maneuvers needed to arrive at consensus, it is a wonder that any of their actions make sense *except* in terms of the politics of the moment. In both situations Congress appeared determined to alter social security substantially, even as it portrayed its reforms as modest in scope.

"Nobody is enamored with this solution," acknowledged James Baker the day after the NCSSR concluded its deliberations. Still, the White House claimed that it had gained from the compromise. Amid rumors that Reagan's administration was in "disarray," Baker hailed the social security package as "a reassertion of leadership by the President" that "knocks down the idea that Ronald Reagan cannot govern this country on a bipartisan basis."[69] At least it helped

defuse his immediate budget problems. Based on the commission's remedies, Reagan and his associates projected a $169 billion
smaller deficit between 1984 and 1989. The six-month delay in
cost-of-living adjustments for social security beneficiaries was
extended to other entitlement items in the budget, including the
food stamp program and black-lung disability program.[70]

The Democrats were also pleased that a compromise had been
reached. All along they had wanted to placate fears that the system
was "bankrupt" or that its flaws could not be remedied. Confirming the nation's commitment to federal old-age insurance meant,
Alicia Munnell believed, that "younger people have gained in an
important respect." Pragmatists put the Democrats' concessions
in as favorable a light as possible. "These are changes in law,"
declared Wilbur Cohen, "but none of them are fundamental changes
or unreasonable in light of the situation."[71]

The parallels I have drawn between the 1930s and the 1980s may
not be predictive of the long run. The 1939 amendments proved
their value by working in the nation's best interest. Yet the 1937–8
Advisory Council and the Seventy-fifth Congress cannot take
full credit for what happened. Postwar America's growth and
prosperity enabled officials to broaden protection and increase
benefits for several decades. This fortuity was not anticipated in
1939. Precisely because growth between 1950 and 1972 came so
easily, policymakers rarely had to make critical choices. They were
increasingly inclined to build on past precedents, confident that
destiny was on their side.

The consequences of the 1983 amendments cannot be forecast
with any degree of accuracy. History, of course, does not repeat
itself. Unlike FDR and his New Dealers, President Reagan and his
administration expressed doubts about the system's future *after* the
amendments they supported became law.[72] When social security
became an issue in the 1984 presidential debates, both sides chose
to score political points based on recent events rather than to say
how they would deal with the program in the future.

Now that social security has come of age, it simply cannot operate as in the past. The cost of maintaining or increasing benefit
levels can no longer be underwritten by extending coverage to
new categories of workers, for nearly every wage earner now contributes to the system. Nor does it still make sense to insist that
social security is self-financed: The public will be outraged if they
are taxed more and more to pay for entitlements that they doubt
they will ever receive themselves. Technical "fixes" may rectify

anomalies that penalize certain sectors of the electorate, but they will not allay nagging doubts about the essential purposes of social insurance in America.

This review of the historical record should provide new insight into how well the various provisions of 1983 mesh with social security's evolution to date. What impact will changing the retirement age have on older workers' employment opportunities? Will taxing social security benefits make it possible to reduce the economic hardships of the needy aged without being unfair to those who pay the new taxes? Are women and disadvantaged minorities treated fairly? Can the health care needs of the elderly still be paid for in the same way that income-maintenance programs are financed? Now that social security is fifty years old, a basis for judgment exists that was lacking in 1939. The time has come to think through hard problems that have never been fully addressed – much less resolved – in order to rejuvenate a vital institution that has come of age in a rapidly aging society. A new vision of social insurance can grow out of 1983's revisions.

PART II

Current social security issues in historical perspective

5

Retirement under social security

In 1983, Congress changed social security's "normal" retirement age in order to save the system itself. After considerable debate and by close margins, lawmakers raised the eligibility age for full benefits from sixty-five to sixty-six gradually by 2009, and then to sixty-seven by 2027. People could still take early retirement at age sixty-two, but with larger reductions in their social security benefits.[1] Two changes in the retirement earnings test were also approved. Starting in 1990, beneficiaries between the ages of sixty-five and sixty-nine would have their benefits reduced by only $1 for every $3 (not $2, as under the present law) they earned over prescribed limits. Higher credits for delayed retirement would commence in 1990, rising from the current 3 percent per year to 8 percent for those who attain the normal retirement age in 2008.

These changes were considered enough to eliminate one-third of social security's projected long-term deficit. Even the higher benefits for workers who postponed their retirement were expected to cost little, or possibly result in some savings. For if healthy and productive workers could be induced to stay in the labor force past the official retirement age, social security's trust funds would accumulate more revenue than anticipated, because fewer workers would be drawing on current reserves.[2]

The retirement provisions of the 1983 amendments conform to the pattern of incremental policymaking that has long served social security. Once again the experts found technical expedients for raising new money without ruffling many feathers. Over the previous decade, blue-ribbon panels had increasingly endorsed a higher retirement age. Vociferous opposition by lobbies for the aged had made the idea a dead letter until the entire social security program appeared to be in jeopardy. The new legislation might not have passed at all, however, had its designers not delayed the full effect of the new retirement age until well into the twenty-first century. By the same token, the new law's incentive for delayed retirement was purposely written in such a way as to preclude an increase in overall expenditures. It looked almost like a free lunch – at least up close. Unfortunately, the cleverness of the solution obscured the fact that larger questions about social security's meaning and purpose had again been postponed until the Greek calends.

A frank, open-ended discussion of what retirement under social security means is long overdue. For behind the smokescreen of cost–benefit analyses and seemingly minor administrative adjustments lingers substantial disagreement about the wisdom of raising the retirement age. Eight members of the NCSSR mustered a variety of arguments to justify the move:

> The major reasons for this proposal are: (1) Americans are living longer; (2) Older workers will be in greater demand in future years; (3) The disability benefits program can be improved to provide cash benefits and Medicare to those between age sixty-two and the higher normal retirement age who, for reasons of health, are unable to continue working; (4) Because the ratio of workers to beneficiaries is projected to decline after the turn of the century, younger generations are expected to pay significantly increased taxes to support the system in the twenty-first century. An increase in the normal retirement age will lessen the increase; (5) Given sufficient notice, coming generations of beneficiaries can adjust to a later retirement age just as earlier generations adjusted to age sixty-five.[3]

The five NCSSR members selected by the Democratic leadership of Congress were not convinced. They wanted to retain the full range of retirement options as they were, and viewed any rise in the retirement age as a benefit reduction. "The cut would be concentrated on those unable to work up to the newly set higher age and on those unable to find jobs. It would cut protection for those now young, the very group being asked to pay in more and for a longer period of time."[4] The Democrats thus appealed to their traditional New Deal base among lower-income workers to block the changes. Advocates for the disabled and elderly also joined the fight during congressional debate. The battle lost, a coalition of interest groups and liberals vowed not to lose the war; they mounted an assault to repeal the 1983 amendments before they go into effect.

The opposition may win yet, because the recent shift in retirement policy goes against long-term American trends and contemporary patterns here and abroad. During the last half century, age sixty-five has taken on a significance far beyond its original administrative utility. Turning sixty-five connotes the onset of old age in American popular culture. People *say* they intend to retire at that age, but senesence defies precise chronology, and most workers now retire "early." Moreover, developments in western Europe have been running quite contrary to the United States' decision to legislate a higher retirement age: France changed it from sixty-five to sixty in 1982; Great Britain and Italy, in a move to counter unemployment, also lowered the age required to receive full benefits; strikes broke out in Germany over the issue.[5] New ideas about old age and retirement may arise once the significance of the arbitrary sixty-five-year benchmark is recognized as just that – arbitrary.

Because earlier retirement is becoming the norm, it is important to ask: Will American workers alter their retirement plans to accord with the new social security rules? Probably not: The link between official policies and retirement behavior is less straightforward than commonly assumed. Hence, the question of when people should become eligible for Title II payments requires further inquiry. Does it make sense to raise the retirement age? Are even bolder steps (elimination of mandatory retirement and the earnings test itself, for example) warranted?

Establishing a "normal" retirement age under social security

Retirement was uncommon until the twentieth century. As late as 1900, roughly two-thirds of all men over sixty-five were still gainfully employed. Most were engaged in agriculture. Since then, there has been a marked departure of older people from the labor force. According to census data, 55.6 percent of all aged men were in the labor force in 1920, 42.2 percent in 1940, 28.9 percent in 1960, 23.9 percent in 1970, and 18.4 percent in 1981.[6] Comparable employment patterns exist for aged women. Despite the fact that more than 50 percent of all women over eighteen are gainfully employed, only 8 percent of all women over the age of sixty-five were in the labor force in 1981.[7] Demographic factors do not explain the decline in the proportion of older people at work. Nor have progressive technological improvements systematically displaced the elderly.[8] Alternate sources of economic support have been paramount. In the 1930s, many older people had to rely on relatives and local agencies to make ends meet; earnings and assets were the major sources of income for the elderly minority with cash income. In 1967, by contrast, 12 percent of the elderly relied on public assistance, and only 27 percent of them earned wages or salaries or were self-employed; 89 percent of all persons over sixty-five received monthly benefits from public and private retirement programs; and 15 percent could count on veterans' benefits. By 1980, social security accounted for 40 percent of all income received by aged households, up from 31 percent in 1962.[9]

Although social security clearly affects the structural context in which the retirement decision is made, one must avoid making hasty inferences about what the statistics just cited reveal. Have OASI entitlements simply reduced the elderly's need and desire to work? Or do they also serve as an instrument of social control – a means to justify the discharge of "superannuated" workers? If retirement under social security has always fulfilled more than one function, as I contend, those functions merit closer examination.

Apparently simple administrative decisions – such as the adoption of age-specific criteria to determine eligibility for social security benefits – often masked genuine disagreements within policymaking circles. The principle of requiring people to stop working or offering them the option to do so because they had reached a certain age had already been established in public and private retirement plans here and abroad.[10] Although the Committee on Economic Security had selected sixty-five as the cutoff for the new social security measure, Congress heard expert testimony challenging this choice. Some witnesses urged that the age of retirement be raised to seventy, but this recommendation did not make much sense during the Depression. During the Senate hearings, a compelling case was made for making retirement benefits available at age sixty. "Old age, in the physiological sense, may not begin until sixty-five or even seventy," observed Thomas Kennedy of the United Mine Workers. "But economic old age, in this age of mechanical conveyors, begins at a much earlier period."[11] William Green, president of the American Federation of Labor, contended that setting the age of eligibility at sixty would not greatly increase the number of potential beneficiaries.[12] Congressional leaders disagreed. They feared that additional costs entailed by expanding the pool of social security recipients might jeopardize chances for enacting the omnibus bill. Thus, selecting sixty-five as the benchmark for "retirement" under social security was the result of compromise; at the center of a range of plausible options, it satisfied policymakers' need for an administrative cutoff point.

Far more intense debate focused on whether or not those entitled to retirement benefits should be *required* to cease working. The bill submitted by the Committee on Economic Security included a provision drafted by its general counsel, Thomas Eliot, stating that "no person shall receive such old-age annuity until . . . not employed by another in a gainful occupation." Middleton Beaman, legislative counsel to the House of Representatives, objected to this requirement because he thought it would be too difficult to administer. As a result, the House Ways and Means Committee did not stipulate that one retire in order to qualify for an annuity.[13] After hearing additional testimony, members of both houses concurred that Title II of the 1935 Social Security Act should not serve as a compulsory retirement mechanism. Because old-age insurance was to replace income "lost" because of retirement, however, the Social Security Board was authorized to regulate the withholding of pensions from those who "received wages with respect to regular employment."[14]

The wording and thrust of the 1939 amendments reaffirmed and sharpened the purpose of the "retirement test" established in the original act. Instead of defining the vague term "regular employment," the law set a limit on how much a person could make each month and still receive a pension. Once again a technical decision followed extensive consideration of opposing viewpoints. Arguments first advanced in 1935 by the Townsendites and by others favoring universal mandatory retirement at some prescribed age were reiterated in the 1939 hearings.[15] Congress also listened to experts who thought that *any* disincentive to employment in late life was counterproductive and who therefore wanted to eliminate the retirement test entirely. "The average elderly person is far happier and healthier if engaged in his usual occupation than he is if he retires from active work," argued Dr. Wilford I. King of New York University's School of Commerce. "One of the outstanding problems before the nation at present is, therefore, how to keep persons over sixty years of age engaged in productive work as long as possible, thus preventing them from becoming burdens upon the younger members of society."[16] The idea that older workers could still be productive, and that their mental and physical well-being could be prolonged through gainful employment, directly challenged the view that the aged constituted a drag on the economy.

If policymakers had wanted to force older people out of the labor force, they could have reversed their earlier stance on the basis of evidence presented in 1939. They declined to do so, but many issues nevertheless remained unresolved. Rather than try to reconcile conflicting assessments of older workers' worth, law-makers pitched the debate on a more pragmatic level. The primary function of the retirement test, in their view, was "to prevent the labor market from being depressed by subsidizing wages by means of the old-age benefit."[17] Imposition of an earnings ceiling was policymakers' response to the concerns of union officials, business executives, and representatives of insurance companies. All these leaders worried that if an appreciable number of social security beneficiaries continued to be employed on a full-time basis, their presence in the marketplace might tempt employers to reduce the going wage rate for younger people.

No subsequent attempts to alter the sixty-five-year-old baseline made any headway until the 1950s.[18] Under the 1956 amendments to the Social Security Act, however, widows became eligible for full-rate benefits at age sixty-two. Retired working women and wives could opt for reduced benefits between the ages of sixty-two and sixty-five.[19] Not surprisingly, once there was a precedent, men pressed for comparable benefits: Beginning in 1961, working men could elect to take "early" retirement between the ages of sixty-two and sixty-five at an actuarially reduced rate equal to that for women. Note that these amendments reinforced the significance of the sixty-five-year benchmark, because only at that age could "full" *retirement* benefits be initiated. Still, these departures from a single age criterion constituted an important departure from the "normal" retirement cutoff.

The murky relationship among disability, superannuation, and retirement under social security

Not every worker is healthy enough to stay in the labor force until the "normal" retirement age. Disability and poor health have always affected employment in late life. Historically, the consequences of "superannuation" depended on occupation. The concentration of older people in the agricultural sector in the eighteenth and nine-teenth centuries, for instance, offered the aged a measure of protection and security.[20] As farming declined as a source of employment, in both absolute and relative terms, workers in failing health found it harder to hang on to their jobs. The situation for factory workers was particularly grim. Some stepped down and assumed more menial or custodial tasks in order to avoid destitution. Even during periods of comparatively stable employment they were often forced into retirement as their health declined.[21]

The Committee on Economic Security commissioned two reports in 1934 on "invalidity insurance." Although the committee recommended an extension of public health services to prevent illness, it urged that consideration of disability insurance be postponed until the matter had been studied more fully.[22] Temporary and permanent disability programs were included in the Wagner-Murray-Dingell bill defeated in the midst of World War II. And because disability insurance was viewed as a Trojan horse to usher in a national health insurance system, proposals during the Truman years met with great opposition from life insurance lobbyists and the American Medical Association.[23]

It was not until the 1950s that proposals for a federal disability program were tied to the nation's retirement system. In the absence of such a link, many potential beneficiaries discovered that they had not become "permanently insured" prior to disability. Thus, they lost all claims to social security benefits. Some disabled people were penalized for their incapacity because their years of disability were counted as years of zero contributions in determining retirement benefits.[24] The case for disability insurance rested heavily on the idea that it involved payments to unfortunate individuals who had to "retire early" because of permanent mental or physical impairment. Social security officials were persuaded that "it seemed eminently fair not to have your Social Security benefits drop because of a period of nonearning resulting from disability. It seemed humane. It didn't cost much. It paralleled a common provision in private health insurance."[25]

Though the fight for further liberalization and expansion of the disability program quickly developed a logic of its own, lawmakers never distinguished sharply between the risks associated with disability and old age. This was a deliberate decision: By associating the causes of retirement with the conditions of disability, reformers were able to surmount long-standing opposition to broadening the concept of social insurance. The disability program further reinforced the significance of age sixty-five as the retirement benchmark.[26] That such an easy transition from one program to the other was institutionalized into the system suggests that the health factors that caused "disability" and "retirement" were closely related in legislators' minds. Ironically, however, seemingly precise age-specific boundaries left significant gaps in protection. All too often, criteria stemmed from political compromises or administrative convenience rather than from a candid assessment of reality.[27] Bureaucratic arrangements thus made it harder to capitalize on social security's transgenerational features in providing continuous protection throughout life.

Confusion over liberalizing the "retirement test"

Congress has periodically liberalized the "retirement test," but only after ensuring that changes would have minimal impact. In the 1950 amendments, for instance, the amount that a person could earn and still collect social security was raised from $15 to $50 per month; beneficiaries over age seventy-five were exempt from any earnings test. Two years later the ceiling was raised to $75 per month. The 1954 amendments increased the ceiling on annual covered wages to $1,200 and permitted beneficiaries over the age of seventy-two to earn as much as they could without affecting their pensions. A 1960 amendment to the Social Security Act retirement test reduced Title II benefits by $1 for every $2 of earnings from $1,201 to $1,500, and $1 for each $1 of covered wages over $1,500. Amendments between 1961 and 1972 gradually raised the ceiling, but in 1972 it was still less than $2,100. The 1973 social security amendments automatically adjusted the annual earnings ceiling, beginning in 1975.[28]

Congress made these changes in part because it faced steady pressure from advocates of increased opportunities for older workers in the labor force. Debate over liberalizing the retirement test, however, did not focus on older people's ability or right to work.[29] The cumulative effect of changes in the retirement test was to make older people calculate the relative advantages of staying on the job or receiving Title II payments. If they wanted to work full time past sixty-five, they had to forgo a significant percentage of their earned social security benefits unless they were fairly "old." Otherwise they had to rely on part-time employment or find a job in which wages were not subject to social security taxes, so that total covered earnings would not exceed the prescribed maximum.

The notion that people over the age of sixty-five should receive credit for each year they postpone collecting Title II benefits also has a checkered legislative history. Beginning in 1940 and terminating in 1950, 1 percent was added to the basic pension for each year of coverage in and after 1937 in which an employee earned at least $200 of creditable wages. This, incidentally, enabled those working after sixty-five to augment the size of the benefit they would have received at that age. The chief justification for this provision was not that it enhanced job opportunities for the elderly; rather, policymakers sought to increase the reserve fund of a still-immature system. To establish a set of "flexible retirement" options around the sixty-five-year baseline, Social Security Commissioner Arthur Altmeyer recommended that the monthly benefit be increased for anyone who deferred retirement after reaching sixty-five.[30] But proposals of this sort did not receive serious attention until the late 1960s. As part of the major changes enacted in 1972, benefits were increased by $\frac{1}{12}$ percent for each month between the ages of sixty-five and seventy-two for which no benefits were received, retroactive to 1970. In 1977 this provision was further liberalized: For each month after 1981 that a worker between sixty-five and seventy-two deferred retirement, his or her Title II benefit would be increased by $\frac{1}{4}$ percent.[31] The retirement-credit principle advanced by the NCSSR and embodied in the 1983 social security amendments, therefore, builds on fairly recent precedents.

The analysis thus far reveals a pattern of policymaking that avoided serious effort to resolve conflicting opinions about the meaning of retirement. Technical amendments masked philosophical differences. Changes were made in retirement-age criteria to advance other social security priorities. Hence, to study shifts in the significance of "retirement" as a social institution it is necessary to go beyond noting *when* changes took place. It remains to be determined which interest groups pressed for particular social security amendments. The assumptions and objectives of major contestants in the policy arena must be compared.

Convergent and divergent meanings of retirement

There is no consistent or persistent cleavage over retirement as an institution, whether between Democrats and Republicans, between "insiders" and "outsiders" in the policy elite, between business and labor, or between young and old. But there have long been differences of opinion *across* segments of the population and *within* special-interest groups. Moreover, specific positions changed over time. Thus, insofar as various groups have viewed retirement in complementary ways, agreement has often been coincidental.

Views expressed by policymakers

Partisan differences are a likely source of friction over social security. It would be reasonable to assume, for example, that the split between NCSSR Republicans and Democrats resulted from a long-standing divergence of opinion. Republicans, who have traditionally extolled the work ethic and urged restraint in public spending, might be expected to support measures that would encourage older people to stay at work. Democrats, who count heavily on the votes of organized labor and older Americans, might well oppose any step that would reduce benefits for these constituencies. The historical record prior to the mid-1970s, however, reveals little precedent for a cleavage along party lines when retirement is at issue. Nor were there serious rifts within bureaucratic circles over the meaning of retirement under social security. Successive changes in the age-specific eligibility criteria for Title II benefits enjoyed overwhelming bipartisan support in both houses.

Moreover, until quite recently, the principle of a social security retirement test has not been subject to much debate. Conventional wisdom held that any "solution" to social security's financial problems required either increasing taxes or cutting benefits. But the experts knew how to avoid these stark alternatives; they were accustomed to recommending technical changes without immediate impact as a way around politically unpalatable choices. It was in this context that raising the retirement age at some future date gained support among policymakers. The 1975 Advisory Council on Social Security, for instance, alluded to the desirability of a gradual increase in the "normal" retirement age, effective about 2005. Two years later, several members of Congress proposed raising the age from sixty-five to sixty-eight, beginning in 2000. J. J. Pickle, who became chairman of the House Ways and Means Subcommittee on Social Security in 1979, doggedly advocated such an increase. With varying degrees of reluctance, every major panel after 1979 endorsed a formula for moving beyond the baseline of sixty-five. Only a narrow majority of the 1979 Advisory Council on Social Security wanted to postpone the payment of old-age insurance benefits for those contributors who were then under age forty-five. The President's Commission on Pension Policy urged in 1981 that managers of private plans voluntarily "increase their normal retirement age in tandem with social security."[32] The report of the National Commission on Social Security (March 1981) recommended that, beginning in 2001, a worker would have to reach the age of sixty-five and a quarter to claim full OASI benefits and Medicare; sixty-eight would become the "normal" retirement age by 2012.[33] The Committee for Economic Development (CED), among other private groups, pressed for legislation along these lines.[34]

Nevertheless, to cite a string of quasi-official endorsements calling for a rise in the "normal" retirement age does not demonstrate that policymakers adopted a cogent position on the issue. On the contrary, equivocation and rhetoric have been the surrogates for a coherent policy on the role of older workers in the labor force. Political developments, in fact, often heightened only the *potential* for debate over the efficacy of social security's retirement test. The Older Americans Act (1965), for instance, promulgated the right of elderly people to "adequate income" and the "pursuit of meaningful activity." Two years later, however, Congress enacted the Age Discrimination in Employment Act, which protected workers between the ages of forty and sixty-five from discriminatory hiring and employment practices – but the law did not apply to workers over sixty-five. It took ten years to amend this act in order to enhance job opportunities of older people. Even then, coverage was extended only to age seventy, and several categories of workers were exempted.[35] Legislators might have altered the retirement age in response to executive-branch initiatives. They did not do so because powerful lobbies backed the current retirement test.

Officials have not yet reached a consensus on the worth of older workers. All the same, federal programs rarely emphasize labor opportunities for the elderly. Government agencies charged with protecting mature workers against age discrimination are understaffed and overwhelmed by cases. The Comprehensive Employment and Training Act (CETA) enacted in 1973, moreover, initially did not require participating employers to provide jobs for older workers. Reagan's Job Training Partnership Act (JTPA), which replaced CETA in 1983, requires states to allocate only 3 percent of federal funds to this constituency. Various federal programs are tailored to the job-related needs of economically disadvantaged groups, but the United States (unlike many European nations) has not promulgated an explicit "national older worker policy."[36] Unless public officials conjoin retirement policies to the broader human-resource needs of our society, it is unlikely that a fight will erupt over the future of older workers. It is easier to pretend that older workers' needs can be neatly separated from those of younger people.

The complementary stances of business and labor

Business executives and labor officials often take divergent positions about workers' rights and benefits, and so they might well be expected to oppose each other over the retirement criteria in public and private pension programs. But business and labor have actually taken complementary positions; both sides saw an advantage in creating and enforcing age-specific criteria inducing workers to "retire." When the interests of the two groups have diverged, their differences are best explained in light of specific challenges facing union negotiators and corporate managers, not because of some larger power play between business and labor. Hence, by 1973, roughly half of the nonagricultural labor force was subject to mandatory retirement. Most employers in the private sector chose age sixty-five, whereas seventy was the common standard for public employees.[37]

Developments during the past fifteen years forced both businesses and unions to reevaluate their post–World War II views on mandatory retirement programs. The rising costs of social security, as well as the passage (and extension) of the Age Discrimination in Employment Act, have led some corporate executives to ask whether or not they can still afford to retire workers at sixty-five. Management chafes at the "hidden" costs of early retirement (particularly if the superannuated worker is to be replaced), because it has to make periodic adjustments in pension benefits for former employees and, in many instances, for their surviving spouses.[38] Human-resource studies indicate that employing people over the age of fifty increases rather than reduces productivity and that chronological age per se is a poor predictor of job performance. Turnover, training, and personal absences usually are much lower among older workers than among younger ones. As a result, more and more companies have experimented with part-time work and "flexi-job" concepts to encourage some of their employees to work past "normal" retirement. Retaining and retraining employees past the age of sixty makes more sense than ever before.[39] Nonetheless, the slow-growth economy, inflation of labor costs, the persistence of negative stereotypes about age – all still restrain the extension of working life.

More than is evident in public debate, personnel managers give diametrically opposed estimations as to how older workers "fit" into broader employment patterns. Corporate America's view of retirement changed as the impact of demographic and technological trends, poor economic performance, and new federal regulations and tax laws became more widely felt. There will probably be even more doubt among business leaders when addressing the future. By 2000, that part of the work force between ages twenty and thirty-four is expected to drop from 45 percent to 35 percent. This demographic trend could create a new need for older workers. Some economists think that the limited education of the elderly makes them less desirable than younger workers; others predict that the decline of the aged in the labor force will be stabilized or reversed as those with higher educational attainment and work experience in the service sector approach old age.[40]

Thus far, unions have been less receptive than business to modifying the social security system in any way that would encourage or force older people to remain in the labor force. Probably the strongest and most cogent defense of the status quo has been made by the American Federation of Labor/Congress of Industrial Organizations (AFL-CIO), which has mounted a campaign against raising the retirement age. Lane Kirkland was influential in convincing Democratic members of the NCSSR to oppose the Republican proposal to raise the retirement age. Even though Congress has raised the "normal" retirement age in the twenty-first century, Kirkland considers the measure a mirage-style reform that can be rescinded before it actually goes into effect.[41]

Organized labor's stance reflects its twofold belief that it can most successfully appeal to younger workers by reducing their competition from older workers for a limited number of jobs and that it can best serve its elderly constituency by pressing for better health care provisions and disability benefits. Nonetheless, in light of declining union representation in the labor force and correspondingly diminishing influence in the policy arena, some unions may soon find it advantageous to modify their stand on social security in order to attract women and white-collar employees to their ranks. The potential for cleavage along these lines within the labor movement is therefore quite real.[42]

The gray lobby's conflicting signals

During the past fifty years, some lobbyists for older Americans have stressed the gains to be secured if the aged were no longer in the work force. Townsendites urged that people over sixty cease to be gainfully employed. Others in the old-age network, however, have rejected this view, contending that meaningful employment and utilization of the talents of the elderly were the best ways to "salvage old age."[43]

Throughout the postwar period, the gray lobby and scholars investigating old-age problems emitted contradictory signals concerning the trade-off between work and leisure in late life. As the trend toward mandatory retirement accelerated and employees and employers alike expressed greater interest in early retirement options, those committed to improving the elderly's place in society demanded more generous social services and social security benefits. When they talked about improving the "quality of late life," such advocates had the needs of retired people in mind. Yet increasing numbers of economists and critics charged that relegating the aged to leisure might harm not only the elderly but also society at large. "Perhaps the fundamental problem of the aged in industrial societies is that they have no definite place in the social structure," declared Wilbert E. Moore. "That is, there are no regular, institutionally sanctioned responsibilities for their care and social participation which square with both traditional values and the requirements of an industrial system."[44] In the midst of the civil rights movement and Great Society initiatives, many called for greater employment opportunities for the aged and claimed that mandatory retirement schemes were discriminatory. In addition, some gerontologists cited data indicating that many older Americans lacked the economic resources to enjoy a period of leisurely consumption and that failure to attain meaningful social roles after retirement posed severe psychological problems.[45]

The depth of disagreement within the gray lobby has become familiar in recent years. All old-age interest groups oppose reduction of existing benefits and urge that more attention be given to the plight of impoverished senior citizens. But they divide over the meaning of "retirement" under social security. This was particularly evident during the debate over the 1983 amendments. Jacob Clayman, president of the National Council of Senior Citizens, said that raising the retirement age to sixty-seven constitutes "a 13 percent cut in benefits, and is particularly unfair to those who have to perform heavy labor . . . Raising the retirement age was not part of the official compromise package and we are very sorry it was included in the final bill."[46] On the other hand, the elderly's right to work has become a clarion call among activists. Groups such as the Gray Panthers denounce the ageist assumptions embedded in early retirement and mandatory retirement provisions.[47] Unlike other old-age lobbyists, moreover, the American Association of Retired Persons (AARP) endorsed a "work promotion strategy" that would give older people who continued working after age sixty-five more than an 8 percent increase in social security benefits.[48] Academic specialists in the Gerontological Society see merits both in the sixty-five-year-old baseline and in measures to encourage older people to stay at work. They nonetheless present longitudinal studies of retirement patterns as a way of underscoring that *any* modification will have minimal effects on the options of the elderly or the timing of their retirement.[49]

Increasing divergence of opinion among senior-citizen advocates is quite likely. Those who represent middle-class interests may take positions antithetical to those of the working class. Those who advocate special consideration for minorities, older women, or public services workers may well criticize the "typically mainstream" views of older white, male workers and their lobbyists.[50] Thus, perceptions and experiences of older people are by no means homogeneous.

The personal dimensions of retirement

Retirement is a social institution, but it is also a personal experience that varies in cause and timing among individuals. Most workers retire before sixty-five. According to government statistics, the average age of retirement has declined since World War II. For men, it declined from nearly seventy to sixty-four between 1945 and 1979; during the same period, the average retirement age for women dropped from about seventy-three to around sixty-four. Nearly a fifth of those who retired with pensions between 1976 and 1979 did so prior to the sixtieth birthday; some 58 percent of that group entered retirement by age sixty-three.[51]

Surveys indicate that mature workers are far more likely than younger workers to make plans for their later years. But because many factors affecting a retirement decision are beyond individual control, *actual* retirement ages have been consistently lower than *planned* ages during the past twenty years.[52] Millions of older men and women withdraw from the labor force during periods of high unemployment. Although official statistics do not include "drop-outs," government reports and independent studies confirm that the unemployment rate among workers over fifty-five exceeds the national average. Once unemployed, older workers face longer periods of idleness and are more likely to become discouraged about searching for a new job. If rehired, they typically must settle for pay cuts that get relatively larger with advancing age.[53] Thus, diminishing employment opportunities constitute an important reason why the timing of older workers' retirement presently is subject to change.

Insofar as current employment practices discriminate against older workers, social norms also affect the timing of retirement. However, the widening gap between "official" and modal retirement ages suggests that mandatory retirement provisions have recently become less salient to retirement behavior. The proportion of workers *forced* to retire because they reached a stipulated age fell from about 13 percent in 1951 to 4 percent in 1969. In keeping with 1977 testimony, instrumental in extending Age Discrimination in Employment Act coverage from sixty-five to seventy, only 3 percent of all employees' retirement decisions were then due to mandatory retirement.[54] Hence, total abolition of mandatory retirement probably would not affect very many older people. Apparently, more and more people are choosing to retire before they are required to quit. A more complex framework for tracing the impact of policy on the retirement behavior of the elderly is necessary to understand why this is so.

A worker's actual or self-perceived health status has proved to be of decisive influence on why and when a person retires. During the last three decades, poor health has accounted for 51 percent of all retirements; 90 percent of all health-related retirements have occurred before employees reached age sixty-five. Declining health has been cited more frequently by workers in low-paying jobs and lower-status positions in explaining their retirement decisions, as compared with the rest of the population.[55] Because of medical advances and improvements in health care, one might have predicted that the proportion of elderly people afflicted by infirmity or disability should have declined. Although there is some evidence to support this hypothesis, no clear-cut, long-term trend emerges from the data.[56]

Health per se not only influences retirement decisions but also clearly interacts with other factors. Researchers have found that those in relatively poor health are more inclined to retire if they are eligible for early retirement benefits under social security or a private pension.[57] Once retired, moreover, few return to work. A study of the employment availability of recently retired men and women between sixty-two and sixty-seven found that half of them were not in a position to seek jobs because of health problems.[58] Of course, not every health problem is bona fide. "Health" is sometimes used as an acceptable excuse in lieu of other reasons, such as boredom and frustration at work.

Many older people retire because they find themselves psychologically unable to stay on the job. Social researchers have found that people at all ages remain committed to the work ethic and acknowledge that one's job is an essential component of one's identity and self-image. Beginning in the 1960s, however, there was a steady, albeit gradual, decline in job satisfaction. To varying degrees, discontent and "burnout" affected men and women, black and white, young and old. Employees have also felt increasingly locked into their jobs: in 1977, only 20 percent of all workers thought they could find positions with different employers that would offer them pay and benefits comparable to those of their current employment.[59] Retirement thus appeals to those who find their work unattractive.

Policymakers who press for raising the retirement age across the board often forget that few derive the same satisfaction from work as they. Working a year or two more may not matter much to people who like their jobs, but it will impose a psychological hardship on those who long for relief from dull work. And those who choose not to prolong their agony will pay a stiffer price than before, because early retirement benefits will have larger actuarial-reduction factors beginning in 2000.

The financial trade-offs people make between work and retirement vary from case to case. Those who voluntarily retire often do so when they believe that they can get the best return on the money they have put into social security, other retirement programs, or savings. In many cases the retirement decision is dependent on market calculations as well as a judgment about the consequences of taking advantage of flexible benefit provisions.[60] Some think they will get more out of social security by collecting reduced benefits, but starting "early." Others claim that it is smarter to work a little longer in order to boost average monthly pensions, especially because Americans today live longer than ever before.

On balance, however, most older people currently think that it makes sense to retire early, even if they will have less money at their disposal.

It is intriguing to note that the incidence of voluntary retirement has increased for *all* categories of workers – although the economic consequences of their decisions differ markedly. Two Louis Harris surveys provide fascinating subjective assessments of older people's financial situations in 1974 and 1981. More than 85 percent of those interviewed believed that "not having enough money to live on" was a somewhat serious or very serious problem for older Americans. Furthermore, because of persistent inflation, more people in 1981 than in 1974 thought that the aged were worse off than they had been a decade earlier. Yet only 40 percent of the elderly in 1981 personally experienced a lack of money as a serious problem. Not unexpectedly, far greater proportions of blacks (80 percent) and Hispanics (71 percent) and people without pensions (61 percent) felt more vulnerable economically than did whites with incomes over $20,000 or those still at work.[61] Retirement income, though modest, was sufficient for most; 58 percent of the elderly even stated that money was "hardly a problem at all." Only 40 percent of people between the ages of eighteen and fifty-four responded the same way about *their* situations!

Now that retirement is a mass experience, most Americans view a healthful and financially secure retirement as a major goal. The available evidence indicates that a comfortable retirement is now perceived as an earned right. The nearly universal coverage provided under social security, OASDHI's rising benefit levels, the increasing availability of supplementary pensions, and IRS tax credits have afforded older people an unprecedented degree of choice between work and leisure. According to the 1981 Harris survey, 62 percent of all retired people over the age of sixty-five chose when to stop working. (The statistics, of course, vary by race, ethnicity, and gender.) Those with more education and those in the upper income bracket are even more likely to retire by choice. Furthermore, 90 percent of those who had looked forward to retirement felt they had made the right decision by quitting when they did.[62]

Not all those blessed with good health and a decent income choose to retire; a significant minority of older Americans stay in the labor force. One-eighth of all persons over sixty-five work; they represent 2.9 percent of all American workers. Nearly 60 percent of this group are employed in retail trade, service areas, or the professions. Half of the men and roughly three-fifths of the women work on a part-time basis; older people are more likely to be part-time workers than any other age group.[63] There are difficulties associated with this "partial retirement." Those who wish to work part time often have trouble finding jobs. They face age discrimination and receive low pay and few benefits, reflecting the limited number of hours they work. But such work is often the only thing available; 54 percent of the elderly doubted that a "greater availability of regular full-time jobs" would help their employment prospects – a suspicion that many experts believe valid, given the way work and leisure are allocated over the life cycle in highly developed nations.[64]

Despite such constraints, most older people, like younger members of society, wish to remain productive. Thus, it is not unusual that 79 percent of all employed men and women between the ages of fifty-five and sixty-four wish to continue in some kind of part-time paid work after retirement. Nearly half would like different kinds of jobs than their current positions. Slightly more than 80 percent of those between sixty-five and sixty-nine still in the labor force have no appetite for quitting. More and more Americans believe that people should not be forced to leave work on account of age if they want to work and are up to the task. Only 37 percent of the population think that the elderly should make way for the young.[65]

Some of those who no longer hold regular jobs nonetheless add significantly to the nation's stock of goods and services. A growing number serve as expert consultants, charging less than market rates. Others contribute through voluntary associations, providing services that cannot be easily or cheaply obtained in the marketplace and that no public agency is equipped to supply. In 1980 there were roughly 13,000 volunteer organizations with 7 million local chapters; surveys indicate that 69 percent of all urban Americans are willing to engage in such activities.[66] Roughly 20 percent of the population over sixty-five are engaged in some political, church-related, or social activity. Participating in community endeavors serves as a prophylactic against role loss in old age.[67]

Retirement at the individual level, in sum, is characterized by countervailing trends and paradoxes. Fewer older people work full time than ever before; yet there seems to be growing interest in part-time opportunities with flexible hours. Older people are doubtless healthier than earlier cohorts, but many legitimately retire for health-related reasons. Half the elderly population seem anxious for retirement to begin, and the other half dread its onset. How can policymakers significantly influence behavior under such conditions?

Toward a new view of retirement under social security

In general, I think the adjustments pertaining to the "official" retirement age were a constructive step, even though they were designed with cost–benefit ratios and OASDI's long-term deficits uppermost in mind. As a result of these changes, social security can continue basic operations on a more secure financial basis. Those directly affected have ample time to revise their retirement plans. Raising the actuarial adjustment for delayed retirement from 3 to 8 percent means that older people working on a full-time or part-time basis will incur a smaller financial penalty and gain greater incentive for staying in the labor force. Thus, the 1983 amendments make possible a fundamental rethinking of retirement policies in the United States.

However, policymakers still do many "good" things without shedding their myopia as to the consequences. If the trend toward early retirement continues, the gap between policy and the real world will widen. Critics have rightly focused, moreover, on the financial hardship disabled workers may encounter if benefits expected at age sixty-two are further reduced beginning in 2000. Such hardship can be avoided if policymakers acknowledge that key provisions of disability insurance no longer need to be linked to Title II eligibility criteria. Congress must discard its anachronistic view of disability as premature superannuation. Only then can it hope to recover the original vision of social insurance as protection covering every stage of life, rather than a loose assortment of remedies for discrete categories of need.

"Age sixty-five is obsolete," contends Alan Pifer, president emeritus of the Carnegie Corporation. "We need to rethink our attitudes toward retirement age so that public and private business policies are better attuned to the realities of our time."[68] Pifer estimates that a third of the population will be between the ages of fifty and seventy-five by 2010; they will be better educated and in better health than any previous generation. To concentrate on the burdens rather than assets of this group means to squander its talent and vigor, incurring a huge cost in social as well as financial terms. "As a nation, we have no choice but to become concerned about the productivity of these citizens. Their capacity to contribute to the general welfare in the years ahead is enormous. It must not be ignored."[69]

Changes in retirement policy, as this chapter has shown, do not operate in a social and economic vacuum. After all, the range in retirement ages currently available was made possible largely by the existence and elaboration of social insurance in the first place. Though they made key changes in eligibility criteria in 1983, policymakers would be foolish to anticipate a sudden influx of elderly Americans into the labor market. Health problems remain an employment factor that policymakers can assuage, not prevent. It is doubtful that any single set of financial incentives or social pressures would induce many to change their plans.

Retirement is an essential element in a complex and ever-changing set of relationships reflected in – and transformed by – the evolution of social security. And yet the "big picture" is still incomplete. In the course of this chapter, other matters have emerged that merit further considerations. To avoid pitting the interests of the retired against the interests of those who still work, for instance, it is imperative to reevaluate the balance between equity and adequacy under social security. This analysis, in turn, requires a clear sense of how programs for income maintenance and health care in both the public and private sectors are coordinated. The status of women under social security presents itself as a useful point of departure.

6

Social security and the modern American woman

Discussing the changes in retirement age has required primary attention to the needs of "typical" wage earners. This kind of analysis is consistent with the basic principles of social security policymaking. In determining Title II benefits, "there seems to be a consensus of response, in America at least, that the starting point in the procedure is the establishment of normal status."[1] Social insurance, in this view, deals with the major risks that Americans are likely to face during their "normal" working lives. But what happens when the needs of subgroups do not conform to such patterns? Can rules keyed to averages take account of the diversity in employment paths and family relationships in the United States?

Critics claim that social security treats women and minorities unfairly.* True, the same rules apply to everybody, but not all groups live by the same "rules." OASDHI's methods of determining eligibility have evolved in ways that militate against the interests of those whose employment and earnings histories differ from those of "average" white males.[2] Moreover, differences in marital status and life expectancy exacerbate the situation; some benefit unduly, whereas others are penalized by formulas that apply a single – admittedly complex – set of criteria to all.[3]

Public officials have been more responsive to women's demands than to those of minorities. As this chapter shows, both the courts and a succession of high-level panels have sought to eliminate gender discrimination. The NCSSR paid scant attention to the pressing needs of aged minorities, but devoted an entire meeting to women's issues. Members of both parties agreed that inequities

---

*I have concentrated on the treatment of women under social security here and in Chapter 9 and have chosen not to devote a separate chapter to the status of disadvantaged minorities. I recognize that racism and nativism no less than sexism pervade nearly every public policy and social relationship in this country. Social security's putative inadequacies in this area pale by comparison with the injustice the American welfare system has dealt many racial and ethnic groups, however. I could not begin to cover this "American dilemma" in a book primarily about OASDHI policymaking.

had to be corrected, but in light of the overriding need to shore up social security's financing, the commission did not recommend any measures that might greatly increase OASDHI costs. Instead, it fine-tuned eligibility criteria in order to serve the needs of select groups of women. Congress accepted the NCSSR's recommendations and promised to further consider social security's impact on women by the end of the decade.

Women's issues seem to have taken precedence for two complementary reasons. First, minorities have had more pressing matters to deal with than possible biases in their treatment under Title II. Social security as currently understood and administered cannot be applied effectively to such problems as unemployment among the young, illiteracy, broken families, drug abuse, urban decay, and the health care needs of the underclass. Second, race has never been a basis for determining benefits under social security, but gender has. Officials have been adapting Title II coverage and eligibility criteria to reflect the changing roles of men and women in American society ever since the 1930s.

In this area, as in others, incremental policymaking has obscured the inherent tension between social security's insurance and welfare objectives. Lawmakers have tried to provide more protection for "dependents" and better returns for workers without acknowledging the anomalies that have been found to result. Officials have consistently defined gender-specific issues as narrowly as possible, but the outcome has been paradoxical.[4] Social security responds well to problems at the margin, but proves intractable in adapting the system as a whole to the needs of modern women.

The evolution of social security policy toward women

In the 1930s, most women expected to marry and raise children, not to seek careers in the same way that men did. Even then, however, there were many whose situations did not fit that pattern. Little or no attention was paid to the likelihood that women's typical work experiences – the type and length of employment, average size of covered earnings, and age at retirement – often would lie outside parameters drawn up with male workers in mind.

It is not surprising, then, that legislators reinforced women's traditional roles in American society in their effort to bolster the family against the Great Depression. "In the last analysis, security for family life, insurance of an environment in which the rights of children are safeguarded, is the principal objective in an economic security program," declared the Advisory Council to the Committee on Economic Security.[5] Mothers – by choice and by default – have typically taken charge of daily familial activities. More than anyone else, they have maintained a semblance of order in the household, provided care to the young and helpless, and, in general, met the demands of spouses and children before attending to their own special needs and desires.[6] "Mothers' pensions," instituted by Progressive reformers to prevent disruption of the family unit by poverty and to enable primary care-givers to stay at home, were already mandated by law in forty-five states in 1934. Most local governments, however, failed to implement such laws, and those that did often provided inadequate support. Older forms of poor relief and private charity also proved unsatisfactory.

Two titles of the 1935 Social Security Act were created to remedy this situation. Title IV, "Grants to States for Aid to Dependent Children," was designed to strengthen and expand mothers' pensions and to provide state-supported and locally sponsored social services for homeless and neglected children. Congress initially appropriated nearly $25 million to underwrite *one-third* of the payments a state made to care for dependent children under sixteen. The term "dependent children" was broad indeed; it covered all those "deprived of parental support or care" residing instead with relatives – including brothers, sisters, uncles, aunts, and stepparents as well as mothers. Policymakers estimated that at least half of the families on relief – mainly those headed by widowed, divorced, or separated mothers – would be eligible for assistance under Title IV.[7] Under Title V, "Grants to States for Maternal and Child Welfare," $3 million was appropriated in fiscal 1936 to enable states to extend and improve "services for promoting the health of mothers and children, especially in rural areas and in areas suffering from severe economic distress."[8] Through this measure, legislators hoped to lower infant mortality rates, reduce the incidence of death for mothers and babies during childbirth, and improve child hygiene and nutrition. By offering categorical assistance to women, Washington intended to serve the needs of children in a family context without undermining traditional institutional supports.

Women were not accorded special treatment under the 1935 Title II legislation, however. The wages of all employees covered by social security were taxed at the same rate. The formula for calculating benefits was straightforward and gender-irrelevant. Nevertheless, Title II eligibility criteria, benefit categories, and financing principles were all altered by the 1939 amendments. Many women benefited directly from the new provisions. The wife of an insured worker who had retired was eligible for 50 percent of her husband's pension when she became sixty-five. For the first time, survivors' benefits were provided for widows, children under eighteen, and dependent parents. Because some feared that such innovations might greatly increase the long-term cost of the program, advocates made a special effort to reassure fiscal conservatives. The Advisory Council that developed the rationale and justification for the 1939 amendments based its recommendations "on the grounds of cost, internal consistency of the program, and administrative feasibility."

Without question, the most disingenuous arguments were those designed to show that the proposed changes in the benefit formula served the "welfare" goals of Title II without violating familiar "insurance" principles. Married couples needed more resources in old age, proponents claimed, than single people. But in the long run, it was said, most women would accumulate their own wage credits. Legislators were assured that "there may not be one citizen out of 100 who will get the advantage of [the spousal benefit]."[9] Such statements raised few eyebrows, even though they were flatly contradicted by readily available demographic and occupational statistics. When Senator Lundeen (D–Minn.) argued that 60 percent of the men and women who reached the age of sixty would be dead within five years, no one bothered to mention that, even in 1900, a sixty-year-old white man could have expected to live another fourteen years, and a white woman at that age could have expected about fifteen more years of life. Did the senator and his colleagues really think that most people would not live long enough to collect old-age benefits? And why should Congress have supposed that women would increasingly become eligible for Title II benefits on the basis of their own earnings records and thus would not draw "supplementary allowances"? Most women were *not* then building up retirement credits – even the 1930 census reported that only 29.4 percent of all women between the ages of twenty and forty-four were gainfully employed.

Contrary to policymakers' expectations, spousal supplements and widows' benefits quickly became important for older women. The proportion of gainfully employed women had been rising since the late nineteenth century, but rates fluctuated sharply. Women

experienced severe job discrimination during economic downturns and tense labor disputes.[10] During World War II, 6 million
of them entered the labor force. Most, like "Rosie the Riveter,"
were over forty. In 1945 there were – briefly – more women than
men in the civilian labor force.[11] Within a year after the war, however, 2.25 million women had voluntarily given up their jobs, and
another million were laid off in anticipation of veterans reentering
the marketplace. Given their episodic employment opportunities
and continuing family responsibilities, therefore, most older women
had to rely on Title II payments keyed to their husbands' earning
histories. As late as 1952, only about 36,000 (some 2 percent of
those over age sixty-five receiving benefits) were eligible for both
spousal benefits and retired-worker pensions in their own right.[12]

   As it became clear that most women were not able to contribute
to their own old-age security through regular gainful employment, Congress amended existing social security provisions to
provide greater protection to spouses, to widows, and (later on)
to divorcées. These changes were part of a broader effort to liberalize the program, but controversy frequently attended the
movement.[13] As early as 1948, some members of Congress pressed
for reducing the eligibility age for women to receive spousal and
survivors' benefits from sixty-five to sixty. Conservatives rejected
the idea. The House of Representatives voted in 1955 to lower the
minimum retirement age for women from sixty-five to sixty-two,
but HEW Secretary Oveta Culp Hobby testified against this change:
It would not help women in their forties and fifties. Worse, it
would threaten the integrity of the OASI trust fund. A compromise was struck in the form of elaborate actuarial adjustments
enacted in 1956.[14]

   It is worth pointing out that such top-down, incremental
policymaking had its limits, even in affluent times. "The guiding
idea in American social insurance is that the *individual earns* the
right to benefit through payment of contributions by himself and
on his behalf. Nevertheless, the act of contributing . . . can only
bind the government morally, rather than legally, to render specified benefits," as Gaston Rimlinger pointed out in 1961.[15] Legislative and judicial landmarks confirm this judgment. The 1935 law
reserved to Congress "the right to alter, amend, or repeal any
provision" of the Social Security Act. The Supreme Court confirmed this interpretation of entitlements in *Helvering v. Davis* (1937)
and *Flemming v. Nestor* (1960). In the latter case, the plaintiff's husband, a Bulgarian immigrant, had qualified for a Title II pension

before he was deported. The Social Security Administration denied Mrs. Nestor a spousal benefit, because in 1954 Congress had excluded from the receipt of social security benefits anyone deported for Communist affiliations. (Twenty years earlier, Ephraim Nestor had been a Party member.) The Court had made it clear – for legal cognoscenti if not for citizens at large – that social security was not an inviolable property right.

The experts, meanwhile, still held sway: Social security policymakers pressed for incremental changes on the basis of new precedents. Under amendments enacted in 1961, working men became entitled to early retirement benefits; husbands could claim "dependent" benefits at age sixty-two, subject to the same actuarially reduced rates in effect for women; widows' and widowers' benefits were increased 10 percent relatively. Four years later, widows (but not widowers) over sixty became eligible for survivors' benefits, reduced $\frac{5}{9}$ percent for each month under age sixty-two. The 1972 amendments sought to increase benefits and introduce greater parity between certain classes of dependents. The maximum amount a widow or widower past sixty-five could receive was increased to 100 percent of the amount the deceased spouse would have been entitled to had the worker retired at sixty-five; in the case of early retirement of the worker, the actuarially reduced benefit became the maximum amount. Widows and widowers first claiming benefits between sixty and sixty-five received actuarially reduced benefits, subject to the aforementioned maximum.[16]

Policy moved in a new direction when divorce surpassed death as the major reason for marital dissolution. Officials gradually became sympathetic to the plight of homemakers who were too old to build up a substantial earnings record but who had lost their right to benefits based on their former husbands' FICA contributions. In 1965, Congress provided a divorcée over sixty-five a monthly pension of 50 percent of her ex-husband's Primary Insurance Amount (PIA), *if* (1) she had been married to that former spouse at least twenty years, (2) she was not presently married, and (3) she could demonstrate that she was dependent on "substantial contributions" from her ex-spouse in order to live. Divorcées between the ages of sixty-two and sixty-five who met these criteria could qualify for an actuarially reduced benefit. Once this measure was enacted, efforts to liberalize it began.[17] "Dependent" benefits for divorced wives were added to the disability insurance program. The 1972 social security amendments raised payments for dependents of disabled-worker beneficiaries and extended coverage under Medicare, thereby giving women additional protection.

Without discounting the improvements resulting from these gender-specific amendments and regulations, it is important to note that this policy tack obscured the widening gap between policymakers' assumptions about sex roles in American society and prevailing demographic and economic trends. As time passed, it made less and less sense to presume that home and work constituted "separate spheres." Marital and employment patterns were changing. Cultural norms and preferences were transvalued as middle-class America questioned "the feminine mystique."[18] Social security officials did try to accommodate the resultant new needs and divergent circumstances. But insofar as status within and outside of the marketplace was used to determine eligibility under OAS-DHI, anomalies were sure to arise. Compartmentalization of policy objectives reduced the likelihood that the experts would achieve an accurate overview. Focusing on the specific needs of certain categories of "dependent" women – such as widows, displaced homemakers, and mothers with young children – was consistent with the overarching goal of using social insurance to reduce major economic hazards. However, this concern sometimes blinded officials to the possibility that they were ignoring the rights of working women, dependent husbands, and unmarried wage earners. "Adequacy" issues could not be neatly separated from questions of "equity." As a result, social security measures aimed at *protecting people* increasingly seemed at odds with existing rules aimed at *providing equal treatment*.

Efforts to solve the policy conundrum were initiated in various quarters during the 1970s. The Supreme Court ruled on several pivotal cases involving gender-specific rights under social security. Perhaps the most significant case since *Flemming v. Nestor* was *Goldberg v. Kelly* (1970), which guaranteed social security recipients the right to due process – in this instance, a hearing before termination of AFDC benefits.[19] Legal *process* had to be observed, but to what end remained Congress's decision. The word was out: Ensuring women's rights under social security was a matter of political influence as well as of disinterested benevolence from administrators, legislators, and judges. In *Weinburger v. Wiesenfeld* (1975), the Court held in favor of a widower who claimed partial entitlement to his deceased wife's primary benefit on his own behalf (in addition to survivors' benefits received by his children), even though he had not been "dependent" on his wife for support.

Granting women automatic entitlement to "mother's insurance benefits" while denying them to men, in the Court's judgment, violated the right to equal protection under the due process clause of the Fifth Amendment. The ruling was intended to overturn "an archaic and 'overbroad' generalization not tolerated under the Constitution, namely, that male workers' earnings are vital to their families' support, while female workers' earnings do not significantly contribute to families' support." Gender discrimination, then, was objectionable regardless of sex. Critics charged that the justices had substituted a legalistic concept of fairness for the prudent insurance principles that had long obtained under social security.[20]

The critics had a point. The Supreme Court had said all along that Congress had the right to set the rules for OASDHI, but now it appealed to a higher authority – the Constitution itself – to defend due process in an unforeseen way. The unanimous verdict in *Mathews v. DeCastro* (1976) upheld a provision denying benefits to women under sixty-two with responsibility for the children of their former husbands. Women in the same circumstances over the age of sixty-two, by contrast, were eligible. This looks like boxing the compass; the Court, however, reasoned that the constitutional question at stake "is not whether a statutory provision precisely filters out those, and only those, who are in a factual position which generated the congressional concern reflected in the statute," but whether or not equal protection under the due process clause has been violated.[21]

By taking due process this seriously, the Court engaged in its own version of incremental policymaking at a time when social security loyalists were more interested in holding the line than in further expansion. The insertion of gender as a constitutional desideratum threatened to explode a financially precarious institution.[22]

Other federal officials were concerned about gender discrimination in OASDHI as well. Beginning in the late 1960s, researchers in the Social Security Administration systematically investigated how well women were faring under the current law, what foreign social insurance systems did to provide for housewives, and what women's work patterns and future social security benefits were like.[23] The 1975 Advisory Council on Social Security investigated long-term changes in women's socioeconomic status; the 1979 Advisory Council spent more time reviewing the treatment of working and nonworking women than on any other issue.[24] In addition, scholars churned out essays and position papers critical of various inequities in the current system. Many urged that benefits be adjusted to new societal trends and cultural norms.[25]

From this surge of interest emerged a consensus about what caused anomalies in the program: "The current Social Security system treats the worker as an individual for the purposes of building an earnings record and as part of a family unit with dependents for the purpose of paying benefits," a 1977 Task Force on Sex Discrimination reported. "Almost all the inequities in the current system can be traced directly to this approach."[26] The amounts most women received from social security depended on whether the system paid them primarily on the basis of their employment records or on the basis of their status as "dependents" or "care-givers." Because of this, it was difficult to reform the system; treating gender issues in isolation would not suffice. Women, more than men, had been the subjects of previous efforts to provide protection in a manner that transcended age-specific guidelines. As the 1979 Advisory Council noted, "The Social Security system touches on some of the most basic institutions and traditions of American life . . . marriage, the family, care of dependents and survivors . . . and the effect of any major changes in this system must be carefully considered."[27]

An opportunity existed, then, to rethink the enduring objectives of social insurance in light of present-day realities. Competing national priorities and OASDHI's shaky financial status, however, forestalled bold action to accommodate women's diverse needs. The 1981 National Commission on Social Security, for example, advocated "incremental reforms rather than a fundamental restructuring of Social Security benefits."[28] In similar fashion, the National Commission on Social Security Reform proposed four changes affecting mainly disabled and divorced widows and widowers; the total cost was estimated at $1.4 billion between 1983 and 1989. Significantly, these were the only NCSSR recommendations for increased outlays; all its other recommendations would reduce them. In addition, both Republican Mary Falvey Fuller and the commission members selected by the Democratic leadership in Congress issued supplementary statements calling for major reforms to achieve "equitable treatment of women in today's world."[29] Congress approved a proposal requiring the secretary of health and human services "to prepare an implementation report on earnings sharing for social security purposes."[30] Some observers interpreted this as a small but necessary step toward major change in the way social security benefits were calculated. At the very least, the agenda for the next round of debate over women's issues had been blocked out.

Major options

Policymakers have an extraordinary range of strategies to choose from in accommodating social security to the needs of modern American women. Some proposals could be instituted piecemeal. Some would call for a radical restructuring of the entire system; others would necessitate less dramatic changes, but nonetheless would require a shift in priorities. Assessment of two proposals in each category will highlight some of the issues that arise from efforts to alter the treatment of women under OASDHI.[31] The challenge of reform is to avoid entrapment in obsolete assumptions and procedures. Policies need to be sufficiently fluid and flexible to facilitate what has to be done – but also sensitive to the unexpected impact of even the best-laid plans.

Two proposals for fine-tuning the current system

Because they believe that an impressive case can be made for the efficacy of technical adjustments, some experts deny that major reform is necessary. "Change is not always necessarily beneficial, and even when it may be beneficial in some ways, the net effect produced may be harmful," contends Robert Myers.[32] In all major respects, Myers and others argue, the current program is objectively nondiscriminatory toward women.

When critics deplore the antifemale bias they find in Title II operations, defenders of the status quo point out that in some regards the system appears to treat women better than men. In the late 1970s, women accounted for about 28 percent of all payments flowing into the system, but some 54 percent of all benefits went to women.[33] This "gender gap" results from three factors. Women tend to live longer than men and thus collect more in the long run. Because of the progressivity of the benefit formula, moreover, wage-earning women often get back relatively more on their FICA contributions than men because as a group they tend to have lower average covered earnings. Finally, far more women than men receive spousal benefits without themselves having contributed to the system.

Social security loyalists, however, do not regard every provision as sacrosanct. Instead, they suggest adjusting the existing benefit structure and eligibility criteria. Nearly a decade ago, for example, Robert Ball devised such a way to reduce the bias in favor of families with only one wage earner.[34] More recently, Robert Myers has proposed that women divorced after at least five years of marriage be eligible for spousal benefits.[35] But his reasoning that "the absence of deferred-benefit rights for very short marriages broken by divorce does not seem vital, because the individuals involved will almost certainly obtain OASDI benefit rights in other ways" begs the issue.[36] Are the contributions spouses make to one another during a brief marriage to be utterly discounted? And if the salient phrase is "very short marriages," then why not specify two years instead of five? Arbitrary assumptions are hidden behind Myers's adroit handling of the numbers.

An apparently more attractive option proposes that the time a parent devotes to raising young children be "bracketed out" when calculating lifetime average earnings to compute initial social security payments. Periods of life devoted primarily to child care are typically times in which a person earns little or no money. Under the present method of determining average earnings, a worker can drop only the five lowest years after 1950 (or age 21, if later). This puts women at a disadvantage, because they are more likely to be the primary care-givers, to interrupt their careers for their children's sake, and to have relatively low-paying jobs. To deal with this problem, the 1981 National Commission on Social Security devised an ingenious proposal based on the law's special proviso for calculating benefits according to workers' total years of coverage rather than their average covered earnings.[37] On further reflection, one uncovers biases that probably doom this option. Would all unemployed parents with young children automatically qualify? Why should parents get credit for caring for children – but not for their own parents or aged relatives? "Spells of caring," after all, exist over the entire life cycle, and many adults prefer that other adults care for them in times of need. Furthermore, not everyone stands to profit equally from credit for child-care dropout years. The better educated and relatively well-off would gain most from this proposal, because with larger increases in annual earnings, they would "drop" their years of lowest income; mothers who must work as well as care for children would not benefit nearly as much. The paucity of formal child-care arrangements when the federal government is not interested in underwriting them poses additional problems.[38] This proposal thus seeks to redress a penalty currently imposed on middle-class women who raised the baby-boom generation and chose not to work outside the home; it is well intentioned, but inequitable in its potential impact on women in different circumstances.

Radical options

Radical proposals typically start from the premise that only drastic changes in the insurance-welfare mix of OASI can remedy its "inherent" flaws. Advocates of a double-decker or two-tier system of social insurance, for instance, reject joining the "equity" and "adequacy" principles to determine eligibility criteria and benefits. They propose instead that the redistributive and insurance functions of social security be clearly separated. They would pursue social adequacy by providing flat demogrants financed through general revenues to every individual who meets broad and universal criteria; this amount would be supplemented by payments directly related to a social security contributor's (or, in some variants, a couple's) prior covered earnings.[39]

This strategy has an impressive pedigree. Many European countries offered universal grants before they enacted contributory insurance programs. Townsendites and other utopian reformers advocated variations on this idea during the Depression. In the late 1930s, Social Security Administration researchers drafted various double-decker schemes for the contingency that Congress might vote down Titles I and II.[40] In the 1960s and 1970s, before OAS-DHI's recent funding problem reached crisis proportions, experts in the liberal camp advanced the notion of a two-tier approach to social insurance in a series of influential publications. Conservatives have lately recommended phasing out Title II and developing autonomous welfare and insurance programs to help "save" the system.[41] The appeal of the double-decker approach lies in its consistency, administrative flexibility, and political-economic efficiency. In the new structure, the bottom tier of social security would fulfill the "adequacy" objective of social insurance, and the top tier would serve that of "equity." It would therefore be easier, advocates maintain, to establish what the public and Congress judge to be a proper balance between these two goals. A double-decker approach, moreover, would facilitate subsequent reform if the nation decided to raise the "minimal" standards of income support or to establish a different ratio between past employment contributions and future old-age benefits.

A two-tier program would eliminate some current benefit categories and disrupt existing arrangements, inviting criticism on several grounds. "Part of the problem is that any structural reform that does not boost costs must cut someone's benefit one dollar for every dollar by which someone else's is increased. This law of arithmetic may well step over the border between truism and banality, but it does carry the useful reminder that improving benefits for one group necessarily entails either lower benefits for another or higher program costs." [42] Many who currently rely on actuarially reduced spousal and survivors' benefits would be forced to wait until they met the "normal" age of entitlement under most two-tier schemes. Cost–benefit analyses of most such plans indicate that divorced women and widows would receive less than they now receive from social security. Hence, it is not at all clear that this radical reform would really improve the overall treatment of women and the family.

Given budgetary constraints, moreover, it is doubtful that lower-tier benefits would ever be large enough to meet a reasonable criterion of "adequacy." Demogrants would have to be far more generous – and costly – than average SSI grants or even the Title II minimum benefit. (It is worth remembering that neither presently guarantees an income above the official poverty line.) Many fear that to keep universal pensions within manageable bounds would eventually entail means testing. Because general revenues would finance these pensions, demogrants probably would not be automatically indexed to protect recipients against inflation, as is currently the case. Without such protection, recipients would be under tremendous pressure to seek employment. Without supplementary support, standards of living among the neediest segments of the population would fall. In this worst-case scenario, a new set of unfair redistribution patterns would quickly ensue.

Another radical reform, advanced by Rita Ricardo Campbell, builds on the notion that both men and women do in fact expect to spend much of their adult lives in the labor force. Contending that it is anachronistic and unfair to treat a woman as if she were "dependent" on a man's earnings, Campbell proposes phasing out dependent spousal benefits over a thirty-year period and eliminating surviving spouses' benefits within the next half century. To help parents nurture their young, she advocates providing three years of earnings credits to the primary care-giver for each of the first two children. [43] The ultimate goal of this plan, nevertheless, is to provide social security benefits solely on the basis of a worker's *individual* contributions. Those who did not work in covered employment would have to look to SSI, public assistance, or private means. The Campbell plan, in essence, would restore Title II to its configuration in the 1935 legislation. The restructured system would clearly address two complaints about the current program: its low return to the second working spouse and its presumed unfairness to single workers.[44] Under Campbell's plan, all one-earner couples would get lower benefits than two-earner couples with the same total earnings. Adopting this reform would save money: Experts have projected that it would generate long-term savings equal to 1.21 percent of taxable payroll – or roughly two-thirds of the "savings" realized in the 1983 amendments over the next fifty years.[45]

The biggest drawback to basing social security benefits solely on individual earnings is that it would reward "equity" at the cost of other needs. Divorced and separated spouses would clearly suffer. Disabled surviving wives with no covered earnings record would get no benefits; widowed homemakers would have very limited disability protection. These are not groups whose needs can be easily dismissed. In 1978, when the Campbell plan was near the peak of its popularity, 46 percent of all women Title II recipients were entitled to benefits only because of their relationship to a covered wage earner. Another 13 percent were dually entitled, but their spousal benefits exceeded their benefits as workers.[46] Given such data, it is difficult to believe that her plan would improve the overall status of women, especially because it aims to gut social security's welfare features. The Campbell plan is a vision of social insurance long on "equity" but short on "adequacy." And because it entails such sweeping changes in other aspects of the program, most reform-minded policymakers prefer to consider less radical alternatives.

Reforming the system by dealing directly with gender issues

The marginal adjustments loyalists propose will not be enough, according to some who seek improved treatment of women under social security. Like those who advocate a double-decker system or the elimination of spousal benefits, they acknowledge that current eligibility criteria and benefit formulas do not mesh neatly with changes in women's employment patterns and family responsibilities. They accept, however, the rationale for balancing equity and adequacy in the OASI system.

One idea issuing from this camp during the past decade has been expansion of Title II coverage to unpaid homemakers in their own right, rather than continually devising piecemeal protection. Representative Bella Abzug (D–N.Y.) introduced a measure that would provide earnings credits, financed through general revenues, to qualified homemakers. Two years later, Representative Barbara Jordan (D–Tex.) proposed mandatory credits to be financed through taxes paid at the self-employment rate. Around the same time, Representative Martha Griffiths (D–Mich.) made a compelling case for the idea that homemaker credits should replace spousal benefits.[47] Without taking the extreme position that all social security entitlements should depend on individual earnings, homemaker credits would bolster the system's emphasis on "equity." Under this arrangement, benefits could be more closely correlated with payroll-tax contributions: Homemakers would be either underwriting the cost of their retirement through paid employment or receiving credit for work that society deems vital. Such credits would provide a continuous earnings record for homemakers who shift to paid employment, as well as for those who do not.

The homemaker-credit idea has its appeal, but trying to implement it poses serious problems. Who, after all, is primarily a "homemaker"? How many hours of work must one do to qualify? Should it matter if people are homemakers because they cannot find – or choose not to seek – jobs outside the home? How should imputed earnings (credits) be calculated – should they be equal to the prevailing minimum wage? Should they reflect the going rate for domestic help in the area? Should they take into account educational attainments or time spent in on-the-job training? Should a wage-earning spouse who assists the homemaker with chores around the house also build up some credits? Devising an acceptable way to finance such a scheme raises another set of difficulties. Financing homemaker credits through general revenues would be anathema to conservatives, but liberals would be unlikely to support additional FICA taxes because of the burden they would impose on low-earning couples. Finally, it is not at all clear that this innovation would help the most vulnerable elderly women in American society; most experts agree that these credits would yield less to widowed homemakers than they currently receive under social security.[48]

An alternative approach, "earnings sharing," invokes the concept of marriage as an economic partnership to argue that the total covered earnings of married couples should be divided equally between them each year.[49] What distinguishes earnings sharing from other reform proposals (and from the current system) is its disinterested approach to the labor-force participation decisions of married women. Unlike other social security benefit schemes, which provide strong inducements for women to work for pay most of their lives, this plan recognizes that care-giving and homemaking are important tasks – even though not rewarded in strictly monetary terms. Whereas the present system typically gives higher benefits to one-wage-earner couples than to single workers or two-career spouses, earnings sharing would assure fair treatment to people in a variety of situations.[50] Moreover, the current system provides no spousal benefits to those whose marriages end in less than ten years, but under an earnings-sharing plan benefits for the divorced would be based on half the family earnings while married plus individual earnings before marriage and after divorce. Spouses who shift between homemaker status and paid employment, moreover, would gain disability and survivor protection based on the new continuity in their individual earnings records.

There are important precedents for introducing earnings sharing into social security. The Napoleonic Code, which serves as the basis of property laws in several states, stipulates that each spouse has "an undivided present equal interest" in earnings and property acquired during marriage.[51] The Internal Revenue Service adopted the community-property method of income taxation in 1948. Finally, advocates cite an important legal case involving spousal entitlements to a private pension: In California, attorneys can be sued for malpractice if they fail to secure a client's community-property interest in a pension plan.[52] Because such precedents dovetail with changing attitudes toward the economic meaning of marriage, the time does seem right for moving in this direction.

For all its attractiveness, however, earnings sharing would require restructuring some social security provisions. It works best when spouses have equal earning potentials. In all cases, policymakers must weigh the trade-offs involved in emphasizing earnings sharing at the expense of the earnings-replacement principle already established in the benefit structure. Earnings sharing poses questions of fairness and of adequacy for married couples in which only one is eligible for benefits on retirement. All other things being equal, earnings sharing would lower current benefits for one-wage-earner couples by an average of 10 percent.[53] To guarantee widows' and widowers' benefits at least as large as current law allows would entail substantial long-range costs. Indeed, the transitional costs of this program are viewed as a negative feature of the proposal. In the short run, this measure would necessarily increase overall expenses – unless, of course, benefits were cut.[54] Finally, new information on marital status would have to be collected and verified, and new procedures to administer earnings sharing and to update individual earnings records would have to be established.

If the earnings–sharing concept should be adopted, it probably would make more sense to do so over a twenty- to thirty-year period than to change existing rules suddenly. As Congressional Budget Office economist Nancy Gordon cogently argues:

> Although some supporters of earnings sharing may be frustrated at the suggestion of such a gradual phase-in, in the long run we will have achieved the advantages that earnings sharing presents and we will have avoided imposing costs on those whose decisions about family and employment roles were made in past years . . . Such a scheme would avoid disrupting the financial plans of people who will retire in the near future. Further, such a transition would minimize the effect on couples in which the wife never worked.[55]

This approach would also be consonant with recent trends in women's employment patterns: It seems increasingly likely that most women will pursue multiple careers entailing both paid and unpaid work. Furthermore, should the Equal Pay Act be strictly enforced and sex discrimination in the marketplace diminish, the choice of earnings sharing would become all the more appealing.

By the end of the 1980s, Congress will once again take account of the changing roles and needs of women in American society. I think the principle of earnings sharing will be the basis of any significant reform in this area. This proposal, more than any other, directly addresses itself to major policy problems without necessitating radical changes in the status quo. Earnings sharing enjoys increasing support across the political spectrum. Congress has already begun further investigation; a report issued by the House Ways and Means Committee in February of 1985 analyzed the costs and relative merits of several earnings-sharing proposals at great length without endorsing any. This study can provide a wedge for bolder action. If the economy permits, policymakers should seize the opportunity to make the needed adjustments in the balance between social security's welfare and insurance goals.

Whatever happens, however, one must remember that social security is not the only source of retirement income. Indeed, in the next chapter, I shall argue that it is impossible to think broadly about social insurance without considering the roles that private pensions, government-employee retirement programs, and individual savings play in providing economic support. All these are important sources of retirement income, but not all segments of the population have equal access to them. It will even be necessary to assess the salience of gender in this area once more. To improve social security's responsiveness to women's needs requires better coordination with complementary retirement institutions, and vice versa.

7

Universal coverage: an either/or proposition?

Although members of the NCSSR were deeply divided over the need to change the retirement-age baseline from sixty-five and were unwilling to make major changes in the treatment of women, most agreed that coverage under social security should be broadened as much as possible. The commissioners called for extending mandatory coverage to all newly hired civilian employees of the federal government as well as to all employees of nonprofit organizations. They also wanted to prohibit withdrawal of state and local governments from social security coverage.[1] It was the need to generate additional revenues, not any fresh new perspective on universal coverage, that led Congress to accept these recommendations with only minor alterations. Implementing them, according to the NCSSR Final Report, would save the system at least $23.2 billion by 1989 and would eliminate about 17 percent of the long-range payroll deficit.

At first glance, the requirement that new federal workers and employees of nonprofit institutions contribute to social security appears to be yet another instance of making marginal adjustments in order to generate more income for the OASDHI program. Actually, addressing the question of universal coverage under social security threatened to destroy the fragile legislative consensus in favor of the NCSSR proposals. Several last-ditch efforts to postpone extending coverage to federal employees were made in the Senate, but many lawmakers feared that any such delay would jeopardize the entire bailout plan.[2] The acrimonious and protracted debate whether or not to require government employees to participate in the social security system raises at least two obvious questions: What has been the basis for claiming that every employee should be covered by the nation's social insurance program? And why were federal employees exempt from this principle for so long?

Historical precedents and exceptions to the universal-coverage principle

Universal coverage of the labor force was a major objective for the architects of social security. Policymakers recognized, however, that it could not be fully implemented at the outset. "All workers face the contingency of dependent old age, whether employed in large factories or in small shops or offices, and only serious administrative difficulties, previous legislation, or constitutional limitations should be permitted to interfere with the provision of basic, uniform protection related to contributions."[3] Thus, the ideal had to be tempered by practical considerations.

The Committee on Economic Security initially recommended covering all privately employed wage earners. Railroad employees were excluded because they were already protected by the federal Railroad Retirement Act of 1934. Applying the same logic, policymakers decided it was not "expedient" to include federal employees, because most of them were covered by the Civil Service Retirement System established in 1920. Constitutional limitations on federal jurisdiction made it seem imprudent to require state- and local-government employees to contribute. Modifications were also made during the legislative hearings. On the advice of Secretary of the Treasury Henry Morgenthau, farm laborers and domestic servants were excluded. The House Ways and Means Committee exempted employees of charitable, educational, and religious institutions.[4]

Once social security had been established, officials extended coverage incrementally. "The proper test of coverage is not the special nature of a worker's employment but the universal nature of the risks he or she faces . . . The national government should, therefore, have the right to enforce the obligation to participate in a system of protection upon those able to do so," explained J. Douglas Brown, who helped to draft the original legislation and served as an advisor through the 1970s. "It should not permit any employer, private or public, to substitute its special, limited program of protection for the universal national system."[5] As a result of seven sets of amendments between 1939 and 1967, the goal of truly universal coverage slowly came into sight. The proportion of the civilian labor force embraced by the whole social security program (OASDHI) grew from 24 percent in 1939 to 55.4 percent in 1959, and to 88.7 percent in 1977.[6]

Yet why were federal employees excluded during social security's first four decades? The irony of the situation was not lost on policymakers, who recommended their inclusion as early as the 1950s.[7] When OASDHI's financial difficulties became more apparent two decades later, calls for coverage of federal employees and other exempt groups became more insistent.[8] Every effort to extend coverage to federal employees before 1983, however, met with insurmountable opposition. Especially the campaigns waged by civil service unions demonstrated the salience of special interests, especially when those affected live and work close to the Capitol.

Even in 1983, the NCSSR's recommendations concerning universal coverage were denounced by representatives of federal employees and postal workers.[9] Those who wanted to maintain the status quo claimed that (1) the federal government had already established a retirement program for its own workers and (2) that system provided more generous pension benefits than were available under the nation's old-age insurance program. These arguments were true as far as they went, but they ignored two other important truths. First, the prior existence of a government-approved pension plan does not preclude the need for worker coverage under social security. This had been established by congressional decision not to adopt the Clark amendment of 1935, which would have exempted from social security those private-sector workers covered under federally approved retirement annuity programs. Mutatis mutandis, the Civil Service Retirement System's pension plan should not exclude federal workers from social security. Second, social security has long been perceived as a necessary foundation for America's retirement system. Even if federal-employee organizations could demonstrate that their own programs were superior to Title II, the *generosity* of a supplemental retirement program does not obviate the principle of universal coverage under social insurance.

In the final analysis, arguments that appealed to people's sense of fairness and to their pocketbooks won out. In Senator John Heinz's view, "The public perception of unfairness comes in part from the sense that civil service retirement provides unnecessary plush benefits to federal retirees at the taxpayers' expense . . . With social security in financial trouble, and only a limited range of unpleasant options available to restore solvency, there has been a growing public sense that continued exclusion of Federal workers from social security is a luxury the taxpayers can no longer afford."[10]

It is a curious feature of the 1983 debates that in their effort to solve short-term financing difficulties and dispel the crisis mentality, policymakers often treated social security as if it operated in isolation. There was remarkably little discussion about other pension programs. Legislators were not oblivious to the fact that America's retirement system consists of many parts. But a succession of blue-ribbon panels and expert witnesses had interpreted "the big picture" differently, and lawmakers disagreed about the long-term advantages and risks of relying on any of its several components. So, many important questions were not asked; some that were posed were left unanswered. What is the proper balance between the private and public sectors in providing retirement income for workers and their families? What impact have recent changes in social security coverage as well as in government regulations and tax provisions had on pensions and individual savings? Could – and should – supplemental programs become an increasingly important resource for older people, or would it be better to concentrate on improving the social security system itself?

Answering such questions requires attention to how the federal government has shaped policy objectives and options in both the private and public sectors. It is also important to assess the extent of coverage and adequacy of benefits under various programs before evaluating recent proposals to change the existing balance in American insurance protection.

Retirement programs that supplement social security

Developments in the public sector

Roughly one of every eight public-sector retirement plans was established before 1930; half of them were in place by 1950. During the past three decades, the number of municipal and county plans for workers who previously lacked coverage has grown markedly. Concurrently, many smaller programs have been consolidated. By 1981, around 9 million public employees participated in approximately 6,000 state and local plans. With total assets in excess of $200 billion, this component of America's retirement system paid out in that year alone over $13 billion to 2.4 million beneficiaries.[11] Under the majority of these plans, benefits are based on an employee's final average pay, usually adjusted for inflation. Though most schemes require financial contributions from their participants, disbursements generally exceed such revenues; current operating costs are partly defrayed through taxes, which is really the employer share of the cost of the program. Because local and state governments have often failed to increase their contribution rates sufficiently to pay for benefit liberalizations negotiated since the mid-1960s, taxpayers will have to underwrite them as well. In addition to their public-employee pensions, nonfederal government workers can usually count on receiving social security; it covers roughly 70 percent of all state and local employees.

Federal workers do not participate in a uniform retirement plan. As a result of historical happenstance, Washington operates fifty-one separate programs, many of which are independent of programs for military and civilian employees – as well as of social security itself. Only the railroad retirement system is fully coordinated with social security.[12] Benefits under the retirement plan for Employees of the Federal Reserve Board, the Foreign Service Retirement System, and the TVA's retirement scheme, for instance, are paid from current-year appropriations. The Civil Service Retirement System, which now covers more than 2.7 million federal workers, is the largest of such autonomous programs. In 1983, approximately 1.87 million annuitants collected $20.7 billion worth of disability, retirement, and survivors' benefits.[13] The formulas used to calculate pensions for federal employees, on balance, are more liberal than those used elsewhere. The military, for example, offers the most attractive retirement package available anywhere today. Participants contribute nothing toward retirement, but after twenty years of service they can depart with a full pension based on their final paycheck. Like pensions for all other federal retirees, veterans' pensions are protected against inflation through a generous cost-of-living escalator. "The current system," according to the Department of Defense, "provides excessively liberal benefits when compared with most civilian sector plans."[14]

Public pensions are an operating cost of government, just as retirement plans maintained by private corporations represent business costs. Public-employee "fringe benefits" make up a third of the government's compensation payments; retirement pensions are the major item in this outlay. Unlike social security, however, federal-employee pension plans cannot be financed on a pay-as-you-go basis. Hence, the present and future costs of benefits and the financial security of reserve funds must be assessed as prudently for federal pensions as for programs operated by the private sector.[15]

The growth of private programs

On the eve of the Depression, only 15 percent of American workers were eligible for retirement programs operated by their companies or unions. Many plans failed to pay benefits during the economic crisis. The 1935 act, however, gave new life to private pensions. Many life insurance executives had testified on behalf of Senator Clark's proposal to exempt from the federal old-age program those corporations offering their employees retirement annuities. However, they quickly saw that their position had been shortsighted. Despite fears to the contrary, the federal initiative did not reduce interest in privately funded insurance; if anything, Title II made Americans more security-conscious than ever. And by not demanding special treatment (on the grounds that life insurance and annuities were alternatives to social security), insurance companies spared themselves administrative intrusions by federal regulators.[16]

In the 1940s, moreover, several factors combined to sustain the growth of private pensions: a sharp increase in corporate tax rates; amendments to the Revenue Act that modified tax qualification standards; and World War II's dramatic revitalization of the economy. In this context, employee pension funds provided a convenient tax shelter, because pension contributions were exempt from wage controls and could be deducted from employers' taxable income. Such contributions also augmented corporate investment portfolios. Besides, more liberal retirement benefits could be cited as a justification for holding wages down. The upshot was that an additional 2.25 million workers gained private pension coverage between 1940 and 1945.[17]

After World War II, organized labor's drive for additional employment protection and benefits helped stimulate further expansion of retirement programs in the private sector. In 1946, the Inland Steel Company unilaterally imposed a mandatory retirement age. The union filed a grievance with the National Labor Relations Board (NLRB), charging that this violated an employment-termination feature of its contract. In its defense, the company contended that the mandatory-retirement clause was an essential feature of its pension program and that pensions were not negotiable. The NLRB in 1948 ruled in favor of the union; the board's decision that employers must bargain on pensions was upheld by the Supreme Court a year later. A Steel Industry Fact-Finding Board in 1949 went a step further: It held that employers had a social obligation to provide steelworkers with pensions along with other fringe benefits.[18] Other unions recognized the need for supplemental retirement income as well, particularly because social security benefits had not been increased since 1939. Labor officials became more sensitive than ever to the need for adequate pensions because of the increased technological displacement of older workers.[19] Thus, when General Motors President Charles Wilson offered to establish a pension fund during his 1950 negotiations with the United Auto Workers, he launched a pension boomlet.

The 1950s witnessed the greatest growth yet in private pension plans in terms of increased coverage, relative gains in assets, numbers of beneficiaries, and benefit payments. The number of workers covered rose from 3.7 million in 1940 to 23 million in 1960 – the latter figure representing nearly 30 percent of the civilian labor force.[20] Amidst the prosperity of the decade, annual contributions rose from $2 billion to $5.6 billion, total benefits grew from $370 million to $1.2 billion, and reserves more than quadrupled to $52 billion. At the same time, multiemployer pension plans – especially in the construction, transportation, trade, and service industries – became more widespread. Many of these new plans were administered by life insurance companies. Experts noted that this infusion of pension-fund money was affecting investment markets, but it was not clear whether or not pension-fund managers might someday secure a controlling interest in major companies.[21]

President Kennedy, recognizing the growing significance of private pension programs, appointed a committee to investigate contemporary developments and to recommend appropriate policies. "This public interest in private retirement plans arises because they provide economic security for millions of workers and their families; are a substantial element in the national savings stream and the financial markets; affect the incentives, mobility, and employment prospects of the labor force; [and] are to a significant degree subsidized by Federal taxpayers."[22] For nearly a decade, Congress considered various ways to protect employees' rights and ensure the financial solvency of private pensions. It finally codified a set of regulations in the Employee Retirement Income Security Act (ERISA) of 1974. Among other things, the law required private plans to conform to minimum vesting standards that essentially guaranteed workers 100 percent of their accrued benefits after ten years of service. Strict funding requirements and fiduciary standards were established. As a further measure of protection, Congress established the Pension Benefit Guaranty

Corporation (PBGC) to monitor existing plans and to collect termination insurance premiums against the eventuality of a firm's bankruptcy or an unforeseen problem in its pension plan.[23]

As an extraordinary period of growth gave way to persistent stagflation, many firms found themselves unable to maintain, much less expand, their pension programs. In addition, some corporations were unwilling to amend their plans to comply with the higher vesting standards and stringent fiduciary requirements of ERISA. Consequently, there was a flurry of pension plan terminations in the mid-1970s. This trend, however, was short-lived. By the end of 1981 there were 696,000 tax-qualified plans in operation. To bolster private initiative, the Reagan administration took steps to ensure parity between corporate and noncorporate plans and to prevent abuse of PBGC funds.[24]

The federal government's involvement in private retirement options has not been limited to employee pensions. Through tax incentives and legislative initiatives, Washington in recent decades has made it much easier and more attractive for individuals and owners of small companies to save for their old age. The Self-Employed Individuals Tax Retirement Act of 1962 permitted professional people, owners of unincorporated businesses, and other self-employed workers to establish "Keogh plans." Such people were thereby allowed to set aside 10 percent of earned income up to $2,500, of which half was exempt from taxes until drawn upon in retirement.[25] By 1977 there were some 649,000 Keogh plans in operation, with assets of $6.5 billion. As coverage has expanded, the ceiling on contributions has risen. The 1982 Tax Equity and Fiscal Responsibility Act, for instance, permitted deductions from taxable income up to 15 percent of total earnings or $30,000, whichever was less; future contribution limits will be increased in conjunction with the ceiling on corporate business plans.[26]

Extending the logic justifying Keogh plans, President Nixon in 1971 sought to address the needs of workers who were not protected by group pension plans or whose coverage was inadequate:

> There is sometimes a tendency for Government to neglect or take for granted the "little man" in this country, the average citizen who lives a quiet, responsible life and who constitutes the backbone of our strength as a nation . . . The fact that a man is self-reliant, however, does not mean that Government should ignore him . . . Self-reliance, prudence and independence are qualities which our Government should work to encourage among our people. These are also qualities which

are involved when a person chooses to invest in a retirement savings plan, setting money aside so that he will have greater security tomorrow.[27]

Nixon's proposal struck a responsive chord in Congress. His recommendations became the basis for the Individual Retirement Accounts (IRAs) authorized under the 1974 ERISA law. Employees not covered by a pension plan who invested in an IRA could deduct up to $1,500 (or 10 percent of their income if they earned less than $15,000) from current income taxes until the money was drawn after age sixty or in retirement.[28]

Subsequent legislation increased the relative importance of IRAs in America's retirement system. Public officials worried about the decline in individual savings compared with disposable income during the 1970s. In an effort to help individuals maintain their standard of living in later years (and to generate sources of capital vital for industrial renewal), Congress made it easier for them to set aside savings for their old age.[29] Under the 1981 Economic Recovery Tax Act, *all* workers – including those covered by pension programs at their places of employment – were eligible to create IRAs; this provision doubled the number of potential participants. Beginning in 1982, any employee could deduct up to $2,000 from current taxable earnings by putting the money into an IRA or by making a voluntary contribution to the company plan; couples in which one spouse did not work could shelter as much as $2,250. Initial studies indicated that IRA contributions exceeded $24 billion in 1982 alone, but well over half of that amount had been shifted from other savings accounts. Thus far, IRAs have had little impact on the nation's overall savings rate.[30]

The development of retirement programs in the public and private sectors parallels the evolution of social security in significant ways. In each instance, much of the growth was inevitable. As more organizations established programs, more of the labor force became eligible for protection. The greatest expansion in coverage took place in times of affluence, when managers and workers alike found this fringe benefit attractive. As with the OASDHI program, retirement options were created incrementally. Ideas that gestated for some time in policymaking circles were tried out on a limited scale. If they worked, officials gradually fine-tuned eligibility criteria and liberalized benefit formulas. Reforms and subsequent expansion increasingly took place at the margins, in part because so many people had such a stake in existing operations that radical change did not seem a viable option.

Yet despite such similarities in development, there has been remarkably little coordination of plans and objectives within America's retirement system: Various programs have been established at different times with distinct purposes in mind. Given the wide-ranging scope of federal involvement and the massive sums of money involved, it is essential to determine the degree to which all of the pieces fit together. In the absence of a central governmental agency to monitor trends in all sectors of the economy, however, students of policy must fashion their own sense of the larger picture.

The shape of America's retirement system

Social security compared with other programs: the employee's perspective

Because patterns of employment and compensation have changed during the twentieth century, the relative importances of various components in the retirement system have shifted over time. Social security represents the major source of money for the elderly today: In 1981 it provided 37 percent of the income available to elderly householders and 46 percent of that available to older persons living alone.[31] Rents, dividends, and interest made up nearly a quarter of the elderly's total income, though this was a notably less significant resource for blacks than for whites. Despite the tremendous growth of retirement programs in both the public and private sectors, employer pensions constituted a surprisingly small portion of the income available to the aged. Depending on race and household status, they provided between 10 and 15 percent of the total.[32] Earnings accounted for 25 percent of elderly householders' income, but only 11 percent of that at the disposal of older singles.[33]

A prime reason why social security is vastly more important than employer pensions in old age is its broader coverage. Although most workers contribute to social security, probably only 50 to 67 percent also participate in another program.[34] Although there is room for disagreement about how many are actually covered by a supplementary pension, there is little doubt that coverage varies considerably by work status, sex, race, income, and place of employment. In addition, those who work more than 1,000 hours per year are more likely to participate in a program than employees who are part-time, seasonal, or under twenty-five. Recent surveys indicate that even among full-time workers, women, minorities, and those earning below the national median are less likely to be covered than men, whites, and highly paid workers. Pension coverage varies by industry: Nearly 40 percent of all jobs exist in trade and services, but workers in this sector make up 58.4 percent of all noncovered employees. Small firms, moreover, are less likely than large firms to have a pension plan.[35]

Fewer workers are covered by other plans than by social security, and so a smaller proportion get supplemental income from their employers in old age. Social security benefits currently reach 91.2 percent of the population over sixty-five, whereas only 40 percent of families with a member between the ages of sixty-five and sixty-eight receive income from another public or private pension.[36] Will the present gap between the elderly's coverage under social security and other pensions narrow in the future? The experts are divided. The President's Commission on Pension Policy concluded in 1981 that no significant change lay ahead. Other analysts, using dynamic-simulation models and making moderate growth assumptions, project far greater coverage. A study prepared by the American Council of Life Insurance, for instance, estimates that the proportion of retired employees receiving supplementary pensions will grow to nearly 80 percent by 2004.[37]

The divergence in expert opinion about the elderly's future receipt of employers' pensions is not simply a result of static or dynamic assumptions about growth. Even if more and more workers participate in pension plans, there will not necessarily be a corresponding rise in the proportion of workers who receive benefits on retirement. Rules that govern the vesting and portability of pensions differ between OASDHI and other retirement programs. Social security permits workers to become eligible for benefits (that is, their future rights to a pension become "vested") after a relatively brief period of covered employment. And if a work history includes periods of noncovered employment, the retiree's prior FICA contributions are "portable" in the sense that the periods when they were made will count when calculating Title II benefits. Most private- and public-sector pension plans, on the other hand, impose more rigorous vesting standards. For example, a minimum of five years of service is required under ERISA guidelines to guarantee at least 25 percent of accrued benefits.[38] Many people technically covered by private- and public-sector plans will not collect all of the benefits they might have expected in old age. According to analyses based on 1972 data from the Social Security

Administration's Retirement History Study, 28 percent of all men and 45 percent of all women once covered by private programs received nothing from them. The situation probably has not improved dramatically during the past decade.[39] Though the portability issue has attracted considerable attention in recent years, little has been done to protect workers' retirement rights. The 1974 ERISA legislation did try to reduce the loss of future retirement payments incurred because of a change in jobs by providing certain tax advantages for transferring vested benefits to an IRA. But the administrative complexity of the rules has discouraged any significant change.[40]

The cumulative effect of differences in coverage, vesting, and portability has a direct impact on the size of the initial average benefits provided under social security and other pension programs. On the basis of a detailed study of 977 private-sector plans, it was estimated that men who retired with thirty years of service in 1974 received an average of $2,700 per year from their former companies. Women in the same situation got $2,000 per annum. The ratio between before-tax gross earnings prior to retirement and private pension income (the "replacement rate") was about 25 percent, though it varied significantly from industry to industry and depended on the nature of the pension arrangement.[41] In contrast, the average replacement rate for a single worker retiring at age sixty-five under social security in 1974 was 51.2 percent. The figure is somewhat lower today because of the impact of the 1977 amendments, but social security still replaces around 41.2 percent of the average single worker's preretirement income.

Comparing early retirement benefits under social security with those of other programs is more complicated. During the 1970s, many firms abruptly amended their retirement programs as their personnel needs changed. For a brief time, workers were permitted to take early retirement without actuarial reduction in benefits. Other companies lowered age and service requirements or devised other incentives to encourage early retirement. For example, some employers today give workers larger checks before they begin to collect social security, then reduce the amount so that total retirement income remains constant.[42]

On balance, however, old-age benefits under social security are far more attractive than those under employer pension plans. Few private pensions automatically index payments; ad hoc increases seldom compensate fully for inflation.[43] Perhaps more significantly, survivors' provisions under the two programs differ markedly. At no extra cost, spouses and other qualified dependents are guaranteed social security benefits based on a worker's imputed pension. Private plans are rarely so generous. Before ERISA, about 20 percent of those covered by private-sector programs could count on no survivor provisions. Since 1974, joint and survivor *options* have become more common, but they need not be exercised. If these options are elected, pensions are typically reduced commensurately; survivors' benefits, moreover, tend to be relatively small and to terminate after a sharply limited period of time (such as five years after the worker's death).

Social security compared with other programs: the institutional perspective

Coverage under private- and public-sector pensions is clearly neither as uniform nor as universal as it is under social security. Hence, America's retirement system divides the working population into two groups. The more fortunate can count on both social security benefits and supplemental resources to finance their old age; the rest must depend on social security alone. Not unexpectedly, income is a good predictor of whether or not a worker has access to supplemental resources, including IRAs.[44] Social security provides roughly half of the income available for approximately 50 percent of the elderly population; it is the only source for roughly 20 percent of the population over sixty-five; 40 percent of all elderly blacks who live alone derive at least 90 percent of their income from social security. These statistics emphasize that not all pensions are created equal. Their structural importance transcends dollar-count measures of well-being in later life. Private- and public-sector retirement plans are a "fringe benefit" that shelters the earnings of higher-paid employees from taxes while laying the groundwork for an old age that is pleasurable, not merely endurable.[45]

Income, however, is not the only salient predictor of pension coverage. From the institutional point of view, a firm's size is an equally important indicator. Nearly 80 percent of all employees covered only by social security worked for companies employing fewer than 100 people. There are several reasons why pension programs have not spread to more small firms. Emerging companies are typically small; most of them die young. The owners of small businesses, moreover, usually are at a financial disadvantage, and so they prefer not to divert capital to pension programs. Nor are they likely to establish retirement plans in order to gain a tax advantage: Successive administrations have reduced the overall corporate tax rate, and anyway, most new firms are not in the higher brackets, where tax deductions become most attractive. Finally, few small firms employ a work force able to demand retirement protection; smaller businesses also have higher rates of employee turnover than do larger concerns.[46]

That small firms usually have no pension programs may affect the future of America's retirement system. For it is the small companies, not the larger ones, that are generating most new job opportunities. Roughly 6.1 million of the 6.9 million jobs created between 1969 and 1976 were provided by firms that employed fewer than 250 people. Companies that hired fewer than 20 people provided about two-thirds of the new positions.[47] Given the high failure rate among new firms, and given the volatility of their labor force, it is difficult to imagine that they will usually be able to provide for their workers' retirement, at least as long as their vesting and financial arrangements remain decentralized.

Another institutional difference merits attention here. Social security's recent financing woes pale in comparison with the unsecured liabilities of most public- and private-sector pension plans. Many state and municipal retirement programs are chronically and dangerously underfinanced. Because tax dollars must be spent on such immediate and visible needs as maintaining roads, fixing bridges, educating children, and paying salaries, legislators rarely have a surplus with which to maintain adequate pension reserves. Officials have exacerbated this problem when resolving labor disputes. Rather than accede to all of the demands of their public workers, negotiators often give smaller pay raises and then sweeten fringe benefits, such as pensions. Government pensions have acquired many of social security's more attractive features – provisions conspicuously missing from most other employee plans. Initial benefits, for instance, usually are based on a worker's years of highest earnings, thereby increasing payments far beyond what would have been the case if all the years of service had been averaged; most public-employer programs also incorporate some sort of cost-of-living escalator. Consequently, it is possible for those who have worked a sufficient number of years to retire with more income than they had while on the job. Indeed, according to the 1981 President's Commission on Pension Policy, the costs associated with inflation-proof early retirement clauses pose the biggest issue facing these plans.[48]

Although no one denies the right of state and local employees to a decent retirement income, the future costs of past compromises and present-day provisions are often overlooked. If liberalized benefits are to be provided, then either contribution rates or taxes must be raised now to meet future obligations. It is dangerous to assume that future taxpayers will fulfill promises made in order to settle a labor dispute in the past or to attract workers to the public sector. Policymakers are not eager to grasp this nettle; the public has been told about the potential crisis, but thus far has not acted.

Thanks to the strict fiduciary standards enacted under ERISA, the acute indebtedness that characterizes most state and local plans does not bedevil programs operating in the private sector.[49] The law establishes standards for administering and managing pension funds; it also stipulates that regular and detailed reports be prepared to ensure that employees know the status of their future benefits and that government agencies can monitor developments. Even so, the vagueness of ERISA terms permits pension managers to set aside fewer reserves than are actuarially prudent. The same imprecision sets corporate lawyers and accountants at loggerheads over the conflicting needs to maintain fiduciary responsibility and minimize tax liabilities.[50]

Given the frequency with which major corporations since the mid-1970s have declared bankruptcy or hovered on its brink, moreover, the question of what happens when a large pension program is terminated has become an issue of more than academic interest. Under ERISA, employers pay plan-termination insurance to the government's nonprofit Pension Benefit Guaranty Corporation (PBGC). PBGC, in turn, will guarantee the first $5 and 75 percent of the next $15 of an employee's monthly benefits per year of service. Between 1974 and 1981, PBGC covered benefit liabilities under 783 multiemployer pension plans that were terminated; the largest single claim was $60 million. At the moment, PBGC is legally responsible for meeting hundreds of millions more dollars of unfunded pension liabilities; it clearly lacks the assets necessary to pay its debts should several large companies in multiemployer pension funds collapse. Indeed, the PBGC has been plagued by operational deficits since 1977. By the end of 1983, its annual shortfall was over $430 million.[51] Technological backwardness, short-sighted investment strategies, inflexible pricing policies, and foreign competition have made it harder for the American steel, textile, apparel, footwear, and appliance industries to sell their products. What happens to workers who find themselves in dead-end jobs in "sunset" industries? Can the PBGC possibly underwrite their retirement if Washington chooses not to bail out their bosses?

And what would happen to workers' retirement security if developments in the international marketplace were to remove their employers from the American industrial landscape? Because of their vested interest in pension funds, workers are technically the legal owners of a large share of U.S. industrial wealth. Yet most of it is concentrated in multinational corporations: 70 percent of manufacturing-sector profits are generated by companies with branches and subsidiaries outside of the United States.[52] As they become more cosmopolitan, these corporations' managers have less incentive to look after the welfare of domestic workers. Just as companies now relocate from one region of the country to another, international enterprises may try to default on their pension promises in their worldwide search for greater profits.

Even without indulging in worst-case fantasies, there are other reasons to be concerned about the security of private pensions. ERISA's architects never envisioned a situation in which cash-hungry managers would terminate existing plans, establish new ones financed in the least costly way to satisfy current legislation, and then use the excess funds to finance acquisitions, fight takeovers, retire debt, or simply make the quarterly report look more attractive to stockholders and potential investors. The House Select Committee on Aging estimated in 1983 that 114 employers had already "raided" pension funds to recapture $443 million.[53] Such "paper profits" benefit the careers of rising managers while undermining employees' retirement security. Nor are corporate executives the only pension managers faced with conflicting interests. Unions have misused pension funds for dubious real estate investments and other transactions. "The critical question," notes Robert Tilove, one of the nation's leading students of pension programs, "is the extent to which various social and political goals can be reconciled."[54]

Finally, it must be remembered that the general health of the economy will largely determine the growth of savings and the value of other retirement vehicles. Roughly 30 percent of all workers participate in defined-contribution plans, which cannot offer a guaranteed level of benefits, because the size of the pension to be paid depends on investment performance. (The same risk applies to IRAs, stocks, bonds, variable annuities, and mutual funds.)

Defined-benefit plans, which cover 70 percent of all those who participate in pension programs, promise either a flat-rate or earnings-related benefit. But if commitments under this type of plan are to be honored, contributions must meet costs. Should inflation persist, fixed-annuity plans and traditional savings schemes would be less attractive, because their earnings potential would be undermined. Because employers' actual pension costs are uncertain and the nation's economic prospects are problematic, employees may have to contribute more to their pension funds, continue working longer to maintain their current standard of living, or accept lower benefits.

The retirement system in wide focus

Two important lessons about America's retirement system stand out from the foregoing analysis of supplements to social security:

1. *The distinction between public- and private-sector programs should not be overdrawn, because the federal government directly or indirectly affects every component that provides economic support for retired workers.* Programs in both sectors share striking operational similarities. Moreover, traditionally private matters have become public issues, and vice versa. The coverage and financing of public-employee systems are greatly affected by public policy decisions, particularly by changes in the federal tax code. The exemption of contributions (by individuals and corporations) to private pension plans and of the interest on these funds cost the government $37.9 billion in uncollected taxes in 1983 alone, according to the Office of Management and Budget (OMB). This was considerably larger than the projected cost of military pensions ($18.4 billion) or of federal civilian pensions ($22.5 billion) for that fiscal year. Partial exemptions for IRA accounts and Keogh plans, OMB estimated, represented another $5.8 billion in lost tax revenues. The special income-tax deduction for people over sixty-five cost $2.4 billion; preferential treatment regarding capital gains for people over fifty-five who sold their principal residences represented an additional $820 million in uncollected revenue.[55]

2. *The function of public and private pensions is not limited to providing income in retirement.* In addition, pensions have long been a convenient way to get rid of putatively superannuated workers and a valuable chip in collective bargaining. The cumulative effect of this legerdemain in the retirement game is now irreversible: Funds invested to pay for workers' retirement presently constitute one

of the greatest sources of financial power in America. As of September 1981, the assets and reserves of major private plans exceeded $472 billion; the value of government-administered plans (excluding OASDI) exceeded $297 billion. The amount spent on retirement income programs, which represented less than 1.5 percent of the GNP in 1950, now approaches 8 percent.[56]

Clearly, then, it makes no sense to embark on social security reform without considering the program's interconnections with other institutions. As a result of the 1983 amendments, all but a tiny fraction of workers will eventually be covered under OASDHI. Having achieved the long-range goal of universal coverage, policymakers must now take steps to ensure that this is a genuinely meaningful achievement. At the very least, the concept of "social insurance" will have to be broadened to coordinate public and private efforts to provide income security while encouraging economic growth.

A multifaceted approach would avoid overdependence on any single component of the nation's retirement system, thus minimizing the risks of failure in a relatively uncharted area of social policy. "There are no simple solutions to the dilemma of today's worker. He could easily consume all his earnings, leaving no claims (either public or private) for future retirement needs. Social policy cannot hope to satisfy all his present and future needs, for they outstrip his lifetime earnings," observed Juanita Kreps in 1970. "All social policy can do is provide a mechanism that allocates aggregate output in some democratically agreed-to-optimal fashion, the optimum allocation in this case having a lifetime as well as a temporary dimension."[57] Kreps's observation remains instructive today; federal policymakers would be wise to act according to her assumptions. Social security must fulfill its long-standing goal of providing an adequate floor of protection for older workers and their families. Doing so will also reinforce the program's intergenerational appeal. But it would be wrong to consider universal coverage under social security an either/or proposition. OASDI must be supplemented by a broad mixture of options: some involving individual workers, others pooling the resources of many; programs that provide defined benefits and others that rely on defined contributions; programs that facilitate capital formation and others that guarantee more than a minimum standard of living in old age.

Thus far, Chapters 5–7 have tried to achieve a broader perspective by focusing on three key changes resulting from the 1983 amendments. The significance of changing the normal retirement age, of studying the pros and cons of structuring Title II benefits in conformity with an earnings-sharing provision, and of enforcing the principle of universal coverage can be fully appreciated only after assessing the broader context in which these seemingly technical adjustments were made or remain to be made. And yet, as the next chapter demonstrates, a wider policy horizon does not necessarily lend support to those who seek program expansion. On the contrary, the Progressive notion that income maintenance and health care programs should be linked under the rubric of "social insurance" may have outlived its usefulness.

8

Federal health care programs and social security

The 1983 social security amendments addressed OASDI's financial problems, but they also dealt with Medicare. Government reports at the time indicated that the Hospital Insurance (HI) Trust Fund would be depleted by the late 1980s. Medicare's anticipated deficits over the next twenty-five years were almost as staggering as those estimated for the old-age retirement program during a seventy-five-year period.[1]

The hearings on the NCSSR's "consensus package" presented a propitious moment to shore up the HI Trust Fund while attending to the OASDI program. Unlike most provisions in the 1983 legislation, however, proposals to stabilize health care financing were not based on NCSSR recommendations. (The problem of the HI Trust Fund was not within the scope of the commission's assignment.) The basis for change was found instead in the 1982 Tax Equity and Fiscal Responsibility Act (TEFRA), which altered payment methods for health care providers and increased beneficiaries' out-of-pocket expenses.[2] To mobilize support for introducing health care issues into debate on the retirement program, lawmakers pledged that Medicare changes would be "budget neutral" through fiscal 1985 – that is, revisions would cost neither more nor less than changes already projected under current legislation.[3] On this understanding, Congress swiftly enacted a new method for reimbursing hospitals.

Instead of paying for inpatient services on a virtually unchallenged "reasonable-cost" basis, as it had done for nearly twenty years, under the 1983 amendments Medicare would adhere over a three-year phase-in period to rates it established for 467 different diagnosis-related groups (DRGs). Recent national averages were to be used for calculating and adjusting DRG rates, but allowances were made for urban/rural differences and specific types of "outliers." If the treatment cost less than the prescribed rates, the hospital could keep the "savings"; if it cost more, the hospitals had to absorb the loss.[4] This change was expected to save the system roughly $33.6 billion in the 1980s.

Even so, the 1983 amendments did not eliminate all anticipated long-term deficits in the Hospital Insurance Trust Fund. The problem of Medicare financing remains unresolved, though concern over social security's fiscal health has generally abated. "The rate of increase in health expenditures today," declared Senators John Heinz and John Glenn (D–Ohio), "constitutes perhaps the single most destabilizing element in the Federal budget on the domestic side."[5] What should be done to prevent a Medicare crisis that might undermine the solutions enacted in 1983?

The fundamental Medicare issue hinges on whether or not it still makes sense to evaluate health care policies in the social security framework. Recent history suggests that lawmakers are disposed to "solve" Medicare's financial woes the same way they shored up OASDI trust funds. Building on the status quo, they will make the technical changes necessary to bring projected cost situations into a fiscally and politically acceptable range. Yet the problem requires attention to issues that go beyond income security provisions. Medicare is not merely an OASDHI program; it is also part of an unwieldy medical-industrial complex whose organization and purpose affect Americans of all ages and stations.

An uneasy alliance: health insurance as part of social security

Support for public health care and "sickness" insurance predates social security. Since the colonial period, local communities had built and subsidized asylums, "pesthouses," almshouses, dispensaries, and hospitals for the sick and poor. Most cities and many states by the early twentieth century had health departments to monitor sanitation and to control disease.[6] During the Progressive period, reformers linked health care issues with income-maintenance schemes; by 1915 there was probably more support for government-supported health insurance than for a system of contributory old-age pensions. California, New York, and Massachusetts considered compulsory health insurance proposals based on ideas formulated by the American Association for Labor Legislation. The American Medical Association suggested management guidelines for such compulsory programs. These initiatives foundered with surprising rapidity, however. American physicians suddenly turned hostile toward mandatory health insurance as they rethought its implications for their professional freedom and economic future. Others denounced the idea as "socialist" and "European." The New York Medical Society, reversing its earlier stance, in 1925 flatly announced that compulsory health insurance "is a dead issue in the United States."[7]

Despite these setbacks, efforts to make medical care more affordable and accessible continued. In 1924 the federal government extended hospitalization coverage to all veterans, even for non-service-related disability or illness.[8] Many of those without access to government health programs sought participating insurance protection. "Group payment of the costs of sickness" (excluding public health expenditures), reported the Committee on Costs of Medical Care, totaled $830 million in 1929. More than 60 percent of this amount was underwritten through federal, state, and local taxes.[9] That same year, Baylor University Hospital in Dallas experimented with a prepaid group hospitalization plan. Although there were only nineteen such programs in effect three years later, the principle of "group hospitalization" insurance soon inspired the creation of Blue Cross.[10] By no means all segments of the population were receiving proper attention, however. Several Department of Labor studies and independent exposés deplored the haphazard and disgraceful treatment of older men and women with chronic illnesses who could not rely on family or friends to provide long-term care. There were more old people in mental hospitals than in almshouses or charitable private homes combined; in effect, lunatic asylums were warehouses for many needing institutional care.[11]

Groping for a proper federal response to health care needs

The health of many Americans suffered during the Great Depression. Experts reported far higher rates of disabling sickness among the unemployed and those who had taken salary cuts than among those who maintained their economic positions. Despite rising mortality rates, per capita expenditures for health in fifty-three major cities declined 18 percent between 1931 and 1934.[12] In 1933 the Federal Emergency Relief Administration (FERA) responded with a program of home medical care, allotting funds through state agencies to pay physicians on a fee-for-service basis. Under the original Social Security Act, Washington increased its responsibility for promoting public health and better delivery of medical services. Title V authorized grants to states for maternal and child welfare; $8 million was initially appropriated under Title VI for public health work. However, no plan for a compulsory health insurance program was included in any draft of the 1935 legislation. President Roosevelt, Labor Secretary Frances Perkins, and CES staff director Edwin Witte feared that such a provision would doom the omnibus measure.[13]

Although the architects of social security issued a number of official statements about health care, they did not formulate a coherent rationale for national health insurance under federal auspices. The case they made for replacing wages lost through sickness or disability and for providing health coverage to wage earners and their dependents was murky. If such protection were not offered as a legitimate function of social security, some experts claimed, then the cost would have to be borne by some other program, like unemployment compensation. Even so, the Committee on Economic Security opposed the merger of health care programs and income-maintenance programs: "The members of our advisory committees and of our staff are unanimously in favor of the separate administration of insurance against wage loss and of insurance against the costs of medical care."[14] Policymakers offered broad guidelines, not programmatic specifics. The federal government should establish objectives and provide some aid, they claimed, but states were to take the initiative in creating health insurance systems. Above all, "the private practice of medicine and of the allied professions should be conserved and strengthened."

The lack of coherent policy goals and a well-defined course of action did not deter Roosevelt from acting to make the federal presence increasingly important in stimulating research, and Washington also became a significant source of funds to defray the medical costs of needy citizens. The National Cancer Act (1937), for example, broadened the scope of the National Institutes of Health to engage in biomedical research. An Interdepartmental Committee to Coordinate Health and Welfare Activities, established in 1938, recommended major changes in public health services and proposed grants-in-aid for constructing new hospitals and health care centers. Two years later, Surgeon General Thomas Parran appointed a National Advisory Committee on Gerontology and organized a unit with the Public Health Service to survey current research on aging.[15] World War II provided additional justification for bold federal action. Roughly a third of all those drafted failed their induction physicals. Thus, it is not surprising that FDR included "the right to adequate medical care and opportunity to achieve and enjoy good health" as part of his "Economic Bill of Rights" in 1944. But it is worth noting that the president and his advisors did not translate political rhetoric into real programs.[16]

After World War II, the federal government continued to broaden its range of activities piecemeal. The Hill–Burton Act (1946) promised huge federal sums for hospital construction and for expanding the number of hospital beds across the nation. Concurrently, Veterans Administration officials attempted to revitalize the country's largest hospital system by building new facilities in urban areas and establishing close affiliations with medical schools. Washington financed sophisticated biomedical research and encouraged technologically based therapeutic intervention. Public policy initiatives remained fragmented, however. Agencies such as the Children's Bureau, the National Institutes of Health, the Veterans Administration, and the Public Health Service had divergent interests and conflicting priorities.[17]

Lacking a blueprint for its own forays into the health care arena, Washington permitted the private sector to assume the dominant role in shaping postwar American health insurance policies. Third-party carriers expanded the principle of group protection against the costs of sickness and hospitalization to employees and (often) to their dependents. By 1945, Blue Cross covered 19 million enrollees. Blue Shield, which was started in 1939 to pay for certain physicians' services, covered another 2 million. Both programs grew dramatically, partly because of the 1948 Supreme Court ruling that made health insurance plans negotiable in collective bargaining. By 1954, 12 million union members and their 17 million dependents enjoyed Blue Cross/Blue Shield coverage. White-collar employees increasingly expected BC/BS insurance to be part of their benefit package. Other prepaid group-practice options, such as the Kaiser plan, capitalized on the increasing marketability and profitability of private-sector health plans.[18] Still, not everyone had access to existing insurance plans and basic health care services. The poor, the retired, and minorities typically did not enjoy the same protection as middle-class, middle-aged white workers and their families. Those who wanted government to play a more direct role in financing insurance and medical programs had to adopt a new approach.

Incremental policymaking by analogy: toward Medicare and Medicaid

In retrospect, it seems inevitable that social security officials such as I. S. Falk and Wilbur Cohen should have selected their own system as the foundation for a government-supported health insurance scheme. Their choice of old people as the most deserving targets of public concern also appears eminently reasonable. Mounting evidence showed that the elderly required more medical care and had fewer economic assets to pay for it than younger members of society. The idea of providing all social security beneficiaries with up to sixty days per year of free hospital care, moreover, had been discussed by Social Security Board officials as early as 1944.[19] Not only would the elderly benefit from such a provision, but so would their adult children, relieved of some of the burden represented by their parents' medical bills. Hence, hospital insurance for the elderly potentially had the same intergenerational appeal that made old-age retirement pensions so popular. And categorical eligibility criteria seemed a convenient way to limit expenditures.

Yet this new strategy – limited benefits (hospital insurance) for a limited group (social security recipients) – did not crystallize overnight. The 1950 amendments, for instance, added means-tested cash benefits for the disabled, permitted old-age assistance (Title I) benefits to be paid to residents of suppliers of health services, and required that such "vendor payments" be made only to nursing homes that were duly licensed by state officials.[20] Note that policymakers arranged the relevant administrative, regulatory, and financing details to conform to the "public assistance" component of social security. This essentially arbitrary choice was soon complemented by linking the "insurance" side of social security to health care as well. In 1951, Federal Security Agency chief Oscar Ewing unveiled a proposal to provide Title II recipients with up to sixty days of hospital care.[21] Increasingly convinced that health insurance should be part of OASI, HEW officials pressed for enactment of disability insurance. Their ultimate goal was comprehensive health care for all.[22] As it became less and less likely that a national health insurance scheme could be implemented in the proximate future, however, federal policymakers settled for a fall-back position. The drive to cover aged beneficiaries and to provide relief for the disabled reflected a desire to provide some protection to groups with especially high medical costs and few resources to meet them.

Incremental policymaking by analogy, then, linked social insurance and health insurance within the parameters of the social security model. This ultimately made it possible for Washington to offer health care to the elderly, but it also rendered a truly universal comprehensive plan difficult if not impossible to develop. Too often in the 1950s and early 1960s their concern for conceptual neatness prevented experts from considering whether or not continued reliance on social security precedents would lead to sound health care policy. Planners exaggerated how easily health care could be allocated according to "insurance" and "assistance" functions. Were nursing homes really similar to almshouses? Was it actually more cost-effective and logical to administer and subsidize long-term care as a "welfare" program? Did only workers require health insurance, or should their dependents be covered as well? Such issues seem not to have been raised at the time. Instead, government experts gathered testimony and statistics to document the need for federal intervention: One of every six senior citizens entered a hospital each year; most stayed twice as long as a younger person; less than half of this vulnerable population had any private health insurance.[23] Policymakers seldom considered the impact that other measures then being implemented would have on federal health care arrangements for the elderly. During the 1950s, for instance, Congress changed the legal status of nursing homes and made new arrangements for their funding. Amendments to the Hill–Burton Act subsidized the construction of new facilities. Nursing homes were brought under the jurisdiction of the Public Health Service, thus making them medical as well as welfare institutions. Further expansion of the proprietary nursing home industry was made possible by federal loans and mortgage guarantees authorized by the Small Business Administration (1956) and the Federal Housing Administration (1959).[24] Just because such developments did not neatly "fit" into the social security paradigm did not mean that they were irrelevant. On the contrary, the anomalies sidestepped in the original Medicare and Medicaid legislation make it necessary to reassess the reforms of the 1960s.

Medicare was expected to make health care more accessible and affordable for older Americans already eligible for Title II benefits. Hospitalization insurance was necessary for retirement security, lawmakers were told, because the cost of medical care varied from time to time and from situation to situation. To underwrite "adequate" insurance protection required a new prepayment approach. By protecting the elderly, policymakers hoped to improve hospital services and bolster Blue Cross and Blue Shield as well.[25] More money and heightened insurance consciousness, they thought, would do the trick.

Nonetheless, some of Medicare's designers were concerned about its fiscal soundness from the very beginning. Several cost projections became outdated even as the measure was under deliberation. "The central fact which must be faced on a proposal to provide a form of service benefit – as contrasted to a cash benefit – is that it is very difficult to accurately estimate the cost," declared House Ways and Means Chairman Wilbur Mills. "These difficult-to-predict future costs, when such a program is part of the social security program, could well have highly dangerous ramifications on the cash benefits portion of the social security program."[26] The safety devices that enabled social security administrators to limit Title II outlays would not control the costs of hospital insurance, even though the beneficiary pools were identical. A 1966 Senate Finance Committee report, for instance, complained that Medicare's hospital reimbursement plan "contains no incentives whatsoever for good management and also begs for bad management."[27] Clearly, Medicare was not as analogous to old-age insurance as originally supposed.

By happenstance no less than by intent, Medicaid was strikingly different from Medicare. Middle-class Americans were the intended recipients of Medicare. Medicaid, appended to the 1965 legislation at the last moment, had manifest welfare objectives: Policymakers at the time were even convinced that it would be perceived as a program for blacks. Just as old-age assistance had been viewed as a necessary supplement to old-age insurance, so Medicaid developed in the shadow of Medicare. Because of variations in state eligibility rules and potential recipients' employment status, however, many poor people were excluded from the "medically needy" category.[28] Medicare provided only limited extended-care coverage; by 1969, officials had further reduced it by tightening eligibility rules. In contrast, Medicaid set only minimal specifications for "custodial" care and provided sketchy guidelines about attendant care for the handicapped and other forms of care for the chronically ill. Such differences in regulations had profound financial ramifications: Whereas legislators tried (with mixed success) to limit the costs of Medicare through deductibles and carefully worded eligibility criteria, they showed little concern for containing Medicaid.[29]

Medicare and Medicaid were not the only efforts to establish a national health program fit for a "Great Society." Medical services for the elderly were integrated with the existing social security structure, but other federal initiatives were not. Grandiose purposes were proclaimed. "We can – and we must – strive now to assure the availability and accessibility to the best health care for all Americans," Lyndon Johnson declared, "regardless of age or geography or economic status."[30] Congress authorized new grant programs for training health care personnel, supported the development and operation of primary, emergency, and mental health care services, and earmarked funds for migrant workers, black-lung victims, and other needy people. States were given more federal tax dollars to improve their public health services. Government at all levels greatly expanded its regulatory powers in an effort to deal with the many health hazards posed by contemporary American life: The Environmental Protection Agency and the Occupational Safety and Health Administration were established; the influence and budgets of agencies such as the Food and Drug Administration and the Centers for Disease Control were augmented.[31] As in the past, Washington crossed new frontiers without coordinating its efforts in any consistent manner.

Efforts to contain health care costs

The 1972 social security amendments in some ways perpetuated this pattern of extending health care and broadening the scope of governmental responsibility. Medicare was permitted to pay for kidney transplants and dialysis for those with chronic kidney failure; Supplementary Medical Insurance (Part B of Medicare) authorized chiropractic, podiatry, and speech pathology services. Nineteen separate provisions related to care in nursing homes under Medicare and Medicaid.[32] Equally noteworthy, however, was the fact that Congress had taken the first steps to contain the unexpected increases in Medicare and Medicaid outlays. Medicare authorized health-maintenance organizations (HMOs) to provide services on a capitation basis.[33] A network of "Professional Standards Review Organizations" was created to monitor the quality and utilization of services. Medicaid permitted states to impose copayment requirements on recipients. States were to reimburse "skilled nursing" and "intermediate care" facilities on a "reasonable cost-related basis" in an attempt to tighten eligibility criteria and encourage cost repayment experiments.

Calls to expand health services in the 1970s were more than balanced by efforts to reduce expenses and fraud.[34] New measures languished, mainly because of mounting concern over programs already in place. A 1970 Senate Finance Committee staff report, for instance, criticized the Social Security Administration for its "costly policy of laissez-faire with respect to physicians' fees under Medicare." Six years later, Treasury Secretary William Simon warned that adopting a national health insurance program "could bankrupt the country."[35] Simon's opinion resonated with the growing "crisis mentality" that was undermining support for most social welfare programs. Between fiscal 1974 and 1977, Medicare and Medicaid outlays doubled. States and municipalities suffered as well as the national government: Medical costs for the poor swelled from 24 to 42 percent of property-tax revenues in Los Angeles between 1968 and 1978.[36] Media and congressional inquiries, moreover, brought national attention to the profiteering, scandals, and shocking conditions spawned by the nursing home industry. Experts noted that much of the abuse was facilitated by the sloppy way in which funds were disbursed.[37]

Key officials in Carter's administration disagreed sharply that there was a "crisis" in American health care, but by the end of his term, cost containment had taken precedence over efforts to improve access and benefits. Raising FICA taxes through the 1977 social security amendments bolstered the Hospital Insurance Trust Fund, giving some lawmakers a plausible reason to press for expansion. Representative Ronald Dellums (D–Calif.) called for a U.S. Health Service whose salaried workers (including physicians) would provide "comprehensive care." Senators Russell Long (D–La.) and Abraham Ribicoff (D–Conn.) renewed their support for "catastrophic insurance." Edward Kennedy proposed a "Health Care for All Americans Act," which he hoped would reduce expenses for existing services through incentives and bargaining, both by individual consumers and by government. Despite political pressure in favor of these and other proposals, the president stressed his reluctance to expand the existing system unless the economy improved and stringent cost controls were imposed.[38]

The Reagan administration chose to frame the debate over health care even more clearly in economic terms. It emphasized the dramatic surge in medical expenses: Overall medical costs rose 165 percent between 1970 and 1982, a period in which the Consumer Price Index grew 149 percent. Hospital room charges increased 283 percent; fees for physicians' services went up 169 percent.[39] To deal with this situation, Reagan sought to slow the growth of benefits, shift some of the burden from the federal budget to state and local budgets, rely on private-sector incentives to foster efficient resource utilization, and increase consumer sensitivity to the drastic rise of medical costs. The 1981 Omnibus Budget Reconciliation Act, the 1982 Tax Equity and Fiscal Responsibility Act, and the 1983 social security amendments all attempted to check the growth of Medicare and Medicaid. Under its "New Federalism," the administration proposed to assume full responsibility for Medicaid – on condition that the states take over other welfare programs such as food stamps. Budget director David Stockman recommended merging twenty-five categorical programs into two block grants that would afford states more discretion but less money for services. These efforts were effective in slowing down the rate of inflation in health care costs.[40] Late in 1984 the administration called for a freeze in Medicare benefits and a requirement that consumers shoulder more of their own medical expenses. Not surprisingly, however, Reagan's effort to reduce the federal deficit by curtailing government-supported medical care was criticized on both economic and philosophical grounds. "We are on a collision course, with federal, state, and local governments trying to cut health expenditures in the face of very rapid inflation in the health sector," argued Johns Hopkins University health economist Karen Davis. "Those who are going to be hurt in the collision are the poor and elderly, who are going to have more of the cost shifting back onto them directly."[41]

Redefining the problem: the elderly, Medicare, and Medicaid

Understanding the Medicare crisis and the efficacy of proposed solutions requires evaluation of other federal health care programs as well, particularly as they affect the elderly. A comprehensive overview reveals factors largely irrelevant to the social security framework onto which Medicare and Medicaid were grafted. Because Medicare and Medicaid financing often does not fit the OASDI model, the health care issue is even more complex than the others associated with social security's fiscal hard times.

By most accounts, Medicare has been a success. Elderly Americans' access to physicians, various specialists, and hospital facilities has increased.[42] Medicare has frequently reduced the elderly's financial burden, especially for acute illnesses that require hospitalization. Prior to the enactment of Medicare and Medicaid, 70 percent of health care expenditures for the aged were privately funded. By 1978, public programs underwrote 88 percent of their hospital expenditures, 59 percent of their physicians' bills, and 46 percent of their nursing home costs. The solution, of course, was only partial – and it had the defects of its virtues.

For the population as a whole, the federal government pays 40 percent of all health care expenditures; Washington also underwrites 65 percent of all medical research and helps cover the cost of training personnel. The magnitude of this commitment in actual dollars is staggering: Health care expenditures swelled from $69 billion to $230 billion between 1970 and 1980, a rise from 7.2 percent to 9.4 percent of the GNP. Even so, it is worth noting that Medicare paid for only 44 percent of the elderly's total 1978 health expenditures. Outpatient drugs, eyeglasses, and dental services, for instance, are largely excluded from coverage. Hence, the aged often purchase private insurance to cover such gaps as well as to cover deductibles and co-insurance amounts required by Medicare.[43]

Like most welfare programs, Medicaid obligates Washington to pay a fixed percentage of individual state outlays. Unlike most welfare programs, however, Medicaid pays for everything the rules permit for eligible individuals. Administrative complexity makes Medicaid more difficult to evaluate than Medicare. There are fifty-three different health plans: each state, territory, and the District of Columbia sets its own income eligibility criteria, cost guidelines, and range of covered services. Unlike Medicare's beneficiary pool, moreover, that of Medicaid fluctuates unpredictably.[44] Experts do note significant gains in life expectancy and dramatic declines in age-adjusted death rates among the aged poor.

But is social security an appropriate framework for delivering old-age health care? I think not. For example, actuaries can provide fairly accurate short- and long-term cost estimates for OASDI, but forecasts about federal health care programs are less trustworthy. Medicare and Medicaid costs are difficult to predict or control because they are generated by the provision of medicines and services, not cash benefits. Program costs *must* rise as access and the scope of benefits grow. This basic difference is compounded by a

host of other dissimilarities between financing income maintenance and health care.

Nearly every American over sixty-five qualifies for federal support to pay for medical expenses. Like OASDI, Medicare and
Medicaid are *entitlement* programs. But most older Americans enjoy
relatively good health. Some 54 percent of them report no significant health limitations.[45] The problems they do have differ, however, from those of younger Americans. Heart disease, cancer,
and cerebrovascular disorders are the elderly's leading health
problems; pneumonia and influenza are reported more frequently
as causes of death than at earlier stages of life. Chronic ailments
(such as arthritis, hypertension, and hearing loss) are common-
place; 80 percent of all Americans over sixty-five have at least one
chronic condition, and many suffer from multiple chronic illnesses.[46] Age-specific differences significantly affect utilization of
health services. Older Americans constitute almost 12 percent of
the population but use nearly 40 percent of acute hospital inpatient
days, make 33 percent of all office visits to internists and other
specialists, and represent 90 percent of the nursing home population.[47]

Federal regulations affect the access and type of health care
available to senior citizens. Some older people use Medicare far
more than others. In 1978, one of every nine enrollees was reim-
bursed at least $5,000 (in 1984 dollars) for medical expenses; this
represented approximately 75 percent of all Medicare expenditure
that year. Roughly 11 percent of the aged population pay 36 percent of all Medicare-related individual costs.[48]

Differences in the elderly's long-term needs further complicate
the picture. Today, less than 5 percent of those over sixty-five are
institutionalized. If past trends continue, however, roughly one in
four of them will enter a nursing home, a state mental or VA
hospital, a "board-and-care" home, or some other type of domi-
ciliary, long-term facility before they die. The typical nursing home
resident is over eighty, widowed, and white and suffers from at
least three chronic ailments. Average residence in a nursing home
is 2.6 years; more than 25 percent of those committed stay longer
than three years.[49] For this subset of older Americans, Medicaid
has become increasingly important, though less than 15 percent of
the elderly presently qualify for the program. This is because
Medicare has an acute-care orientation, providing only minimal
coverage for long-term care. Medicaid, on the other hand, makes
nursing home care available to all those who meet its criteria. As

a result, 28.5 percent of all Medicaid outlays underwrite nursing home costs; this figure represents half of all payments made to such institutions. In contrast, poor children and single-parent families, who compose nearly two-thirds of the Medicaid beneficiary pool, account for only about one-third of the program's costs.[50] In addition, terminal care is a major cost under both Medicare and Medicaid. Acute-care costs for the last year of a typical patient's life are extraordinary; 30 percent of all Medicare dollars (1 percent of GNP) are spent on the dying.[51]

The graying of American society thus affects the distribution and cost of health services profoundly because of the way expenditures are skewed in the latter part of the life cycle. To address the challenges posed by a rapidly aging population necessitates a new look at current wisdom: Better care probably will allow the elderly to live longer, but they will not necessarily be healthier.[52]

Unlike the ethical choices typical for OASDI, policy issues concerning health care are literally matters of life and death. One of the lessons to be learned from the debate over government funding of abortions is that medical procedures can polarize the nation in ways neither laws nor litigation can resolve. Determining what constitutes "proper" care of moribund old people poses a similar problem. Do the elderly, if very ill, have a "duty to die"? Should euthanasia be permitted? What percentage of the GNP should be earmarked for health care in general – and, more specifically, for the very old? Is 20 percent too much, for example?[53] Should costly resources be allocated to the fittest? To the youngest? Who should determine priorities?[54]

It will be more difficult to transform the nation's "medical-industrial complex" than its income-maintenance system because of major structural differences between them. Washington does not reimburse Medicare and Medicaid beneficiaries directly; instead, it pays for a portion of the services and medicines that they use. Thus, third-party reimbursement rules and regulations dominate the federal health care system in ways alien to OASI and unmatched by the disability insurance appeals process. Since the inauguration of Medicare, experts have stressed that this arrangement is a major inflator of medical costs. Nursing home reforms endorsed by government, insurance companies, and care deliverers have created a situation wherein the public sector is the largest buyer of health care services: Consumers (not to mention providers) are not free, nor always able, to make informed choices about the services they receive.[55]

Furthermore, Medicare and Medicaid are not the only federal

programs financing medical services for the elderly. The Administration on Aging in the Department of Health and Human Services underwrites demonstration projects that involve older people in long-term care facilities. In fiscal 1983, the Veterans Administration spent $4.9 billion for hospitalized veterans; it disbursed another $150 million for long-term care. As those who saw duty in World War II enter old age, the number eligible for veterans' benefits will soar.[56] Private-sector organizations like Blue Cross/Blue Shield, philanthropies, and corporations play an important role in providing health care services and in supplementing federal benefits. Other institutions – the media, schools, voluntary agencies, charities, churches, and the family – make referral and delivery of services possible.[57] The differing perspectives of these groups will make institutional changes difficult.

Finally, the technology available to meet the aged's health care needs is by no means value-neutral. The issues at stake are central to health care policy, but once again they are less salient for OASDI. Sophisticated medical innovations are often cited as a major source of inflation in health costs, and with good reason. But is such technology always essential for the long-term needs of an aging society?[58] Projected demographic patterns combine with institutional arrangements, consistently underestimated expenditures, and the high cost of scientific progress to assure that medical care in America will become ever more costly. What can be done so that these increasing sums are spent wisely?

Policy options

Just as loyalists rushed forward with proposals to "save" OASDI, so there was no dearth of ideas on how to "reform" Medicare. The Advisory Council on Social Security issued its report on *Medicare: Benefits and Financing* in February of 1984. "The most critical problem" facing Medicare, declared the council, was "insolvency." It expected the Hospital Insurance Trust Fund to have a cumulative deficit of between $200 and $300 billion by 1995. The panel opposed increases in FICA taxes or the use of general revenues to bridge this gap. It rejected an idea that Medicare operate on a means-tested basis.[59] Instead, it recommended taxing employer-provided health insurance and increasing federal excise taxes on alcohol and tobacco. To reduce costs, the council proposed that the Medicare eligibility age be raised from sixty-five to sixty-seven by 1990 and that schedules be developed for physicians' fees. It wanted to restructure Medicare benefits and increase Supplementary Medical Insurance premiums.

The 1984 council trusted "the politics of incrementalism"; in format and tone, its Medicare study resembled the final report of the NCSSR.[60] It argued that its proposals dovetailed with ideas supported by the Reagan administration, key figures in Congress, and private-sector groups, and it cited precedents for every modification it contemplated.[61] This approach was a time-tested maneuver, but likely to prove shortsighted. If the challenge of reforming Medicare is as urgent as the council's report indicates, continued adherence to the social security framework will prove counterproductive.

The recommendations set forth by the 1984 Advisory Council on Social Security may serve as a starting point for new discussions, particularly because they built on the Reagan administration's preferences.[62] But no measure presently under consideration is likely to be adopted intact. A bipartisan "consensus" package probably will be pieced together; once again, the word will be that benefits need to be cut or that taxes have to be increased. Because neither alternative is palatable, policymakers will adopt plans designed to relieve immediate fiscal pressures on the OASDHI system. Another special commission may well be formed in time to issue a report shortly before the Hospital Insurance Trust Fund goes bankrupt.[63] Nineteen eighty-three was the last "High Noon" the nation can afford. *Festina lente* must be the watchword for the future, because the health care crisis will not yield to eleventh-hour solutions. The situation is simply too complex.

Some would-be reforms march under the banner of "cost containment." The 1984 Advisory Council, for instance, recommended a cap on current entitlements and sought to decrease the eligibility pool by raising the Medicare age to sixty-seven, meanwhile increasing beneficiaries' financial liabilities. Such "cost sharing," however, would do nothing to slow the rapid growth in the cost of care itself. It ignores the considerable out-of-pocket expenses that the elderly already pay – a burden that falls disproportionately on the financially and physically weakest members of society.[64] The unrestrained "free-enterprise" ideology in vogue under Reagan has inspired other suggestions. Alain Enthoven, a Carter administration official who has advised Reagan's health care experts, is convinced that a "voucher" plan would reduce waste and encourage competition.[65] Critics charge that this might be a roundabout way of passing costs to beneficiaries, because vouchers might not keep pace with rising medical prices. Nor is it clear that consumers know how to pick the health care plans that best fit their needs.[66]

More promising are proposed regulations that would decrease reimbursement to providers, monitor services, and increase the efficiency of the health care delivery system in general. DRGs, if effective, should be extended in scope. Additional efforts in this direction would require professionals in all health areas to develop new ways of organizing and providing care. Fee-for-services plans are still unpopular in the United States, but experience in Canada and elsewhere indicates they may soon become naturalized, as it were.[67] Other ideas include a "stepdown" system of long-term care: Only individuals afflicted with moderate-to-severe cases of senility or other mental disorders, if entirely bedridden, would be placed in nursing homes for constant medical attention.[68] Those requiring less intensive supervision would be treated in a variety of elder-care facilities and HMOs, congregrate housing centers, and hospices. Reimbursement for home care would add to public outlays, but it is worth serious consideration. Homemakers and family members provide vital support for the elderly, including half of those afflicted with Alzheimer's disease.[69]

Hospitals are a focus of most reform proposals. Some doubt that sweeping improvement in this area is possible. Others note that hospital organization has changed profoundly in recent years, as business considerations have spurred the growth of multihospital systems.[70] Hospitals today do seem aggressively profit-oriented – almost like the trucking and banking industries. Today's innovative, regional multicare health centers may well become tomorrow's best market investment.[71] America's elderly, poor, and sick, however, would not be likely to benefit from such a transformation.

The eventual reform of government medical care programs will depend on when and under what conditions it is enacted. "If the deficit is reduced to manageable levels by, say, fiscal 1989, the debate on Medicare is likely to take place as part of a broad national examination of how to organize and pay for medical services. If the overall deficit lingers at or near its current size, the debate on Medicare inevitably will be enveloped in a continuing effort to bring overall spending and taxes into line."[72] Under either scenario, Washington's role in the health care area will continue to be an essential one.

Radical changes in the balance between private and public sectors in paying medical costs would pose serious problems for the aged. Allocating responsibilities among various levels of government and between purchasers and providers of medical services would require major changes in the medical-industrial complex. Hence, the architects of the present system advocate incremental changes in federal responsibilities. "Efforts to put into effect any large-scale program in one fell swoop can lead to major administrative difficulties and extensive disappointment," stresses Wilbur Cohen. "Unforseen [*sic*] problems develop; errors of judgment occur; costs rise; and local, state and individual problems develop that require time for solution."[73] Yet the analysis of health care policies for the elderly carried out in this chapter makes it clear that incremental solutions based on the OASDI model are inadequate.

For much of this century it made sense to view health insurance as a major component of social security itself. Linking the elderly's case for hospital insurance to Title II was a brilliant political move in its time. But the social security paradigm and apparatus are no longer adequate for the health needs of our aging society. The "health care crisis" is so acute and complex as to demand a new conceptual framework – one that makes it possible to think clearly about what to do and why to do it.

9

A vision renewed: individual needs and mutual responsibility

Constructive debate over the fundamental issues besetting social security is essential for the nation's political and social, as well as economic, well-being. OASDHI began, after all, as a vision of individual needs and mutual interdependence that would change and grow in response to America's own evolution. FDR knew that he was only laying the cornerstone for a new federal venture intended to harmonize individual need with mutual responsibility. He thought that by requiring workers to contribute to his program, "no damn politician" could scrap it. He did not foresee that a new generation would come of age, largely ignorant of or oblivious to the fruitful inspiration that gave birth to social security.

In the past, it really did not matter that politicians and the public did not understand how OASDHI operated. Social security was a good deal and seemed to work – and that was all that counted. The system proved resourceful in adapting itself, by piecemeal reform and incremental policymaking, to the challenges posed by its first half century. Lawmakers largely managed to avoid making tough choices that would cost them votes. Using euphemisms and technical jargon became part of the policymaking process, not because social security's architects wanted to mislead the public but because the experts (many of whom had dedicated their careers to the cause) presumed that this was the best way to sustain growth and bolster confidence.

How ironic, then, that the future of social security hangs in the balance because of its past successes. Partisan palaver during Reagan's presidency reached levels of disingenuousness not witnessed since the 1936 election, when Landon dismissed the fledgling program as a "fraud." There are no easy votes. And now there is little system – and too many systems – in the welter of regulations and reforms that constitute social insurance's answer to unforeseen public- and private-sector developments. Confusion over OASDHI's goals and financing invites demagoguery and shortsighted remedies. Incipient gridlock, however, poses opportunities as well as hazards, but only if politicians and the public realize that reforming social security is not a zero-sum game.

The 1983 amendments to the Social Security Act leave policymakers two choices, broadly speaking. If the legislation is treated as just another patchwork compromise designed to stave off imminent collapse, it will soon disappear into that genteel obscurity reserved for obsolete reforms. Resentment between classes, sexes, ethnic groups, and generations will continue to disturb the citizenry, tearing at the fabric of American society. Given the vast sums of money associated with social security financing, it is inevitable that politicians eager to reduce the federal deficit will be sorely tempted to change the rules of the game, jeopardizing OASDHI's long-term integrity in order to solve an immediate political problem. Late in 1985, the Reagan administration acknowledged manipulating social security trust funds and payroll-tax receipts to keep federal borrowing below the statutory debt limit – actions that could cost the OASDI trust funds $1.1 billion by 1990. The huge social security surpluses that will accrue between 1990 and 2010 pose a different threat: Politicians seeking reelection might be tempted to liberalize benefits, thereby eliminating the cushion intended to support the baby-boom generation in their old age and burdening younger workers with greater liabilities. The danger of a "legitimation crisis" can be averted, however, by seizing on the 1983 amendments as precedents for a long-overdue reworking of social policy. A coherent framework for this task can be derived from the Ninety-eighth Congress's "artful work."

The times demand a renewed vision of social insurance in this country. The observation and recommendations that follow build on the historical narrative in Part I and the analysis of present-day problems in Part II. A historical perspective is indispensable. Most Americans have never endured economic hard times; to them, the Great Depression and New Deal are ancient history. Yet it is difficult to appreciate the long-run political and normative issues at stake without understanding social security's origins and unexpected developments as the program has come of age. The best way to reconstruct the lessons of the past, I believe, is to recast social security's original vision and subsequent revisions into plain language, showing OASDHI's vital pertinence in the years ahead. Coming clean with the issues and posing the choices in straightforward language, to be sure, would violate a tradition in social security policymaking. But any backlash that results from candor is bound to be less risky than proceeding any longer under a self-imposed veil of ignorance. Eventually, and sooner rather than later, politicians of all political persuasions and American taxpayers must see the self-interested advantages that accrue by doing good through social security.

Back to basics: economic protection for the elderly

When social security was enacted in 1935, the risk of old-age poverty was of paramount concern, given the destitution many elderly then suffered and still more feared. Other parts of the legislation provided help to categories not restricted to old age, of course, and policymakers stressed that even Titles I and II had important transgenerational features: Because a majority of the population probably would live to retirement age or beyond, those still young during the Depression could anticipate a pension – or at least federal-state financial assistance should they need it – in old age. Younger people stood to gain in the present or near future by the way society promised to relieve them of some expenses they might be ill-able to afford for their aged family members.

All the same, thoughtful commentators were concerned that the new federal program might pit the legitimate immediate claims of the old against the equally legitimate future interests of the young.[1] But social security's initially small beneficiary pool and rising number of contributors, the "freeze" on payment levels prior to 1950, and postwar prosperity largely averted generational conflict for nearly four decades. By the late 1970s, however, analysts were warning that policies adopted to meet the demands and problems of an ever-growing elderly population might be "busting" the U.S. budget.[2] Indeed, many predicted that the situation would only get worse as the graying of America continued. More than 25 percent of the federal budget was already being allocated to underwrite the nation's old-age retirement and health care systems by 1980. As the number of Americans living past seventy-five climbs, so, too, medical costs will inevitably rise for at least the next half century. Some younger people even argue that the current rules are rigged to give senior citizens far more than was originally intended. As Phillip Longman, commenting at age twenty-six, put it, "In enforcing their claims of generational privilege, the old undermine the younger generation's opportunity to enjoy the prosperity of its elders. That portion of the nation's limited wealth squandered on its unneedy old must be subtracted in equal measure from what can be invested toward future economic growth. The magnitude of these entitlements thus compromises the young's very ability to finance them."[3]

The likelihood of intergenerational warfare can be exaggerated, of course. The assets, interests, and needs of the elderly population are too diverse to foster their mobilization as a monolithic, single-minded political force. Inequalities among the elderly are greater than between the aged and non-aged populations.[4] Nevertheless, if current entitlements even *seem* unduly generous, support for social insurance becomes commensurately precarious; the belief that one age group benefits at the expense of another will hamper rational consideration of the nation's welfare priorities and resources en bloc.[5]

A number of neoliberals, as well as neoconservative critics – many of them in the vanguard of the baby-boom cohort – suggest that it is now politically and economically feasible to reduce federal expenditures for old-age and survivors insurance. But providing continuous protection over the life cycle does not necessitate arbitrary trade-offs between young and old. Rather than dwell on the competing interests of different age cohorts, it would be wise to transcend the rigid boundaries of categorical programs, building on the fact that the life cycle has become "fluid" in modern society. Becoming sixty-five no longer means becoming "superannuated." Indeed, in an *aging* society – one in which two-thirds of all the increases in life expectancy at birth have taken place since 1900 – the future needs of the aged can most effectively be addressed by enhancing people's opportunities earlier in their lives. Current definitions of "risk," which presume that "normal" hazards occur at predictable stages of life, are too inflexible. The goal of social insurance today must be to provide economic security – "a living wage" – for people who find themselves in very different circumstances at the same age.

Social security must be seen as the principal vehicle for facilitating individual and collective efforts to achieve security against the risks of modern times. Policymakers must also take account of the roles played by other institutions in America – the family, the church, voluntary groups, banks, and insurance companies. Social security and these other mediating structures afford the average person an extraordinary range of options, thereby promoting greater individual choices at successive stages of life. Social security is not – and should not be – treated as the only way to provide for the vicissitudes of life. What is needed is better coordination among these institutions and between them and existing programs. Indirect guidance – for example, IRAs and other incentives provided through the tax codes – can help as well.

As a first step toward revamping the nation's social insurance, then, it is vital for policymakers to *embrace the fact that social security is the foundation for guaranteeing adequate financial support for all Americans*. A mélange of private programs will not suffice. Social security is the only nationwide federal program that covers – now or in years to come – virtually every worker or worker's dependent in the country.

It is therefore the logical bedrock on which to erect a genuine "floor" of income security for all, regardless of age. The best way to proceed is to adhere unequivocally to a policy chosen in the late 1930s. Reinhard Hohaus, vice-president and actuary of the Metropolitan Life Insurance Company, provided a strong justification for using social security's "insurance" features to effect "welfare" objectives. The principle of "equity" has its place in social insurance, Hohaus argued, but it should be secondary to the goal of assuring "social adequacy":

> Just as considerations of equity of benefits form a natural and vital part of operating private insurance, so should considerations of adequacy of benefits control the pattern of social insurance . . . Consistent with this philosophy, [social insurance's] first objective in the matter of benefits should, therefore, be that those covered by it will, so far as possible, be assured of that minimum income which in most cases will prevent their becoming a charge on society. Not until this is accomplished should financial resources (whatever, if anything, may remain of them) be considered as available to provide individual differentiation aiming at equity.[6]

Capitalizing on this tradition, social security pensions for the lowest-paid former wage earners should guarantee a retirement income above the "official" poverty level. Those who do not have IRAs or other sources of supplementary retirement income tend to be those who were the poorest paid and who had irregular work histories. If only because this nation values the work ethic so highly, no one who has made a contribution to the country's wealth should be denied at least a minimally adequate standard of living in old age.

What about those whose gainful employment has *not* earned them the right to a Title II pension? The original vision of social security provides guidance: From the very beginning, "assistance" was deemed an integral part of the umbrella of protection it offered. It is worth remembering that social security benefits, skewed since 1935 to provide a higher rate of return for lower-income workers, were subsequently broadened to provide extra support to survivors and dependents whose contributions to the economy were not always fairly remunerated. The 1972 amendments replaced Title I (Old-Age Assistance), Title X (Assistance to the Blind), and Title XIV (Aid to the Permanently and Totally Disabled) with the SSI program. SSI is supposed to guarantee the "minimal standards of decency and health" this nation feels it owes to the needy. But its recipients are not assured an income above the poverty line, and the program excludes children, who have little recourse beyond AFDC, a program that began as part of the original Social Security Act. Thus, social security's "assistance" component not only fails to measure up to the aspirations expressed in 1935, it does not even meet the government's own standard of "adequacy."

This appalling situation demands straight talk and decisive action to put it right. After fifty years it is time to acknowledge openly that the true linchpin of social security is that the adequacy of benefits should take strict precedence over the principle of individually accumulated equity.

It follows from this axiom that all federal assistance programs must put into practice the vision that inspired social security in the first place. For example, Congress should increase SSI payments to the point that dependents of those with minimal covered earnings and irregular career patterns are guaranteed benefits at least equal to the poverty level. If this were done, there would be no need for "special" minimum Title II benefits, such as those enacted in 1972; even in the worst case, no one would be denied humane conditions of life.[7] Achieving these objectives requires better coordination among various income-maintenance and antipoverty programs. That coordination could best be provided by a Department of Income Security, as I shall argue later.

"And justice for all": women's work, children's welfare, and minority rights

Social insurance must be adjusted to the changing situation of the modern woman. Despite resistance from fiscal conservatives, earnings sharing should be adopted: It promotes security for the career homemaker without being unfair to the working wife.

Closely tied to the gradual implementation of this reform should be a phaseout of the 50 percent "spousal" benefit. Today more than ever, marriage is an inadequate vehicle for preventing economic adversity. Eliminating "dependent" benefits, it will certainly be claimed, puts large segments of the population at risk. To allay such fears, a secure "safety net" must be in place. Improving SSI benefits for aged women who are divorced or widowed could serve this purpose in the short run, but more radical steps will also be necessary.

The most important of such steps is provision for "care-giver" credits, credits that would count toward the "average earnings" used in determining social security benefits. Despite the administrative difficulties associated with identifying "care-givers," there should be no penalty for people who choose not to engage in full-time employment in order to care for family members. Present trends suggest that four-generation families will increasingly become the norm: By the end of the century, more and more working people will rely on nonfamilial institutions to help not just with care for children but also to provide meals, housekeeping, and daycare for dependents, especially the frail elderly. Some of these services will be purchased in the private sector. Others will have to be subsidized by taxpayers, though in an age of fiscal austerity the public sector's ability to provide adequate support is questionable.[8] It is therefore important to acknowledge that the care that family members provide is a time-tested, generally unpaid service that can be quite expensive if bought in the marketplace or financed by government. Underwriting this intergenerational service through social security would be less costly than total reliance on private-sector or government provision. Pretending that this need is already adequately met entails costs that far exceed purely monetary considerations.

The proposals advanced so far tie together many of the principles set forth in Part II. Rather than compartmentalize the adequacy and equity functions of social insurance, they seek to mesh them in a more coherent manner. Rather than presume to resolve the tension between individual rights and family responsibilities, they offer a way of providing benefits that is neutral in its treatment of marriage without undermining the critical role families play in American society. Corroborating the principles underlying OASDHI, they treat social security as an essential expression of community that at once transcends and links generational interests.

I believe that these reforms represent a balanced response to important demographic, social, and economic changes of the past half century. Of course, the dynamics of our time make it certain that the balance between "equity" and "adequacy" reached today may prove ephemeral tomorrow. And some will be outraged by the thought that a contributory system like OASDHI can be strengthened by linking it philosophically and bureaucratically with programs that primarily assist the poor. Nevertheless, viewing social security as the nation's welfare "floor" clarifies options even as it presents limits to policy initiatives. It no longer makes sense to subsidize the middle class, but it would be foolhardy to disregard their claims of entitlement. By the same token, it would be economically and morally culpable to deny the wherewithal for a decent existence to the nation's neediest on fiscal grounds. Any scheme that deals fairly with all is likely to require increased outlays in certain categories.* Critics are bound to think that certain segments of the population – divorced or widowed women, ethnic and racial minorities, for example – benefit disproportionately from the changes that become necessary. Such opposition can be attenuated, however, by making it absolutely clear that social security has always had a significant "welfare" function, and rightly so.

Social security is one of this nation's primary weapons in the continuing struggle against poverty; it provides a basis for the economic well-being of all Americans regardless of age, gender, race, or national origin. Nevertheless, in their present form, neither OASDHI nor SSI nor AFDC addresses a major welfare problem of our time adequately: This nation has proportionately fewer children than ever before, and yet a greater percentage of them live in disadvantaged circumstances than in the past. Nearly half of the children born today will become eligible for child support before reaching age sixteen. Roughly 50 percent of all children living in female-headed households are poor; only 11 percent of the absent fathers of young AFDC beneficiaries pay any child support.[9]

Policymakers do not have, nor should they wish, carte blanche

---

*I have deliberately omitted cost estimates for my proposals. Actuaries expect that OASDI will be fiscally sound for the next fifty years and that the HI component is not in imminent danger of collapse. Some of the proposals I make in this chapter – care-giver credits and earnings sharing – will cost additional money. But others – eliminating mandatory retirement and helping workers to retrain by borrowing against their future pensions – will save money. The bottom line will not be radically above or below current projections.

in addressing this problem. Yet at no time since the Great Depression have greater opportunities existed to rationalize and overhaul the American version of the welfare state. Traditional liberals have been forced by their conservative critics to recognize the limits of time-tested methods for moving the nation. On the other hand, rumors about the demise of the New Deal legacy and reports about the utter futility of Great Society initiatives are greatly exaggerated. A viable social policy can still be built on existing measures.

For instance, reform of AFDC and other means-tested schemes must begin by integrating them with OASDHI's overarching coverage. A proposal for "child support insurance" developed at the Institute for Poverty Research offers a case in point. Under this program, all parents who live apart from their children would be liable for a child-support tax on their gross income. Just as workers now pay FICA taxes into a pay-as-you-go system that benefits survivors, so, too, child-support insurance is designed to protect the vulnerable: It would increase the economic security of the very young while reducing case loads and welfare costs.[10] For the sake of the future – not just to placate contemporary critics – benefits and services must be scrutinized carefully to ensure that social insurance serves the young and middle-aged as well as the old.

Readjusting the balance between social security's insurance and welfare functions, however, involves more than questions of gender and age. Conspicuous by its absence in the social security legislation of 1935 and later is any specific reference to the high incidence of old-age dependency among underprivileged minorities. The program's architects and reformers have been wise not to introduce differential treatment along racial or ethnic lines. The potential for discord in such "compensatory" laws is illustrated by contemporary friction over "quotas" under affirmative-action programs. Nevertheless, no realistic assessment of poverty – at whatever age – can overlook the role discrimination plays in its genesis and perpetuation.

Blacks, for instance, were heavily concentrated in agriculture and domestic service jobs during the 1930s and 1940s – occupations not covered under social security until 1950. As a result, blacks "lost" earnings credits and benefits they otherwise would have garnered if employed in other areas.[11] And although less than 3 percent of all blacks are engaged in farming today, they still suffer occupational disadvantages compared with whites. Nearly three-fifths of all white males, but only one-third of all black males, were employed in the four highest-paid occupations in 1980.

Regardless of age, black males are less likely than whites to work on a full-time, regular basis. Given such employment patterns, it is not surprising that blacks continue to have considerably lower average incomes.[12] Differences in black and white life expectancies at various ages, moreover, put minorities at a disadvantage throughout the life course.

Comparable information on Hispanics is more difficult to obtain, but the data available point up similarities in their situation.[13] With the rapid growth of the Hispanic population, the degree to which various ethnic groups are entitled to a "minimal" standard of living is bound to become a major item on the OASDHI agenda.

American social insurance must provide equitable treatment for minorities in a country in which some people are more equal than others. Once again, the most sensible means to this end is to frankly embrace the primacy of "adequacy" over "equity" in social security – and insist that complementary programs do likewise. Assuring universal coverage in order to take full account of the diversity of the American population, in turn, is the best way of securing justice for all.

E pluribus unum: universal coverage, integrated programs

Paradoxically, although public philosophers have been vociferous lately in debating the merits of distributive justice, Americans on the whole have not been much inclined to talk about what they owe one another. "Our sense of citizenship, of social warmth and a shared fate," laments George Will, "has become thin gruel."[14] Has the ideal of "mutual responsibility" long associated with social insurance become so anemic that it can be regarded as irrelevant to the "me generation"? On the contrary: Social security does not undermine the pursuit of private ambition by honoring this country's commitment to mutual responsibility. A great deal of today's apparent indifference stems from incomplete understanding of what social insurance can and should do. "Our welfare system is not just social security, unemployment insurance and food stamps," Robert J. Samuelson notes, "private employer welfare, from health insurance to pensions, is also intended to minimize economic insecurity."[15] To embrace the logic of the original act and to grasp the strengths and weaknesses of its component programs in their present form is to glimpse the outline of a welfare continuum that deals not just with poor people but with the resources of all. The vision of social security advocated here – one that highlights its intergenerational features and underscores the provision of a socially acceptable minimum standard of living – should become the basis for all future discussions of American "welfare" in the broadest sense of the term.

To make social security the basis for a bolder and more comprehensive agenda, policymakers should at the very least adopt a recent congressional panel's suggestion that "to assure a coherent operational mission, a newly independent social security agency should be responsible for administering the old-age, survivors, and disability insurance and the supplemental security income programs."[16] Particularly as the veterans of World War II enter their retirement years, it will become critical to coordinate health care programs and social services underwritten by the Veterans Administration with OASDHI and SSI. If Americans really want less government and more efficiency, they need to go further: Congress and the president should establish a cabinet-level Department of Income Security. Integrating the other income-maintenance components of America's retirement system with social security would eliminate the artificial distinction still made between "public" and "private" policies. Flexibility and coordination are what the system needs at this stage. The General Accounting Office estimates that 119 of the 306 congressional committees and sub-committees have some responsibility for income-maintenance programs.[17] If one central agency were charged with planning, evaluating, and coordinating various programs in the social insurance complex, a more coherent system would emerge over time, with each part functioning according to the principles that befit its manner of financing and relationship to the others.

Under this scenario, social security would remain a universal program. Its mandated payroll-tax rates and eligibility requirements would remain intact. The 1983 amendments included several "stabilizers," which should protect the OASDI trust funds from bankruptcy. It would be worthwhile – if daring – to find alternatives to the current indexing formulas, however. Automatically expanding benefits may have made sense when resources seemed infinite and long-term economic prospects were ebullient, but this does not mean that it still makes sense today.

Because the practice of automatic indexing was reaffirmed in the 1983 amendments to the Social Security Act, it will be difficult to control OASDHI or any other "entitlement" spending. The decision in 1984 to grant the elderly automatic cost-of-living increases even when the CPI falls below 3 percent in any year raises the possibility that politicians will engage in a bidding war to win the elderly vote by adding supplements to automatic increases.[18] Conversely, the effort by the Reagan administration in 1985 to reduce the federal deficit by freezing COLAs is merely an accounting sleight of hand: Limiting mandatory increases in Title II benefits is just another ploy to limit the scope of this program. And disguising cuts to make them look like increases under an elaborate set of contingency rules would ultimately hurt the poorest among the elderly. Policymakers have boxed themselves into a corner by reifying technical formulas rather than thinking through their purposes.

Future increases in entitlements do not have to conform to some formula that is itself a product of a particular historical moment. Congress probably cannot – and should not – return to liberalizing benefits on an ad hoc basis. If the automatic trigger that adjusts for increases in the CPI of 3 percent or more were eliminated, a fair solution would be to acknowledge that social security is intended to replace "lost" wages. The benefit formula should therefore be more closely related to changes in current workers' average wages. That, after all, is the best way to maintain a balance between the interests of those paying taxes and those receiving pensions. Social security's faithful supporters must not resist these changes simply because they were first advocated by fiscal conservatives. Of course, the growth of benefits cannot be altered independent of other developments in the economy. But if there must be a trade-off between "equity" and "adequacy," it is preferable to put a ceiling on benefits received by the wealthy to ensure that the benefits of those who depend most heavily on social insurance afford them at least a decent standard of living. Rather than "cap" all benefits, as proposed by some members of the Reagan administration,[19] policymakers should rely prudently on Congress's power to tax income, including social security benefits.

The contemporaneous maturing of social security and graying of America, some commentators predict, will make it harder in the future to maintain the rate of return that beneficiaries have enjoyed thus far. Experts disagree, however, on the extent to which the baby-boom generation may get its money's worth. If "money's worth" means that former workers will get benefits roughly equal to their employer/employee contributions, then it appears that single *female* workers with maximum covered earnings will be in a favorable position, because women tend to live longer than men and thus can expect to receive greater lifetime benefits. High-income, single male workers, on the other hand, are unlikely to get a full return after 2000. And "if the pay-roll tax rates are increased to a sufficiently high level so that the system will be on a self-supporting basis, the failure to receive one's 'money's worth' will also apply to the average wage-earner."[20] In plain English, if social security financing is made self-contained and OASI is treated as if it is the only source of retirement income, the course is set for disaster. But such worst-case forecasts overlook or underestimate the extent to which workers with above-average earnings can and will rely on personal savings, IRAs, and private pension plans to supplement their OASDHI benefits. They ignore the protection offered by Disability Insurance and the availability of survivors benefits if tragedy curtails a person's ability to work. They also tend to discount the role that an expanded SSI program might play for the lower-income retiree.[21]

Properly underwriting the insurance and welfare functions of OASDHI requires that fail-safe mechanisms be in place across the board. For this reason, all employer pension programs in the public and private sectors should be monitored and financed in accordance with ERISA regulations. Because it is desirable to provide individuals greater opportunity to save for their old age, policymakers can create incentives that foster a fairer allocation of resources and that help shape priorities as economic conditions warrant. As is now the case for employer pension programs, IRAs, and Keogh accounts, a certain percentage of employer and employee contributions to social security should be excluded from current taxable income. This would make it easier for lower-income workers to supplement their anticipated social security benefits through savings. It would also permit higher-income workers to ensure a greater replacement ratio on retirement. To prevent abuse of this "tax shelter" would require setting a maximum percentage of total annual income that could be set aside.[22]

Policymakers should build on the retirement precedents set by the 1983 amendments and other federal legislation, as well as developments in the private sector. In the interest of individual dignity and freedom of choice, as well as of economic efficiency, mandatory retirement should be eliminated. Admittedly, this will not greatly alter the trend toward earlier exit from the labor force. Far bolder and more effective would be elimination of discrimination against older workers in employment and job training pro-

grams. Only 3.1 percent of all Americans over sixty-five participated in adult education programs in 1981, compared with 12.8
percent of the entire population over seventeen.[23] With few exceptions, corporate training programs are geared to introductory-level
workers and employees under forty. To capitalize on the intellectual resources of aging workers also requires greater emphasis on
preparing people to pursue two or more careers during their
working years. Universities, vocational schools, and other post-
secondary centers should try harder to recruit mature students for
general education and specialized courses – even if they do not
matriculate for a degree. In addition, government officials and
corporate planners should facilitate older people's entry or reentry
into the marketplace. Public policy should encourage experiments
with work programs. Greater priority should be given to federally
seeded volunteering and public service initiatives, such as those
already under way through the Retired Senior Volunteer Program
and the Federal Senior Community Service Employment Program. Surely private enterprise can find better ways to solve
employees' grievances than helping them to qualify for disability
benefits or encouraging them to take early retirement. Work
schedules and benefit packages could be adapted to increase the
chances for men and women in the third quarter of life to earn
money or increased health care protection through part-time
employment. Corporate planners ought to learn from major companies such as McDonald's and Atlantic Richfield that have created a climate in which both employees and employers benefit
from the maturity and reliability of men and women in their sev-
enties. These pacesetters have created job banks, job sharing, and
flexi-time arrangements and have used corporate associations and
newsletters to enhance utilization of their older workers' skills.[24]

Consonant with the transgenerational features of social insurance, workers should be permitted to borrow against their future
pensions to pay for training that will enhance their worth and longevity in the labor force. Particularly in its experimental stages,
policymakers would have to impose strict limits on such an initiative. Workers should not be permitted to take out for educational
purposes more than a fraction of what they have already set aside
for OASDHI protection, because future benefits to people who
opt for this provision will have to be based on FICA contributions
adjusted for educational outlays. Critics probably will charge that
this scheme will only result in lower benefits for many of those
with poor wage histories by the time they retire. The merits of

this idea outweigh its drawbacks, however, because intelligent investment in the future is cheaper in the long run than compensating for past mismanagement of the nation's human capital. At a time of rising tuition and increased pressure on workers to upgrade their skills, this new source of money could make the difference between job burnout and career advancement. The measure could serve as yet another way to coordinate job training and retirement policies.

Changing the tax code and benefit structure in the broad fashion outlined here would encourage more, not less, flexibility in America's retirement system. Administratively, this move would be easier to implement if existing federal agencies dealing with retirement were centralized in a Department of Income Security. Rearranging bureaucratic functions, moreover, would force a reassessment of existing arrangements. Making public-employer pension programs conform to standards established under ERISA, for example, would impose new limits on how to meet existing obligations and liberalize benefits for retired state and municipal workers.[25] Furthermore, special-interest groups in the private sector, such as life insurance companies, would naturally insist on helping to determine how regulations were designed and executed. Because so many of the future economic resources of the elderly are linked to profitable maintenance and growth of private-employer pension funds, such representation would facilitate constructive action. Once a Department of Income Security were established, it would be easier to implement the National Commission on Social Security Reform proposal calling for a bipartisan board of public officials and private experts to monitor the financial health of OASDI. This advisory board should be charged with overseeing developments in all components of the retirement system. Only in this way can American social insurance realize its full potential in guaranteeing economic security.

A Department of Income Security would separate income security and health-related programs. This idea is consistent with notions circulating in both liberal and conservative quarters. "Both for better cost control and management, and for more thoughtful financial arrangements, we ought to sever Medicare entirely from the Social Security system over time," contends Hale Champion, who was undersecretary for Health and Human Services in Carter's administration prior to becoming executive dean of Harvard's Kennedy School of Government.[26] Many liberals agree with President Reagan that Medicaid should become an exclusively federal program. Federalization, in their view, would facilitate an integrated approach to allocating resources and ensuring equitable financing for both acute care and long-term care.[27] There is an important precedent for this idea: In 1977, the administration of Medicare was taken out of social security and put with Medicaid under the aegis of the Health Care Financing Administration. Now that actuaries are persuaded that the "Medicare" crisis has been postponed because of changes in hospital reimbursement under the 1983 amendments, the moment is propitious to disengage health care from income-maintenance programs. Thereafter, the Department of Health and Human Services would be responsible for developing health care programs for Americans of all ages. High on the list of priorities must be adjusting for the long-term care needs of the nation's oldest citizens and the development of some special funding provision to underwrite needed services in a period of spiraling medical costs and growing numbers of potential beneficiaries.

Such a reform would not eliminate rancor over thorny policy issues. For example, it would not solve the problem of how to define or implement "socially acceptable criteria" in designing, administering, and evaluating health care programs. If social insurance is indeed to evolve into a fully intergenerational system, a greater share of public resources will have to be devoted to younger people. Ethical issues surrounding the long-term care of very old citizens and the basis for allocating limited and expensive high-tech medical resources surely will not be resolved merely by changing the government's administrative bureaucracy. Taking HI out of social security, in fact, would guarantee more, not less, potential controversy over such matters at the federal level. Nonetheless, this change would foster a bolder vision of social insurance in America, thereby making it possible to confront difficult choices with a clearer grasp of the situation.

A vision renewed

Treating social security not as a contract but as an expression of community reaffirms some of its most important traditional values. It reinforces the familiar claim that all Americans have a stake in the program. It underscores social security's central role in American life: No other bureaucracy is so well positioned to assure everyone, regardless of race, gender, or age, the financial wherewithal for a decent standard of living. At the same time, it sets an agenda that acknowledges that mutual interdependence in the national community presupposes both a shared past and a common future. For if social insurance is to promote flexibility and a prudent investment in the future, thereby maximizing each person's options in a highly fluid, uncertain, and technocratically driven society, social security bears major responsibility for ensuring fundamental protection across public and private sectors alike.

Under a reformed and renewed system of the sort I have sketched, people who currently get lost in the shuffle would have more protection – which in turn might make them more productive. Think about the plight of Ron, a fifty-five-year-old unemployed steelworker. After working steadily from 1950 to 1982, Ron received a modest pension from his company, but his prospects for reemployment in Pittsburgh are grim. He is too young to qualify for an old-age pension and too healthy to collect disability. His unemployment benefits have run out, and he does not want to leave his hometown. Remarried, with two children under sixteen, Ron could live apart from this family so that they could qualify for AFDC. What he really wants to do is get paralegal training so that he can reenter the job market. But Ron lacks funds and cannot qualify for a student loan or the GI bill. Under my scheme, Ron could become "dependent" on social insurance, borrowing from the government against the collateral of his future Title II pension to finance his schooling. Investing in Ron makes sense: With a steady job, he can support his family, stay productive, and regain faith in his abilities.

Or consider the case of Thelma, a forty-three-year-old black woman who is desperate. She may never collect social security. She was married too briefly to qualify for spousal benefits. And Thelma is about to lose her claim for a disability entitlement. Very obese, she tells a judge considering her petition that "My backs and legs hurt me so bad. I hurts all over . . . I vomits." The state disability-determination office, the judge declares, "says that you could operate a feather-cutting machine. Could you do this?" "What's a feather-cutting machine?" she answers.[28] Rather than put Thelma in a Catch-22 situation, it would be wiser to let her earn Title II credits while receiving welfare: Let Thelma join the working poor by taking care of her aged mother, who would otherwise have to move into a nursing home – at public expense. The mother benefits from the support of kin in a familiar environment. Thelma benefits by carrying out meaningful, if nonremunerated, work while on public assistance. At the same time, she earns a modest pension for a dignified old age of her own. Here, too, the government makes an excellent investment. It reduces its overall welfare costs. At the same time, it avoids forcing Thelma into an unsuitable workfare program. Best of all, it nurtures the spirit of mutual responsibility in a family setting.

Can the nation afford such compassion? It cannot well avoid it. And to be honest, as the day of reckoning approaches, the humanitarian impulse works to the enlightened advantage of all. Americans consider it in the national interest to spend billions on defense and to rebuild roads and bridges. Surely it makes at least as much sense to pay for the revitalization of precious human resources. Helping Ron and Thelma through imaginative uses of modest social security outlays will benefit their children and parents and will protect society at large by promoting "the general welfare."

The "community" embodied in social security is fragile; yet it is integral to the nation's fabric. As a people, Americans must constantly renew their adherence to the long-standing value of mutual responsibility by reshaping their most successful domestic policy. The treatment of fellow citizens under social security mirrors, for better and for worse, the essential quality of the American experiment.

Notes

Introduction

1 *Social Security Bulletin* 47(July 1984):40–1, 57–9; "47% of Households Receive Federal Benefits, Census Bureau Says," *New York Times,* April 17, 1985, p. 9.

2 Paul Light, *Artful Work* (New York: Random House, 1985), p. 42; Congressional Panel on Social Security Organization, *A Plan to Establish an Independent Agency for Social Security* (Washington, D.C.: Government Printing Office, 1984), p. 96.

3 John Kenneth Galbraith, "The Heartless Society," *New York Times Magazine,* September 2, 1984, p. 44.

4 *Report of the National Commission on Social Security Reform* (Washington, D.C.: Government Printing Office, 1983), p. 2-2.

5 See *Congressional Record* 129(March 21, 1983):S3488. The full text is in letter from Thomas Jefferson to Samuel Kercheval, July 12, 1816, *The Writings of Thomas Jefferson,* ed. Albert Ellery Bergh (Washington, D.C.: Thomas Jefferson Memorial Association, 1907), vol. 15, pp. 40–1.

6 Gary Hart, *The New Democracy* (New York: William Morrow, 1983); Paul Tsongas, *The Road from Here* (New York: Knopf, 1981); Robert B. Reich, *The Next American Frontier* (New York: Times Books, 1983).

7 *Congressional Record* 129(March 24, 1983):S4098.

1 Social security: the early years

For general background material, I relied heavily on Edward D. Berkowitz and Kim McQuaid, *Creating the Welfare State* (New York: Praeger, 1980); Stuart Brandes, *American Welfare Capitalism* (University of Chicago Press, 1975); Robert Bremner, *From the Depths* (New York University Press, 1956); Roy Lubove, *Struggle for Social Security* (Cambridge, Mass.: Harvard University Press, 1968); James T. Patterson, *America's Struggle Against Poverty, 1900–1980* (Cambridge, Mass.: Harvard University Press, 1981); Paul Starr, *The Social Transformation of American Medicine* (New York: Basic Books, 1982); Carolyn L. Weaver, *The Crisis in Social Security* (Durham, N.C.: Duke Press Policy Studies, 1982); and Daniel Nelson, *Unemployment Insurance* (Madison: University of Wisconsin Press, 1969). Classic primary sources include I. M. Rubinow, *Social Insurance* (New York: Henry Holt, 1913); idem, *The Quest for Security* (New York: Henry Holt, 1934); and Abraham Epstein, *The Challenge of the Aged* (New York: Vanguard Press, 1928).

For European precedents, see Hugh Heclo, *Modern Social Politics in Britain and Sweden* (New Haven, Conn.: Yale University Press, 1974); Peter A. Köhler and Hans F. Zacher, eds., with Martin Partington, *The Evolution of Social Insurance* (New York: St. Martin's Press, 1982).

Basic documents for the original social security legislation include U.S. Committee on Economic Security, *Social Security in America* (Washington, D.C.: Government Printing Office, 1937) [abbreviated in notes as CES], which presented the case for the 1935 law; U.S. Congressional Hearings before the Committee on Finance, U.S. Senate, 74th Cong., 1st sess., on S. 1130 (January 22–February 20, 1935); and Hearings before the Committee on Ways and Means, House of Representatives, 74th Cong., 1st sess., on H.R. 4120 (January 21–February 12, 1935) [notes refer to these documents as "Hearings on S. 1130" and "Hearings on H.R. 4120," respectively]; U.S. Social Security Board, *Social Security Bill, Summary of Provisions, Comparison of Text of Original Bill, and Ways and Means Redraft, Compilation of Proposed Amendments, etc., for Committee on Finance* (Washington, D.C.: Government Printing Office, 1935) [abbreviated as *Comparison of Text*]; and *The Public Papers and Addresses of Franklin Delano Roosevelt*, 13 vols., ed. Samuel I. Rosenman (New York: various publishers, 1935–80) [cited in notes as *FDR Public Papers*].

Essential books by those who helped to create social security: Arthur J. Altmeyer, *The Formative Years of Social Security* (Madison: University of Wisconsin Press, 1963); J. Douglas Brown, *The Genesis of the American Social Security System* (Princeton University: Industrial Relations Section, 1969); idem, *Essays on Social Security* (Princeton University: Industrial Relations Section, 1977); Edwin E. Witte, *The Development of the Social Security Act* (Madison: University of Wisconsin Press, 1963).

On the changing status of the elderly, see W. Andrew Achenbaum, *Old Age in the New Land* (Baltimore: Johns Hopkins University Press, 1978); Irving Bernstein, *A Caring Society* (Boston: Houghton Mifflin, 1985); Michel Dahlin, "From Poorhouse to Pension: The Changing View of Old Age in America, 1890–1929" (unpublished PhD dissertation, Stanford University, 1982); David Hackett Fischer, *Growing Old in America* (Oxford University Press, 1977); Carole Haber, *Beyond Sixty-Five* (Cambridge University Press, 1983); Gail Buchwalter King and Peter N. Stearns, "The Retirement Experience as a Policy Factor," *Journal of Social History* 14(Summer 1981):589–625; and Tamara K. Hareven, "The Last Stage: Historical Adulthood and Old Age," *Aging, Death, and the Completion of Being*, ed. David D. Van Tassel (Philadelphia: University of Pennsylvania Press, 1979), pp. 175–8.

For old-age retirement programs, see William Graebner, *A History of*

Retirement (New Haven: Yale University Press, 1980); Murray Webb Latimer, *Industrial Pension Systems in the United States and Canada,* 2 vols. (New York: Industrial Relations Counselors, 1932); idem, *Trade Union Pension Systems and Other Total Disability Benefits in the United States and Canada* (New York: Industrial Relations Counselors, 1932); U.S. Bureau of Labor Statistics, *Public Old-Age Pensions and Insurance in the United States and Foreign Countries,* bulletin no. 561 (Washington, D.C.: Government Printing Office, 1932).

The rise of the "gray lobby": Jackson K. Putnam, *Old-Age Politics in California* (Stanford University Press, 1970); Richard L. Neuberger and Kelley Loe, *An Army of the Aged* (Caldwell, Ind.: Caxton Printers, 1936); Committee on Old-Age Security, *The Townsend Crusade* (New York: Twentieth Century Fund, 1936); Allen Brinkley, *Voices of Protest* (New York: Vintage, 1982); and Henry J. Pratt, *The Gray Lobby* (University of Chicago Press, 1976).

1 The impetus, timing, and development of specific unemployment insurance measures and old-age pensions varied from place to place. Some policymakers abroad cited the need to respond to increasing demographic pressures and the unfortunate consequences of industrialization. Others hoped that replacing punitive poor laws with measures that gave citizens benefits as a matter of "right" would strengthen their government's legitimacy and win their party support among key (interest) groups in the population.

2 This theme is graphically depicted in a cartoon in *American Labor Legislation Review* 9(March 1919):48.

3 Lobbyists, particularly those affiliated with the American Association for Labor Legislation, hoped to build on the passage of workmen's compensation laws in various states. Enacting compulsory insurance against industrial accidents, they argued, seemed analogous to offering protection against sickness and old-age poverty. Others called for federal initiatives, invoking the British National Insurance Act (1911), which provided mandatory insurance and unemployment coverage to all employees between sixteen and seventy who earned less than three pounds per week. Teddy Roosevelt's 1912 "Bull Moose" party platform affirmed the need for a nationwide system of old-age pensions. Similar pleas were made thereafter in each session of Congress.

4 Business lobbies – like the Pennsylvania State Chamber of Commerce in 1924 – characterized old-age pensions as an "insidious experiment in paternalistic government" that would sap the self-respect and destroy the moral fiber of thousands of people, besides costing the taxpayers millions of dollars.

5 "The vast amount of human suffering and the enormous relief costs, which inevitably will result in increased taxes, show conclusively the folly of failure to give thought to the security of men, women, and children." Hearings on S. 1130, p. 27.

6 In addition to more general works, see Solomon Barkin, *The Older*

Worker in Industry (Albany: J. B. Lyon, 1933); and Johanna Lobsenz, *The Older Woman in Industry* (New York: Scribner, 1929).

7 Marjorie Shearon, "Economic Status of the Aged," *Social Security Bulletin* 1(March 1938):5–16. Since at least the nineteenth century, wealth had been strongly correlated to age. See Lee Soltow, *Men and Wealth in the United States, 1850–1870* (New Haven: Yale University Press, 1975).

8 Joel F. Handler, ed., *Family Law and the Poor* (Westport, Conn.: Greenwood, 1971), especially ch. 5.

9 In 1929, some 82% of all beneficiaries of public and private plans were recipients of war-related survivor and disability pensions; 80% of all money distributed through pensions came exclusively from this source. U.S. Bureau of Labor Statistics, *Care of Aged Persons in the United States*, bulletin no. 489 (Washington, D.C.: Government Printing Office, October 1929), pp. 2–3; see also William Glasson, *Federal Military Pensions in the United States* (Oxford University Press, 1918); and Donald L. McMurry, "The Political Significance of the Pension Question, 1885–1897," *Mississippi Valley Historical Review* 9(June 1922):19–36.

10 Edgar Sydenstricker, "Existing Agencies for Health Insurance in the United States," in U.S. Department of Labor bulletin no. 212, *Proceedings of the Conference on Social Insurance* (Washington, D.C.: Government Printing Office, 1917), pp. 43–75; *Report of the Health Insurance Commission of Pennsylvania* (Harrisburg, Pa.: J. L. L. Kuhn, 1919).

11 Hence, the boundaries distinguishing old age, unemployment, and disability here and in other industrial nations were fuzzy even before the enactment of social security.

12 Graebner, *Retirement*, pp. 92–3; *Pension Facts* (Washington, D.C.: American Council of Life Insurance, 1982), pp. 35–6.

13 The system originally provided pensions for workers over age seventy with at least fifteen years of service. In an effort to merge existing programs, different retirement criteria were set for several categories of workers: Mechanics, letter carriers, and post-office clerks could retire at sixty-five; railway clerks were eligible for full benefits at sixty-two.

14 In 1875, the American Express Company became the first private firm to grant some workers past the age of sixty employer-financed compensation on retirement. The earliest manufacturing-sector pension plan was begun by the Carnegie Steel Company in 1901; two years later, an informal arrangement was set up by the Standard Oil Company of New Jersey. The Granite Cutters Union has the distinction of being the first trade union to establish a fund (1905) that paid retirement benefits; the International Typographical Union was the first large union to adopt a formal plan.

15 The 1921 Revenue Act excluded from current taxation all income derived from stock-bonus and profit-sharing plans that benefited "some or all" workers in a company. (Partly in response to the new

market that this change in the tax code created, the Metropolitan Life Insurance Company issued the first American group annuity contract; other insurance companies quickly followed suit.) The 1926 Revenue Act accorded preferential tax treatment to pension trusts. Consistent with the principle that a program need not cover all workers, the 1928 Revenue Act made it legal and advantageous for companies to establish retirement pension funds for owners and managers – excluding rank-and-file employees. See Sylvester J. Schieber, *Social Security* (Washington, D.C.: Employee Benefit Research Institute, 1982), p. 46.

16 There was considerable variation in eligibility criteria and average benefits. Roughly half the states adopted age sixty-five as the minimum age for receiving a pension; the other half selected seventy. Most states imposed residency requirements and set income and/or property limits, though three jurisdictions established no "means test." (A means test establishes eligibility criteria based on demonstrable economic needs. One must "prove" that one's total of earnings, assets, savings, and any other available means of support counted by administrators does not exceed a specified dollar amount.) The typical Maryland senior citizen on relief received a monthly pension worth $29.90, nearly five times greater than that paid in Indiana; the 1933 nationwide average was $19.25.

17 Statistics from James T. Patterson, *America in the Twentieth Century* (New York: Harcourt Brace Jovanovich, 1976), pp. 198–203; and Lester V. Chandler, *America's Greatest Depression, 1929–1941* (New York: Harper & Row, 1970), pp. 3, 15, 36, 48, 127.

18 According to the Federal Emergency Relief Administration, the average monthly relief benefits per family rose from $15.15 to $29.33 between May 1933 and May 1935. See *FERA Monthly Report* (February 1936):8. The number who really needed help was probably even greater than indicated earlier: About 80% of Philadelphia's 280,000 unemployed, it was estimated, received no help whatsoever in 1932. See Hearings on H.R. 4120, p. 19.

19 Robert S. Lynd, *Knowledge for What?* (Princeton University Press, 1939), pp. 11–12.

20 Paul H. Douglas, *Social Security in America* (New York: McGraw-Hill, 1936), pp. 6–7.

21 A Massachusetts Census for Unemployment (1934) indicated an overall unemployment rate of 25.2%; the percentages for those aged sixty to sixty-four and sixty-five to sixty-nine were 27.2% and 29.8%, respectively. See Industrial Research Department, *Unemployment in Philadelphia Families, April 1931* (Philadelphia: Wharton School of Finance and Commerce, 1931), p. 20; and *Monthly Labor Review* 43 (November 1936):1157–61.

22 "Old Age Pensions," *Encyclopedia of Social Sciences,* 15 vols. (New York: Macmillan, 1937), vol. 11, pp. 456–7.

23 Sonia Kay and Irma Rittenhouse, "Why Are the Aged Poor?" *Sur-*

vey 75(September 15, 1930):486; I. M. Rubinow, *The Quest for Security* (New York: Henry Holt, 1934), p. 250.

24 Frank G. Dickinson, "New Class War," *Saturday Evening Post* 210 (August 7, 1937):23, 81; Richard Lowitt and Maurine Beasley, eds., *One Third of a Nation: Lorena Hickok Reports on the Great Depression* (Urbana: University of Illinois Press, 1981), pp. 169, 227; Federal Writers' Project, *These Are Our Lives* (Chapel Hill: University of North Carolina Press, 1939), pp. 90, 374.

25 Robert S. McElvaine, ed., *Down and Out in the Great Depression* (Chapel Hill: University of North Carolina Press, 1983), pp. 84, 105–8; and David M. Kennedy, ed., *The American People in the Depression* (New York: Pendulum Press, 1973), pp. 165–6.

26 McElvaine, *Down and Out,* p. 100.

27 Despite their differences, it is worth noting that each of these measures promised a flat grant at a level deemed "adequate" to permit an older person a comfortable life. Such generosity was to be made possible by utilizing the taxing authority of the central government.

28 Louis Leotta, "Abraham Epstein and the Movement for Old Age Security," *Labor History* 16(Summer 1975):364–82.

29 Several corporate executives served on Roosevelt's 1934 Committee on Economic Security, which helped draft the first social security bill; those with ties to the Department of Commerce's Business Advisory Council, including the United States Chamber of Commerce and the National Retail Dry Goods Association, testified in favor of the 1935 bill. The National Association of Manufacturers and various state-level manufacturing groups, however, opposed the legislation, For more on business and union views in 1935, see Jill S. Quadagno, "Welfare Capitalism and the Social Security Act of 1935," *American Sociological Review* 49(October 1984):632–47; and Wilbur J. Cohen, "Attitude of Organized Groups toward Social Insurance," in *Readings in Social Security,* eds. William Haber and Wilbur J. Cohen, 1st ed. (Englewood Cliffs, N.J.: Prentice-Hall, 1948), p. 130.

30 Senator Clarence Dill (D–Wash.) offered several proposals between 1930 and 1932 to authorize federal grants-in-aid equal to one-third of a state's total expenditure for old-age assistance. Representative William Connery, Jr. (D–Mass.) joined in sponsoring similar bills during the 1933–4 session. Senator Robert J. Wagner (D–N.Y.) and Representative David J. Lewis (D–Md.) introduced a bill in February 1934 that would have fostered the creation of unemployment insurance programs at the state level. For the significance of the Railroad Retirement Act, see Graebner, *Retirement,* ch. 6.

31 "Objectives of the Administration," June 8, 1934, in *FDR Public Papers,* vol. III, pp. 291–2.

32 This theme appears in "Address to the Advisory Council of the Committee on Economic Security," November 14, 1934, in *FDR*

Public Papers, vol. III, p. 454; Hearings on S. 1130, pp. 104–5; and the president's letter of transmittal of the report of the Committee on Economic Security, January 17, 1935. For more on the need for a centralized polity to administer a complex welfare state, see Harold L. Wilensky, *The Welfare State and Equality* (Berkeley: University of California Press, 1975), ch. 2; Barry Karl, *Executive Reorganization and Reform in the New Deal* (Cambridge, Mass.: Harvard University Press, 1963). For the development of the intellectual case for this move, see Sidney Fine, *Laissez-Faire and the General Welfare State* (Ann Arbor: University of Michigan Press, 1956).

33 For more on this, see James Holt, "The New Deal and the American Anti-Statist Tradition," and Ellis W. Hawley, "The New Deal and Business," in *The New Deal: The National Level,* eds. John Braeman, Robert H. Bremner, and David Brody (Columbus: Ohio State University Press, 1975); and Barry D. Karl, *The Uneasy State* (University of Chicago Press, 1983), especially ch. 7.

34 "Roosevelt Bars Plans Now for Broad Social Program; Seeks Job Insurance Only," *New York Times,* November 15, 1934, p. 1.

35 Because reliable accounts of this political history are already available, I have chosen here and throughout the book not to be exhaustive in recounting details.

36 CES, pp. 189–90; Hearings on S. 1130, p. 1338; and *Congressional Record,* April 16, 1935, p. 5789.

37 Title I, *Social Security Act,* 49 Stat. 620 (1935), ch. 531. It was not known how many elderly Americans actually needed assistance. The Committee on Economic Security assumed that at least 50 percent of the population over sixty-five was "dependent"; this figure was accepted by the lawmakers. See CES report, pp. 149, 154.

38 For the original wording of Title I, *Comparison of Text,* p. 7. For Witte's defense and others' criticisms, see Hearings on S. 1130, pp. 70–1, 517, 917. Consequently, it was inevitable that states' old-age assistance laws would continue to differ concerning the maximum amount of personal and real property, income, and child support an aged person could possess and still qualify for relief.

39 After January 1, 1942, people over sixty-five who had a sufficient amount of cumulative covered wages would be able to collect a monthly pension (in amounts eventually up to $85 – though the maximum at the time rarely exceeded $25.00). This approach, the Senate Finance Committee noted, at once "represents a minimum of what the American People have a right to expect" and would "go far toward realizing 'the ambition of the individual to obtain for him and his a proper security'." See U.S. Senate, 74th Cong., 1st sess., *Report of the Senate Finance Committee on the Social Security Bill,* no. 628, p. 28. As will be seen, the financing and benefit structure Title II was altered by the 1939 legislation.

40 Roosevelt's guidelines are cited in Arthur M. Schlesinger, Jr., *The*

Coming of the New Deal (Boston: Houghton Mifflin, 1958), pp. 308–9. In the original act, legislators separated titles pertaining to revenues and those related to appropriations. Hence, employee and employer taxes were levied under Title VIII, not Title II. This was done to avoid a possible confrontation with the Supreme Court, which in 1935 had ruled the Railroad Retirement Act unconstitutional for contravening the due process clause of the Fifth Amendment. The crux of the matter was the compulsory nature of participation in – and contributions to – the retirement fund.

41 For policymakers' concerns, see Hearings on H.R. 4120, pp. 901–2; and Brown, *Essays,* p. 61. For the impact of this decision, see Douglas, *Social Security,* pp. 30–1; and W. S. Woytinsky, *Labor in the United States, Basic Statistics for Social Security* (Washington, D.C.: Social Science Research Council, 1936), pp. 3–4, 26. The impact of exclusion of federal workers and those elderly already covered by private pensions is discussed in Chapter 7.

42 CES, p. 203. For a fine historical analysis of some of the economic issues at stake, see Mark Leff, "Taxing the 'Forgotten Man': The Politics of Social Security Finance in the New Deal," *Journal of American History* [*JAH*] 70(September 1983):359–81. See also the exchange between Robert J. Myers and Leff on the "regressive" and "progressive" features of the law in *JAH* 71(June 1984):212–16. The 1939 amendments to social security altered this formula before the first benefit was paid out.

43 Canada, New Zealand, and Scandinavia had all inaugurated their social security programs by paying a flat pension to all who attained a certain age; later on, these nations added a contributory social insurance scheme, basing pensions on past earnings and contributions. See U.S. Department of Health, Education, and Welfare, *Social Security in a Changing World* (Washington, D.C.: Government Printing Office, 1979). In this country, one can trace the idea of universal grants back at least to the 1920s and 1930s, when reformers such as Francis Townsend, Abraham Epstein, and I. M. Rubinow rallied support for nationally funded old-age pensions that did not rely on a means test or prior work experience to determine eligibility or benefit levels. Actually, Thomas Paine was the first person in America to propose the idea, but it received scant attention at the time (1797).

44 Brown, *Essays,* pp. 28–31. See also Edwin E. Witte, "Old-Age Security in the Social Security Act" (1937), in *Social Security Perspectives: Essays by Edwin E. Witte,* ed. Robert J. Lampman (Madison: University of Wisconsin Press, 1962), p. 146.

45 There is some evidence to suggest that using the retirement mechanisms created in Title II to reduce unemployment was an objective of some policymakers. For instance, Barbara Armstrong leaves no doubt that she believed that no one over the age of sixty-five should

get "retirement" benefits unless he or she had left the labor force. Several witnesses appearing before the House Ways and Means Committee and Senate Finance Committee recommended using old-age provisions as a way to reduce unemployment rates. Philip Ickler submitted a pamphlet, "Old-Age Pensions and the Solution of Unemployment," which recommended that all men over the age of sixty who worked for a salary or in any paid position should be "retired within 30 days and automatically pensioned from then on continuously until death." Professor Armstrong's memoir is part of Columbia University's oral history collection at Butler Library. Ickler's testimony appears in Hearings on S. 1130, p. 1238. Graebner relied heavily on Armstrong's oral history and congressional testimony to support his argument that social security was designed primarily as an instrument of social control, an employment tool to help the young by forcing the aged to stop working. As will become evident here and in Chapter 5, I think that Graebner overstates his case. Still, his provocative interpretation is essential reading.

46 U.S. President's Research Committee on Recent Social Trends, *Recent Social Trends*, 2 vols. (New York: McGraw-Hill, 1933), vol. I, p. 818; Abraham Epstein, "Old Age Security – A National Issue," *The World Tomorrow* 12(October 1929):418–20; Dwight L. Palmer and John A. Brownell, "Influence of Age on Employment Opportunities," *Monthly Labor Review* 48(April 1939):780–2. See also Daniel Nelson, *Managers and Workers* (Madison: University of Wisconsin Press, 1975), pp. 151–6.

47 For the original House draft concerning a "retirement test" and Section 202(d) of the final law, see *Comparison of Text*, pp. 4–7, 23, 29.

48 CES, p. 381; Hearings on S. 1130, p. 1337.

49 Sections 301, 401, and 1001 of the act.

50 Sections 501, 511, 521, 531, 601, and 603 of the act.

51 "Presidential Statement upon Signing the Social Security Act, August 14, 1935," in *FDR Public Papers*, vol. IV, p. 324.

52 "A Message on Social Security to Congress, January 17, 1935," in *FDR Public Papers*, vol. IV, p. 44.

53 CES, p. 496.

54 Established under Title VII, the Social Security Board was the federal agency responsible for administering the fledgling program. It was also charged with "studying and making recommendations as to the most effective ways of providing economic security through social insurance." As late as July 1, 1936, there were only fifty-three employees staffing the Bureau of Federal Old-Age Benefits.

55 CES, pp. 161–71; New York State, New York Laws, 159th sess. (1936), ch. 693.

56 "Almshouse Care and the Old-Age Assistance Program," *Social Security Bulletin* 1(March 1938):42–3. See also Chapter 8 in this volume.

57 Jerry R. Cates, *Insuring Inequality: Administrative Leadership in Social Security, 1935–54* (Ann Arbor: University of Michigan Press, 1983), p. 29–35; Kenneth S. David, "The Birth of Social Security," *American Heritage* 30(April/May 1979):49–51.

58 Actually, it is not hard to figure out the worth of contributions. A worker who was sixty years old in 1937 and who earned an average of $600 per year during the next five years could have expected a pension of $15.00 per month. Even had that worker earned five times as much, the pension would have been only $25.00 per month. To put these amounts into perspective, the average *weekly* earning for production workers – the very class of people to be covered by social security at the outset – was $23.82; by 1942 the figure had risen to $36.68. U.S. Department of Commerce, *Historical Statistics of the United States, Colonial Times to 1970* (Washington, D.C.: Government Printing Office, 1975), p. 162.

59 In drawing up the 1935 measures, legal draftsmen had eschewed any indirect taxing device that might be perceived as pressuring states or industrial concerns to submit to a federal program. They deliberately separated titles pertaining to revenues from those related to appropriations; thus, taxes on employees and employers were levied in Title VIII, not Title II. This concern also explains why the unemployment compensation benefits set forth in Title III were separated from the taxes imposed in Title IX. See Brown, *Genesis,* pp. 5–8; Martha Derthick, *Policymaking for Social Security* (Washington, D.C.: Brookings Institution, 1979), p. 214n.

60 Charles McKinley and Robert W. Frase, *Launching Social Security: A Capture-and-Record Account, 1935–1937* (Madison: University of Wisconsin Press, 1970), p. 453.

61 Richard L. Neuberger and Kelley Loe, *An Army of the Aged* (Caldwell, Id.: Caxton Printers, 1936); Putnam, *Old-Age Politics,* pp. 89–115; Frances Fox Piven and Richard A. Cloward, *Regulating the Poor* (New York: Vintage, 1971), pp. 100–4; Alan Brinkley, *Voices of Protest* (New York: Knopf, 1982). For policymakers' concern, see Cates, *Insuring Inequality,* pp. 104–5.

62 Edwin C. Rozwenc, *The Making of American Society* (Boston: Allyn & Bacon, 1973), vol. 2, p. 362; Robert S. Lynd and Helen M. Lynd, *Middletown in Transition* (New York: Harcourt Brace & Co., 1937), pp. 128–9, 246.

63 "Text of Governor Landon's Milwaukee Address on Economic Security," *New York Times,* September 27, 1936, p. 31. Immediate reaction to Landon's speech was mixed. The *New York Times* declared that it was "the kind of address deplorably infrequent in political campaigns." See "Landon on Social Security," ibid., September 28, 1936, p. 18. Whereas Democrats predictably seized on the speech to win votes, it was somewhat surprising that John G. Winant, the former Republican governor of New Hampshire, resigned his posi-

tion as chairman of the Social Security Board so that he could attack Landon and defend the program. See "Wagner Assails Landon as Vague," *New York Times,* October 4, 1936, p. 39; "Winant Resigns So He Can Attack Landon and Defend Security Act," ibid., September 29, 1936, pp. 1, 23; "Winant Denounces Pay-Slip Warning," ibid., October 27, 1936, p. 18.

64 "Landon Based His Attack on Security Act on Report to Group Backed by Filene," *New York Times,* October 1, 1936, p. 1. The Fund had first become interested in this topic early in 1935, when its chief benefactor, Edward A. Filene, proposed that a comparative study of the Long, Coughlin, and Townsend movements be undertaken. See Edward A. Filene, "Report of the President for Year ending February 28, 1935," in *Twentieth Century Fund Executive Minutes,* vol. 1, p. 125. The story of the Fund's involvement in this project can be reconstructed through the minutes of the executive meeting, in ibid., vol. 1, pp. 140–1 (December 28, 1935); p. 153 (April 10, 1936); p. 178 (March 25, 1937); p. 192 (May 11, 1937); and the minutes of "Special Meeting of the Board of Trustees," p. 164 (June 4, 1936). The minutes of the Fund's Committee on Old Age Security have been lost, but pertinent details can be found in "Security Data Row Carried to London," *New York Times,* October 2, 1936, p. 3. Further information on the controversy can be found in "Research Report Text on Which Governor Landon Based His Milwaukee Speech on Security," *New York Times,* October 1, 1936, p. 18. Also, "Security in Politics," ibid., October 2, 1936, p. 24; and "A Judas Kiss for Social Security," *The New Republic* 88(October 14, 1936):268. I found that the changes between initial draft and final report were merely editorial. See *More Security for Old Age* (New York: Twentieth Century Fund, 1937), pp. 73ff.

65 In May 1937 the Supreme Court validated the social security program in two landmark decisions. In *Stewart Machine Company v. Davis,* five liberal justices accepted the unemployment excise tax on employers and approved the federal-state funding apparatus. In *Helvering v. Davis,* the Court upheld (again by a 5-to-4 decision) the statute's old-age insurance tax and retirement benefit provisions. Delivering the majority opinion, Mr. Justice Cardozo noted that because the old-age problem was "plainly national in area and dimension," Congress had the right to "spend money in aid of the general welfare." See U.S. Congress, Senate, *Constitutionality of the Social Security Act,* doc. no. 74, 75th Cong., 1st sess., pp. 32–5; Alfred H. Kelly and Winfred A. Harbison, *The American Constitution,* 4th ed. (New York: Norton, 1970), pp. 767–8.

66 These data are taken from George Gallup, *The Gallup Poll: Public Opinion, 1936–1971,* 3 vols. (New York: Random House, 1972), vol. I, pp. 9, 76, 292–3. Most Americans, however, did not fully understand the difference between the government's old-age assis-

tance and old-age insurance programs. "Despite the numerous articles which have been written," lamented Edwin Witte, "the two parts of the old age security program are confused and many of the essential features have been grossly misrepresented." Quoted in Michael E. Schiltz, *Public Attitudes toward Social Security, 1935–1965,* Social Security Administration research report no. 33 (Washington, D.C.: Government Printing Office, 1970), p. 34.

67 *Congressional Record,* vol. 81, January 29, 1937, p. 548. To mobilize support for this position, the senator wrote a stinging piece in one of the nation's major periodicals. See "The $47,000,000,000 Blight," *Saturday Evening Post* 209(April 24, 1937):5–7, 101–2, 104.

68 When the Twentieth Century Fund issued *More Security for Old Age,* 188 news items, 39 articles, 40 book reviews, and 143 editorials dealing specifically with it appeared between July and December 1937. CBS broadcast a coast-to-coast radio program on the book on June 30. These statistics are found in "The Director's Report," Twentieth Century Fund (1936–7), pp. 4–5. See also Witte's pointed critique in *Social Service Review* 12(March 1938):34–40.

69 Abraham Epstein, "Killing Old Age Security with Kindness," *Harper's Magazine* 175(July 1937):192. See also Daniel S. Sanders, *The Impact of Reform Movements on Social Policy Change* (Fair Lawn, N.J.: R. E. Burdick, 1973), pp. 70–9, 145–8.

70 William E. Leuchtenburg, *Franklin D. Roosevelt and the New Deal, 1932–1940* (New York: Harper & Row, 1963), pp. 244–53; Albert M. Romasco, *The Politics of Recovery* (Oxford University Press, 1983), pp. 226–34.

71 See U.S. Social Security Board, *Economic Insecurity in Old Age* (Washington, D.C.: Government Printing Office, 1937), pp. 12–13. The board was careful to note that its perception of "dependency" was not the only way to define the situation. Nonetheless, its report presented the first "conclusive" evidence that a majority of older people in the United States were dependent.

72 Memorandum from Altmeyer to Roosevelt, September 11, 1937, reprinted in Altmeyer, *Formative Years,* pp. 295–6. Congress had authorized the Social Security Board and Senate Finance Committee to appoint an advisory council in May, but because House Democrats on the Ways and Means Committee and members of the Roosevelt administration were suspicious of the conservatives' intentions, the Social Security Board purposely delayed setting a date for the Advisory Council to meet. See *Congressional Record,* May 10, 1937, pp. 4262–3.

73 The Advisory Council was presented with a list of eight matters to consider in the course of amending Titles II and VIII in its charter. See the foreword to the *Final Report of the Advisory Council on Social Security,* reprinted in J. Douglas Brown, *Essays on Social Security* (Princeton, N.J.: Industrial Relations Section, 1977), appendix, pp. 3–4. The council offered ten recommendations on ways to liberalize

benefits, eleven proposals about financing, and a number of sugges-
tions for future action. For reactions expressed by Roosevelt, Van-
denberg, and Senator Henry Cabot Lodge (among others), see
Congressional Record, April 8, 1938, pp. 5050–1; Altmeyer, *Formative
Years,* p. 91; and Edward D. Berkowitz, "The First Social Security
Crisis," *Prologue* 15(Fall 1983):133–49.

74 Ibid., p. 17.

75 By substituting a dollar figure for the vague term "regular employment," policymakers hoped to give the aged clearer guidelines in
deciding whether or not to work. Because only wages in *covered*
occupational categories counted, older people could seek gainful
employment in positions not specifically subject to social security
taxes. Self-employment, for instance, was a legitimate option.
Although the $15-per-month ceiling was low, it was not as ridicu-
lously low as it might seem today. After all, the median income of
all full-time workers in 1939 was $92.67 monthly for whites and
$38.33 for blacks and other minorities. The median annual salary for
farmers and farm managers was $373. Laborers earned about $56
per month; the median wage for farm laborers was $309 per annum.
(Figures derived from *Historical Statistics,* p. 304.) By imposing an
earnings ceiling, policymakers were responding to the concerns of
labor-union officials, business executives, and representatives of
insurance companies, who worried that if an appreciable number of
social security beneficiaries continued to be employed on a full-time
basis, their presence in the marketplace might tempt employers to
reduce the wage rate for younger people. See Wilbur J. Cohen,
Retirement Policies under Social Security (Berkeley: University of California Press, 1957), p. 69. For more on this, see Chapter 5 in this
volume.

76 *Congressional Record,* June 10, 1939, p. 6964.

77 Federal grants-in-aid for dependent children, for instance, were raised
to a 50: 50 basis, rather than depending on the states to provide 67
percent of the relief as the 1935 law had stipulated.

78 J. Douglas Brown, "Economic Problems in the Provision of Security Against Life Hazards of Workers," *American Economic Review*
30(March 1940):67; Frank Bane, "Social Security Expands," *Social
Service Review* 13(December 1939):608–9.

79 *Final Report of the Advisory Council on Social Security,* December 10,
1938, p. 18.

80 *Final Report,* pp. 26–7. To minimize the likelihood of cheating and
unfair windfalls, moreover, the Advisory Council suggested that
spousal benefits be awarded only if the marital status had existed
prior to the husband's attainment of age sixty. Widows' benefits
were to be contingent on proving that marriage had taken place before
the husband reached age sixty and at least one year preceding his
death.

81 Ibid., p. 26; Berkowitz, "First Crisis," p. 142. This argument was

partially true, but Carolyn Weaver rightly notes that the "money-back guarantee" promised in the 1935 act was eliminated in the 1939 amendments, and in some instances "promised" benefits appear to have been cut. See Weaver, *The Crisis,* pp. 116–17.

82 *Congressional Record,* July 13, 1939, Senate p. 9012; but see the entire debate on this point, pp. 9011–18. For more on the unreasonableness of these assumptions, see Chapter 7 of this volume.

83 More on Roosevelt's statement and these changes in operational titles can be found in Weaver, *The Crisis,* p. 123.

84 *FDR Public Papers* (New York: Macmillan, 1941), vol. 8, p. 79.

85 *FDR Public Papers* (New York: Macmillan, 1941), vol. 9, p. 411.

86 *Report of the Advisory Council,* December 10, 1938, p. 18.

2 Social security matures, 1940–1972

In addition to the general works cited in Chapter 1, the argument here relies on themes and citations found in my earlier work, *Shades of Gray: Old Age, American Values and Federal Policies Since 1920* (Boston: Little, Brown, 1983), and in Walter I. Trattner and W. Andrew Achenbaum, eds., *Social Welfare in America: An Annotated Bibliography* (Westport, Conn.: Greenwood Press, 1983). Indispensable overviews include Martha Derthick, *Policymaking for Social Security* (Washington, D.C.: Brookings Institution, 1979); Peter Flora and Arnold J. Heidenheimer, eds., *The Development of the Welfare State in Europe and America* (New Brunswick, N.J.: Transaction Books, 1981); Alonzo J. Hamby, *Liberalism and Its Challengers* (Oxford University Press, 1985); Ronald L. Numbers, ed., *Compulsory Health Insurance* (Westport, Conn.: Greenwood Press, 1982); William E. Leuchtenburg, *In the Shadow of FDR* (Ithaca, N.Y.: Cornell University Press, 1983); and Edward D. Tufte, *Political Control of the Economy* (Princeton University Press, 1978). As the number of references to data and articles in the *Social Security Bulletin* suggests, I consider the statistics and studies provided by the Social Security Administration's Office of Research and Statistics essential to reconstructing the history of American social insurance. Readers should also consult U.S. Department of Health and Human Services, *Basic Readings in Social Security* (Washington, D.C.: Social Security Administration, 1980), which annotates 2,593 academic publications and government reports.

1 Roughly 255,000 Americans received Title II benefits in December 1940; nearly a million workers or their survivors qualified by December 1950. Expenditures rose from $40.4 million to $784.1 million over the decade. The statistics and amendments described in this and the following paragraph are taken from U.S. Department of Health and Human Services, *Social Security Bulletin: Annual Statistical Supplement, 1982* (Washington, D.C.: Government Printing Office, 1983), pp. 22–3, 58–9, 92–3.

2 William P. Browne and Laura Katz Olson, eds., *Aging and Public Policy* (Westport, Conn.: Greenwood Press, 1983).

3 The best analysis along these lines is Martha Derthick's *Policymaking for Social Security* (Washington, D.C.: Brookings Institution, 1979).

4 Nearly 8 million employees were brought *nolens volens* into the system as a result of these amendments. Voluntary coverage was extended to another 2.5 million workers. New beneficiary categories, reduced eligibility requirements, and a revision in the benefit-calculation formula afforded more people a higher level of "basic" protection than ever before. Average benefits for current recipients were increased 77.5%. This was the largest single increase in social security benefits ever enacted, but it needs to be placed in perspective. It exceeded the rise in prices since 1937 by 1.5 percentage points, though it represented only two-thirds of the increase in wage levels. See *Annual Report of the Federal Security Administration: 1951* (Washington, D.C.: Government Printing Office, 1952); Arthur J. Altmeyer, *The Formative Years of Social Security* (Madison: University of Wisconsin Press, 1963), p. 185.

5 In brief, increments were authorized in September 1952 (12.5%), September 1954 (13%), January 1959 (7%), January 1954 (7%), February 1968 (13%), January 1970 (15%), January 1971 (10%), September 1972 (20%), March 1974 (7%), and June 1974 (4%); automatic cost-of-living adjustments for inflation, enacted in 1972, began in 1975. It is probably not accidental that many of these increases appeared in social security checks shortly before elections. See Edward D. Tufte, *Political Control of the Economy* (Princeton University Press, 1978), pp. 29–36.

6 Sweden's national insurance system was also influential in the NRPB's creation. See Hugh Heclo, "Toward a New Welfare State," in Flora and Heidenheimer, eds., *Development of the Welfare State*, pp. 395–6; Otis L. Graham, Jr., *Toward a Planned Society* (Oxford University Press, 1976), ch. 2; E. Wright Bakke, "America and the Beveridge Plan," *Yale Review* 33(June 1944):644–57; Marion Clawson, *New Deal Planning* (Baltimore: Johns Hopkins University Press, 1981).

7 Arthur J. Altmeyer, quoted in *Current Biography* (New York: H. W. Wilson Co., 1946), p. 15; idem, "The Desirability of Expanding the Social Insurance Program Now," *Social Security Bulletin* 5(November 1942):3–8. Ellen Woodward, another member of the SSB, amplified Altmeyer's stance. See Carolyn L. Weaver, *The Crisis in Social Security* (Durham, N.C.: Duke Policy Studies, 1982), p. 125.

8 The 1943 poll data came from George H. Gallup, *The Gallup Poll* (New York: Random House, 1972), vol. 1, p. 400. Similar support was registered in 1944 and 1948; see ibid., pp. 482, 783.

9 Monte M. Poen, "The Truman Legacy," in Ronald Numbers, ed., *Compulsory Health Insurance* (Westport, Conn.: Greenwood Press, 1982), p. 98.

10 "Message on the State of the Union," January 11, 1944, in *FDR Public Papers*, vol. 13, p. 41.

11 James Gilbert, *Another Chance: Postwar America, 1945–1968* (New

York: Knopf, 1982); Alonzo J. Hamby, *Liberalism and Its Challengers* (Oxford University Press, 1985), pp. 61–4.

12 Edwin E. Witte, "Social Security – 1948," *Social Security Perspectives,* ed. Robert J. Lampman (Madison: University of Wisconsin Press, 1962), p. 31.

13 Robert M. Ball, "Social Insurance and the Right to Assistance," *Social Service Review* 21(September 1947):343; Altmeyer, *Formative Years,* pp. 169–70; Raymond M. Hilliard, "Public Institutions in Our Social Insurance Structure," *Social Service Review* 20(December 1946):492–3. See also Jerry Cates, *Insuring Inequality* (Ann Arbor: University of Michigan Press, 1983), pp. 104–5, 155. I think Cates overstates the degree to which social security experts viewed Title I as a "prime policy competitor with social insurance" (p. 20). Rather than compete for support, OAI and OAA were thought to serve different, albeit complementary, functions.

14 See Poen, "Truman," pp. 102–5; Daniel M. Fox, "The Decline of Historicism," *Bulletin of the History of Medicine* 57(Winter 1983):607. On British developments, see Gordon Forsythe, *Doctors and State Medicine* (London: Pitman Medical, 1973).

15 The 1946 amendments, for instance, altered the stringent marital-status eligibility criteria, allowing benefits to an elderly wife who had been married to a worker insured for as little as three years. Four years later, benefits were extended to divorced survivors *under age sixty-five* of retired-worker beneficiaries who were caring for a child eligible for support. Husbands and widowers over sixty-five who were dependent on insured women workers also became eligible for benefits. Amendments enacted in 1957, 1958, and 1960 further liberalized definitions of "marriage" so that more women could qualify for spousal benefits. See U.S. Department of Health, Education, and Welfare, *Report of the HEW Task Force on the Treatment of Women under Social Security* (Washington, D.C.: Government Printing Office, February 1978), pp. 106–11. For Eisenhower's sense that such amendments demonstrated that his administration was "forward looking," see Fred I. Greenstein, *The Hidden-Hand Presidency* (New York: Basic Books, 1982), p. 51.

16 *Annual Report of the Federal Security Administration: 1951* (Washington, D.C.: Government Printing Office, 1952); Altmeyer, *Formative Years,* p. 185; Wilbur J. Cohen and Robert J. Myers, "Social Security Act Amendments of 1950: A Summary and Legislative History," *Social Security Bulletin* 13(October 1950):3–14.

17 For a careful account of the legislation, see Charles I. Schottland, "Social Security Amendments of 1956: A Summary and Legislative History," *Social Security Bulletin* 19(September 1956):3–15ff. See also the interview (1968) with Roswell B. Hess in the oral history collection, Columbia University, pp. 25–6; Derthick, *Policymaking,* especially pp. 308–15. Edward D. Berkowitz will add to our under-

standing of the historical dimensions of disability insurance as a public policy issue in his forthcoming Twentieth Century Fund study.

18 Altmeyer, *Formative Years,* pp. 206ff; Derthick, *Policymaking,* pp. 144–57.

19 Most recipients between 1940 and 1960 were elderly, but at least a sixth of all recipients in this period were under the age of sixty-two.

20 Wilbur J. Cohen, "Income Maintenance for the Aged," *Annals of the American Academy of Political and Social Science* 279(1952):153–60; Gilbert Y. Steiner, "Reform Follows Reality," *The Great Society,* eds. Eli Ginzberg and Robert M. Solow (New York: Basic Books, 1974), pp. 47–65.

21 J. Douglas Brown, "Social Insurance: A Problem in Institutional Economics," *American Economic Review* 47(part 2)(May 1957):464.

22 See Derthick, *Policymaking,* pp. 278, 351–4.

23 U.S. Senate, 74th Cong., 1st sess., *The Economic Security Act: Hearings on S. 1130,* pp. 179, 989, 1238, 1269; Murray Webb Latimer, "Notes on Retirement," pp. 3–5 in Wilbur Cohen papers, University of Michigan, Ann Arbor. It was not a distinctively American practice to require that beneficiaries attain a certain age to qualify for pensions. In Europe, South America, and Oceania, different eligibility ages (ranging from fifty to seventy) have been established; different criteria often apply for men and women. Bismarck's 1889 social legislation had provided for contributory old-age pensions at age seventy and "invalidity" benefits even earlier; the age requirement for pensions was reduced to sixty-five in a 1916 amendment. In 1908 the British government had established age seventy as a requirement for noncontributory old-age pensions; seventeen years later it inaugurated a program for contributory pensions payable from age sixty-five. See Barbara Nachtrieb Armstrong, *Insuring the Essentials* (New York: Macmillan, 1932); for a list of the studies made by staff members of the Committee on Economic Security between 1934 and 1935, see U.S. Social Security Board, *Social Security in America* (Washington, D.C.: Government Printing Office, 1937), pp. 525–7.

24 The 1956 amendments imposed a six-month waiting period before a worker could receive disability benefits. An applicant's incapacity for work had to be verified. No such rules, however, regulated the shift from receipt of disability benefits to a retirement check at age sixty-five. That such an easy transition from one program to the other was institutionalized into the system suggests that the health factors that caused "disability" and necessitated "retirement" were closely related in legislators' minds. The way the two categories dovetailed is indicative of prevailing views about an older worker's value in the 1950s.

25 As early as 1948, some members of Congress, sensitive to the plight of retired couples unable to make ends meet and of widows refused

assistance because they were under sixty-five, urged that the eligibility age for women for spousal and survivors' benefits be reduced to sixty. A conservative Congress rejected the idea. Finally, as a result of the 1956 social security amendments, insured women workers who retired between the ages of sixty-two and sixty-five received benefits reduced $\frac{5}{9}$% for each month under age sixty-five. Wives of retired workers could receive at age sixty-two benefits actuarially reduced $\frac{25}{36}$% for each month they were under sixty-five. Widows over sixty-two, on the other hand, were insured (at 75% of their husbands' primary insurance amounts, which was the rate established in the 1939 amendments for widows over age sixty-five). Children under eighteen were covered, though a series of changes since the mid-1960s introduced broader age-specific options; a "dependent child" could receive benefits up to age twenty-two if enrolled in school. Finally, special cash benefits and earnings-test criteria applied to individuals and couples over seventy and seventy-two. For more on this, see "History of the Provisions of the Old-Age, Survivors, Disability, and Health Insurance Program," *Social Security Bulletin, Annual Statistical Supplement* (1983).

26   See David E. Stannard, "The Dilemmas of Aging in Bureaucratic America," *Aging and the Elderly*, eds. David D. Van Tassel, Stuart Spicker, and Kathleeen Woodward (Atlantic Highlands, N.J.: Humanities Press, 1978), pp. 9–20; and W. Andrew Achenbaum, "Societal Perceptions of the Aging and the Aged," in Robert H. Binstock and Ethel Shanas, eds., *Handbook of Aging and the Social Sciences*, 2nd ed. (New York: Van Nostrand Reinhold, 1985), pp. 129–48.

27   Lloyd A. Free and Hadley Cantril, *Political Beliefs of Americans* (New Brunswick, N.J.: Rutgers University Press, 1967), pp. 20–30, 178; James A. Patterson, *America's Struggle Against Poverty* (Cambridge, Mass.: Harvard University Press, 1980), pp. 82–5; Cates, *Insuring Inequality*, pp. 139–40.

28   J. R. O'Meara, *Retirement: Reward or Rejection* (New York: Conference Board, 1977); Graebner, *A History of Retirement*, ch. 8.

29   Solomon Barkin, "Union Policies and the Older Worker," *The Aged and Society*, ed. Milton Derber (Champaign, Ill.: Industrial Relations Research Association, 1950), pp. 75–92; David Greenstone, *Labor in American Politics* (New York: Knopf, 1969). See also Chapter 5 in this volume.

30   At no point did either party explicitly challenge the retirement test. For the years between 1936 and 1952, see John J. Corson and John W. McConnell, *Economic Needs of Older People* (New York: Twentieth Century Fund, 1956), pp. 133–6; for 1952 through 1968, see Arthur M. Schlesinger, Jr., *History of American Presidential Elections, 1789–1968* (New York: Chelsea House, 1971), vol. 4; for the 1972 platforms, see vol. 30 of the *Congressional Weekly Record*.

31 In a technical study of social security for the Ways and Means Committee (1945–6), for instance, experts concluded that the "entire removal" of the retirement test "would profoundly affect both the fiscal and conceptual aspects of Old Age and Survivors Insurance." See *Issues in Social Security, A Report to the House Committee on Ways and Means* (1946), p. 144.

32 The "insiders" were hardly oblivious to "outside" pressures. Representative Wilbur Mills (D–Ark.), a pivotal figure on the House Ways and Means Committee during social security's formative years, was sensitive to the fact that many of his colleagues did not approve of the trade-off involved in saving money by applying the retirement test in order to increase average benefits. During the 1950s and 1960s, for instance, the Senate Finance Committee was more receptive to proposals to raise earning ceilings than was Mills's committee. North Dakota's Democratic Senator William Langer viewed the liberalization of the retirement test as a "holy war." Other lawmakers shared their constituents' view that Title II benefits were earned old-age annuities and thus should not be subject to an earnings test. See Derthick, *Policymaking,* pp. 42n, 46, 48, 226.

33 Edwin E. Witte, "Changing Roles in the Quest for Security" (1955), in *Social Security Perspectives,* p. 76.

34 John Kenneth Galbraith, *The Affluent Society* (Boston: Houghton Mifflin, 1958), p. 115.

35 J. Douglas Brown, "The American Philosophy of Social Insurance," *Social Service Review* 30(March 1956):3.

36 James N. Morgan et al., *Income and Wealth in the United States* (New York: McGraw-Hill, 1962).

37 Kerr-Mills expanded the purview of Title I, but it had little immediate impact. Few states took advantage of the provisions; in 1963, five states were receiving 90% of the funds. Critics also charged that patients received haphazard care and that their right to privacy was violated. See Richard Harris, *A Sacred Trust* (New York: New American Library, 1966), pp. 99–114, 125.

38 They could have justified their political judgment by invoking the authority of the judicial branch, for according to the Supreme Court, current and future beneficiaries were entitled to receive only what Congress decided it could afford to pay them. In a landmark case, *Flemming v. Nestor* (1960), the Supreme Court extended its line of reasoning in *Helvering v. Davis* (1937) by reaffirming Congress's right to determine the precise nature of governmental benefits under social security – as long as the legislative body operated within consitutional bounds. See *Flemming v. Nestor,* 80 Sup. Ct. Rep. 1367ff. See also Jeremy Rabkin, "The Judiciary in the Administrative State," *Public Interest* 71(Spring 1983):75–7; Charles A. Reich, "The New Property," *Public Interest* 3(Spring 1966):86; and Chapter 6 in this volume.

39 Council of Economic Advisers, "The Problem of Poverty in Amer-
    ica," *Economic Report of the President* (Washington, D.C.: Govern-
    ment Printing Office, January 1964), pp. 56–60; George H. Dunne,
    S. J., ed., *Poverty in Plenty* (New York: P. J. Kenedy & Sons, 1964);
    and Michael S. March, "Poverty: How Much Will the War Cost?"
    Social Service Review 39(June 1965):141–55. For judicious overviews
    of policymakers' assumptions, see Patterson, *America's Struggle*, ch.
    8; and Carl M. Brauer, "Kennedy, Johnson, and the War on Pov-
    erty," *Journal of American History* 69(June 1982):98–119.
40 For a contemporary analysis of these different standards of poverty
    and how they changed between 1900 and 1960, see Oscar Ornati,
    Poverty Amid Affluence (New York: Twentieth Century Fund, 1966),
    ch. 1. Deciding what constituted a "minimum standard of ade-
    quacy," as opposed to a "subsistence standard of living," was prob-
    lematic, of course; no criterion was likely to gain universal accep-
    tance among the experts.
41 At that time, the only reliable social indicators for establishing a
    socially acceptable standard of subsistence dealt with the relative cost
    and nutritional value of various foods. Hence, Orshansky built her
    index around two data sets: a 1961 Department of Agriculture econ-
    omy food plan, and a 1955 household food-consumption survey,
    which measured the national average ratio of family food expendi-
    tures to total after-tax income. She then ran statistical analyses of
    special tabulations of the March 1964 Current Population Survey
    obtained from the Bureau of the Census. By controlling for such
    factors as family size and number of children in a household under
    the age of eighteen and the race, gender, age, and occupational and
    employment status of the head of the household, as well as regional
    farm/nonfarm and urban/rural differences, Orshansky was able to
    count the number of families and unrelated individuals above and
    below her poverty cutoff points. For more on her methods, see Mollie
    Orshansky, "Counting the Poor: Another Look at the Poverty Pro-
    file," *Social Security Bulletin* 28(January 1965):3–29; and "Study of
    the Measure of Poverty," ibid. 39(September 1976):34–7.
42 Orshansky, "Counting the Poor," p. 4. For her later refinements of
    the index, see Mollie Orshansky, *The Measure of Poverty*, technical
    paper no. 1 (Washington, D.C.: Office of the Assistant Secretary
    for Planning and Evaluation, HEW, 1976); Mollie Orshansky and
    Judith S. Bretz, "Born to be Poor: Birthplace and Number of Brothers
    and Sisters as Factors in Adult Poverty," *Social Security Bulletin*
    39(January 1976):21–37; and Mollie Orshansky et al., "Measuring
    Poverty: A Debate," *Public Welfare* 36(Spring 1978):46–50.
43 Archibald Cox, "The Supreme Court – Foreword," *Harvard Law
    Review* 80(November 1966):119.
44 Council of Economic Advisers, "The Problem of Poverty," p. 73.
45 Juanita M. Kreps, "Employment Policy and Income Maintenance
    for the Aged," *Aging and Social Policy*, eds. John C. McKinney and

Frank de Vyver (New York: Appleton-Century-Crofts, 1966), pp. 136–56.

46 Public Law 89-73, July 14, 1965.

47 It is one thing, of course, to set "objectives," and quite another to execute the law so as to attain them. And as I tried to demonstrate elsewhere, the preamble of the Older Americans Act is riddled with outmoded images of age that often work at cross-purposes. See my *Shades of Gray*, chs. 4–5.

48 Quoted in *Science News Letter* 83(June 1, 1963):339.

49 For the legislative background of the 1965 legislation, see the interpretations set forth in Wilbur J. Cohen and Robert M. Ball, "Social Security Amendments of 1965," *Social Security Bulletin* 28(September 1965):3–21; Theodore Marmor, *The Politics of Medicare* (Chicago: Aldine Press, 1973); and Herman M. Somers and Anne R. Somers, *Medicare and the Hospitals* (Washington, D.C.: Brookings Institution, 1967). For evidence of popular support, see George Gallup, *The Gallup Poll: Public Opinions, 1935–1971*, vol. 2, pp. 1, 759, 1,932. See also Chapter 8 in this volume.

50 Even the name affixed to the program had a long and involved history. "Medicare" was a term first used by Congress in 1956 for a measure that provided medical care for the dependents of service personnel.

51 Quoted in William E. Leuchtenburg, *In the Shadow of FDR* (Ithaca, N.Y.: Cornell University Press, 1983), p. 141.

52 Hence, in 1965, when transitionally insured workers over the age of seventy-two became eligible for $35 per month, a widow over seventy-two who survived such a worker became entitled to the same amount; a wife over seventy-two could claim a monthly benefit worth half the worker's benefit. Furthermore, when divorce surpassed death in the 1950s as the major reason for marital dissolution, public officials became increasingly sympathetic to the plight of the homemaker who was too old to build up a substantial earnings record but who had lost her right to benefits based on her former husband's FICA contributions. See Social Security Administration, *Annual Statistical Supplement*, 1981, pp. 19, 21; and Chapter 6 in this volume.

53 Ida C. Merriam, "Young Adults and Social Security," *Social Security Bulletin* 31(August 1968):8.

54 Lenore Epstein Bixby et al., *Demographic and Economic Characteristics of the Aged*, SSA report no. 45 (Washington, D.C.: Government Printing Office, 1975), p. 138.

55 Marilyn Moon, *The Measurement of Economic Welfare* (New York: Academic Press, 1977), pp. 113–14. See also Robert D. Plotnick and Felicity Skidmore, *Progress Against Poverty* (New York: Academic Press, 1975), pp. 73–4; and James Schulz, *The Economics of Aging*, 2nd ed. (Belmont, Calif.: Wadsworth, 1980), ch. 2.

56 "Paul A. Samuelson on Social Security," *Newsweek*, February 13,

1967, p. 88. In the 1982–3 debate over social security, this reference to Ponzi schemes came back to haunt liberals.

57 Robert M. Ball, "Is Poverty Necessary?" *Social Security Bulletin* 28(August 1965):19–20, 24.

58 While serving as assistant secretary of labor, Daniel Patrick Moynihan wrote his controversial report, *The Negro Family: The Case for National Action* (Washington, D.C.: Department of Labor, 1965). From the start, Moynihan's data and interpretations were challenged by social scientists, historians, and policy analysts. For present purposes, it is worth noting that Moynihan's defenders often accused his critics (expecially in the Department of Health, Education, and Welfare) of opposing the report in order to protect their own vested interests. See Lee Rainwater and William L. Yancy, *The Moynihan Report: The Politics of Controversy* (Cambridge, Mass.: M.I.T. Press, 1967).

59 Wilbur J. Cohen, "A Ten-Point Program to Abolish Poverty," *Social Security Bulletin* 31(December 1968):3–13. Cohen's social security proposals appear on pp. 7–8.

60 *Social Security Bulletin, Annual Statistical Supplement* (1982), p. 252.

61 Heather L. Ross and Isabel V. Sawhill, *Time of Transition* (Washington, D.C.: Urban Institute, 1975), ch. 5; Frances Fox Piven and Richard A. Cloward, *Regulating the Poor* (New York: Vintage Press, 1971), part 3; and Wayne Hoffman and Ted Marmor, "The Politics of Public Assistance Reform: An Essay Review," *Social Service Review* 50(March 1976):11–22.

62 Quoted in Patterson, *America's Struggle,* p. 173, but read all of the fine interpretation in ch. 11.

63 Part of the explosion in AFDC expenditures occurred because a few states took advantage of loopholes in the law. California, for instance, claimed 25–36% of all federal dollars for social services between 1967 and 1971; Illinois tried to turn the grants into "backdoor revenue sharing." See Martha Derthick, *Uncontrollable Spending for Social Service Grants* (Washington, D.C.: Brookings Institution, 1975); Neil Gilbert, *Capitalism and the Welfare State* (New Haven, Conn.: Yale University Press, 1983), especially ch. 3.

64 Moynihan was then serving Nixon, but he had been a prime source of ideas in previous administrations. An architect of some Great Society initiatives, Moynihan believed that technical advancements, such as econometric modeling and new budgeting formulas, enabled the federal government to design social programs that reached target populations in a more efficient manner. See Daniel Patrick Moynihan, *The Politics of a Guaranteed Income* (New York: Random House, 1973), pp. 543–9.

65 Under FAP, every unemployed family of four would receive at least $1,600 from the federal government. The working poor also would be assured $1,600; they would receive benefits on a sliding scale until

their income reached $4,000. To be eligible for assistance, able-bodied people (including women with no children under the age of three) had to work or enroll in a job-training program. See Walter I. Trattner, *From Poor Law to Welfare State,* 2nd ed. (New York: Free Press, 1979), pp. 260–2.

66 This panel (often called the Heineman Commission, after its chairman) was appointed by President Johnson in January 1968. See President's Commission on Income Maintenance Programs, *Poverty Amid Plenty* (Washington, D.C.: Government Printing Office, 1969). The commission recommended a negative income tax (NIT), which would provide a family of four with $2,400. This was a low "floor," to be sure, but it was more generous than the one provided by the Family Assistance Plan.

67 Liberal Democrats, after all, had long advocated guaranteed-income schemes, but it was a conservative Republican administration that advocated FAP. Milton Friedman, a conservative University of Chicago economist, had elaborated the best case for a welfare system based on a negative income tax in *Capitalism and Freedom* (1962), yet it was the liberally oriented Heineman Commission that advanced the NIT recommendation.

68 The full Republican plank on social security appears in *Congressional Quarterly Almanac* 24(1968):990. See also 1971 Advisory Council on Social Security, *Reports on the Old-Age, Survivors, and Disability Insurance and Medicare Programs* (Washington, D.C.: Government Printing Office, 1971), pp. 7–15. For more detailed legislative histories of the 1972 amendments, see Robert M. Ball, "Social Security Amendments of 1972: Summary and Legislative History," *Social Security Bulletin* 36(March 1973):3–25; and Vincent J. Burke and Vee Burke, *Nixon's Good Deed* (New York: Columbia University Press, 1974).

69 By the late 1960s, liberals and conservatives alike felt seriously constrained by Myers's "level-earnings" actuarial technique. For an early criticism of the level-earnings assumption, see Charles C. Killingsworth and Gertrude Schroeder, "Long-Range Cost Estimates for Old-Age Insurance," *Quarterly Journal of Economics* 65(May 1951):199–213; see also the influential analysis in Joseph A. Pechman, Henry J. Aaron, and Michael K. Taussig, *Social Security: Perspectives for Reform* (Washington, D.C.: Brookings Institution, 1968).

70 "Elders' Lib . . .," *New York Times,* December 1, 1971, p. 46. See also White House Conference on Aging, *Toward a National Policy on Aging, Final Report,* 2 vols. (Washington, D.C.: Government Printing Office, 1971).

71 "20% Social Security Rise Is Voted by Both Houses; Nixon Approval in Doubt," *New York Times,* July 1, 1972, pp. 1, 13; see also "The Biggest Raise Ever," ibid., July 2, 1972, sect. IV, p. 2. The president, fearing that such a large increase in social security benefits would

be inflationary and swell mounting federal deficits, had tried to limit the increment to 10%. Wilbur Mills, the conservative chairman of the House Ways and Means Committee with presidential ambitions, initially proposed the 20% increase. See "Excerpts From President Nixon's Budget Message as Presented to Congress," *New York Times,* January 25, 1972, p. 17; "Mills Asks 20% Rise in Social Security Aid," ibid., February 24, 1972, p. 19. Once maneuvering in Congress failed, however, Nixon signed the bill into law on July 1. In hindsight, it is revealing – some would prefer to call it a cruel omen of things to come – to note that the 20% benefit hike was attached to a bill the administration had sponsored to raise the national debt ceiling to $450 billion.

72 In order to help to finance such benefit increases, the legislators stipulated that the maximum earnings base subject to social security taxes would also rise with the overall growth of the wage level. Most federal officials, armed with "expert" opinion and actuarial forecasts, believed that the increased revenues from extended coverage, rising wages, and higher tax rates on earnings would be sufficient to continue paying for disbursements on a "pay-as-you-go" basis.

73 "President Signs $5-Billion Bill Expanding Social Security," *New York Times,* October 31, 1972, pp. 1, 36. The total cost of the first full year's benefits under the new provisions was to be offset by yet another increase in payroll deductions. The tax rate levied on employees and employers would go from 5.5% to 5.85%. This meant that an employee's maximum contribution, which had been $468 in 1972, would rise to $608.40 in 1973 and to $704 in 1974. The government was expected to assume an increasing share of welfare costs, because funds for the SSI program were to come from general revenues. As is shown in Chapter 3, subsequent amendments altered the actual dollar amounts of both payroll tax rates and benefits paid.

74 "Social Security – Forty Years Later," *Social Security Bulletin* 27 (August 1975):1; Wilbur J. Cohen, "The Social Security Act – 1935–1975: Forty Years of Progress," *Public Welfare* 33(Fall 1965):6.

75 Historically, "entitlement" referred to the preferential treatment accorded members of the titled nobility; when nineteenth-century and early twentieth-century American politicians invoked the word, they usually referred to abstract philosophical principles – such as the rights to "Life, Liberty, and the pursuit of Happiness." After the New Deal, "entitlements" were no longer construed simply as privileges; in the public policy arena they had become vested *rights*. Entitlements referred to cash payments mandated by law; they had to be paid to all who met the statutory requirements. Increasingly these social benefits were processed by a federal bureaucracy and guaranteed unless Congress changed the eligibility criteria and payment levels authorized by a program like Title II. The earliest printed evi-

dence for this sense of "entitlement" is found in U.S. Code Congressional Service, *Laws of the 78th Congress* (August 1, 1944, to September 5, 1944), p. 2.274. See Henry E. Vizetelly, ed., *New International Year Book, 1951* (New York: Funk & Wagnalls, 1952), p. 171. Social security officials adopted the term in the mid-1960s. See Kathi V. Friedman, *Legitimation of Social Rights and the Western Welfare State* (Chapel Hill: University of North Carolina Press, 1981), chs. 8–9.

76 A prototype of the purchasing-power guarantee in wage agreements had been part of the 1948 General Motors/United Auto Workers settlement; it was a feature of some other private pension arrangements, notably the TIAA/CREF plan for college teachers. Cost-of-living provisions were already part of major public retirement plans: Amendments in 1962 to the Civil Service Retirement Act included a provision for increasing annuities automatically as the consumer price index (CPI) rose; the Uniformed Services Pay Act of 1963 provided similar benefits for military veterans and their dependents. Fourteen other (mostly industrialized) countries had introduced cost-of-living provisions. See Daniel N. Price and Robert O. Brunner, "Automatic Adjustment of OASDHI Cash Benefits," *Social Security Bulletin* 33(May 1970):1–12; Max Horlick and Doris E. Lewis, "Adjustments of Old-Age Pensions in Foreign Programs," ibid., pp. 12–15.

3 The mid-life crisis of American social security

Good analyses of America's political economy in the 1970s include Joseph A. Califano, *Governing America* (New York: Simon & Schuster, 1981); David P. Calleo, *The Imperious Economy* (Cambridge, Mass.: Harvard University Press, 1982); Samuel P. Huntington, *American Politics: The Promise of Disharmony* (Cambridge, Mass.: Harvard University Press, 1981); Dennis Ippolito, *Congressional Spending* (Ithaca, N.Y.: Cornell University Press, 1981); Morris Janowitz, *The Last Half-Century* (University of Chicago Press, 1978); John Myles, *Old Age in the Welfare State* (Boston: Little, Brown, 1984); and Lester C. Thurow, *The Zero-Sum Society* (Baltimore, Penguin Books, 1980). A more detailed summary of major changes in social security during the period can be found in monthly issues of the *Social Security Bulletin* and in Robert J. Myers, *Social Security,* 3rd ed. (Homewood, Ill.: Richard D. Irwin, 1985).

I began to reconstruct OASDHI's recent history by systematically reading every pertinent article in the *Congressional Quarterly, The Gerontologist,* the *National Journal,* and the *New York Times.* My narrative was enriched by insights and clues offered by several distinguished public servants who shaped social security policy. A complete list of the people I interviewed appears in the bibliographical essay for the notes to Chapter 4; whenever possible I have used quotations in the public record.

1   Edwin L. Dale, Jr., "The Security of Social Security: The Young Pay for the Old," *New York Times Magazine,* January 14, 1973, pp. 8, 45.

2   Hugh Heclo, "Toward a New Welfare State" in *The Development of Welfare States in Europe and America,* eds. Peter Flora and Arnold J. Heidenheimer (New Brunswick, N.J.: Transaction Books, 1981), p. 403.

3   Quoted in William Greider, "The Education of David Stockman," *Atlantic Monthly* 248(December 1981):43.

4   To finance this benefit hike, H.R. 11333 raised the payroll wage base subject to FICA taxes to $13,200. The bill also increased the size of initial benefits to be paid under the new Supplemental Security Income program, eliminated unintended reductions in welfare recipients' payments, and liberalized regulations in several other categorical social security programs. See *Congressional Quarterly Almanac* 29(1973):570.

5   Alfred M. Skolnick, "Pension Reform Legislation of 1974," *Social Security Bulletin* 37(December 1974):35–42; idem, "Private Pension Plans, 1950–1974," *Social Security Bulletin* 39(June 1976):3–17; "Congress Clears Bill to Regulate Pensions," *Congressional Quarterly Almanac* 30(1974):244–53. See also Chapter 7 in this volume.

6   Average monthly payments to OAA recipients in thirty-seven states were less than $80 in mid-1973. In contrast, SSI at its inception in 1974 guaranteed an income floor higher than those that existed in twenty-six of the nation's poorer states; its combined minimum and supplemental benefits ranged from 90% to 170% of the poverty line for couples. Statistics from Bruno Stein, *Social Security and Pensions in Transition* (New York: Free Press, 1980), p. 48; and Thomas Tissue, "The Survey of Low-Income Aged and Disabled," *Social Security Bulletin* 40(February 1977):7. See also *Congressional Quarterly Almanac* (1974):508–9; Department of Health, Education, and Welfare, "Social Service Programs for Individuals and Families," *Federal Register* 40(June 27, 1975), part II, pp. 27352–66.

7   For a broader discussion, see Sylvester J. Schieber, "First Year Impact of SSI on Economic Status of 1973 Adult Assistance Populations," *Social Security Bulletin* 41(February 1978):18–46; and Lawrence E. Lynn, Jr., "Poverty Developments in the Income Maintenance System," in *A Decade of Federal Antipoverty Programs,* ed. Robert Haveman (New York: Academic Press, 1977), pp. 55–117.

8   Thomas Tissue, "Response to Recipiency Under Public Assistance and SSI," *Social Security Bulletin* 41(November 1978):8. The welfare stigma did not apply because SSI was viewed as an old-age entitlement.

9   John A. Menefee, Bea Edwards, and Sylvester J. Schieber, "Analysis of Nonparticipation in the SSI Program," *Social Security Bulletin* 44(June 1981):7, 13, 16, 19.

10 See, for instance, U.S. Senate, Special Committee on Aging, *The*

Multiple Hazards of Age and Race, report no. 92-450 (1971); Gayle B. Thompson, "Blacks and Social Security Benefits," *Social Security Bulletin* 38(April 1975):30–40; Sar A. Levitan, William B. Johnson, and Robert Taggart, *Still a Dream* (Cambridge, Mass.: Harvard University Press, 1975), pp. 201–21; Lenore E. Bixby, "Women and Social Security in the United States," *Social Security Bulletin* 35(September 1972):11; and "Rights Panel Charges Programs to Help Women Actually Hurt Them," *New York Times,* June 20, 1974, p. 44; see also Chapter 6 in this volume.

11 "Quadrennial Advisory Council on Social Security: Summary of Major Findings and Recommendations," *Social Security Bulletin* 38(August 1975):32.

12 Ibid., p. 33. To correct the modest short-term imbalance, the Advisory Council suggested making a technical adjustment to the new automatic benefit formula, and proposed financing more than half of the Medicare program out of general Treasury revenues; the council's report added that shortly after the turn of the century it might be necessary to consider raising the retirement age.

13 "Social Security Cost-of-Living," *Congressional Quarterly Almanac* 41(1975):689–90.

14 "Ex-Officials Back Pension System," *New York Times,* February 11, 1975, p. 23. The incumbent commissioner, James B. Cardwell, characterized the trustees' projections as "cause for concern but not alarm." Representative James Burke (D–Mass.), who chaired the House Ways and Means Subcommittee on Social Security, viewed the problem as "substantial but not by any means insoluble." See "Social Security Funds: Gloomy Forecast," *Congressional Quarterly Almanac* 31(1975):690.

15 See the president's state-of-the-union message, January 19, 1976, reprinted in *Congressional Quarterly Almanac* 32(1976):4-A. See also memorandum from Jim Cannon to the president, May 16, 1975, in Spencer Johnson papers, box 10, social security file at Ford Library (Ann Arbor, Mich.). For Congress's response, see "Social Security Hike," *Congressional Quarterly Almanac* 32(1976):378; and "Medicare Amendments," ibid., p. 563.

16 The data and interpretation are based on my reading of Lester C. Thurow, *The Zero-Sum Society* (Baltimore: Penguin Books, 1980), pp. 43–6, 85, 191; Robert Weibe, "Modernizing the Republic," in *The Great Republic,* 2nd ed., eds. Bernard Bailyn et al. (Boston: Heath, 1981), pp. 922–3; and David P. Calleo, *The Imperious Economy* (Cambridge, Mass.: Harvard University Press, 1982), especially chs. 3 and 6.

17 See my *Shades of Gray,* pp. 128–34; Morris Janowitz, *The Last Half-Century* (University of Chicago Press, 1978); Samuel P. Huntington, *American Politics: The Promise of Disharmony* (Cambridge, Mass.: Harvard University Press, 1981).

18 Juanita M. Kreps, "Social Security in the Coming Decade: Ques-

tions for a Mature System," *Social Security Bulletin* 39(March 1976):22. Cf. Martha Derthick, "How Easy Votes on Social Security Came to an End," *Public Interest* 54(Winter 1979):94–105.

19 Robert S. Kaplan, *Indexing Social Security* (Washington, D.C.: American Enterprise Institute for Public Policy Research, 1977), p. 16; Dean Leimer and Ronald Hoffman, *Designing an Equitable Intertemporal Social Security Benefit Structure* (Washington, D.C.: Social Security Administration, November 1976).

20 Martin B. Tracy, "Maintaining Value of Social Security Benefits During Inflation: Foreign Experience," *Social Security Bulletin* 39 (November 1976):33–42; International Labour Office, *Pensions and Inflation: An International Discussion* (Geneva: ILO, 1977); Stanford G. Ross, "Social Security: A Worldwide Issue," *Social Security Bulletin* 42(August 1979):3–10; Lillian Lui, "Social Security Problems in Western European Countries," ibid. 47(February 1984):17–22.

21 "Carter Signs Social Security Tax Rise for 110 Million," *New York Times,* December 21, 1977, p. A19. It is worth noting that the 1977 amendments passed in the Senate by 56 to 21. The vote in the House was even closer, 189 to 163; significantly, Democrats supported the measure 174 to 54, whereas Republicans opposed it 15 to 109.

22 "Plans for Raising Personal Taxes Expected to Reduce Purchasing," *New York Times,* January 12, 1978, sect. IV, p. 1; see also "Social Security Tax Rises for Nearly Every American Worker," ibid., January 1, 1978, p. 14.

23 "O'Neill Wants to Cut Social Security Tax," *New York Times,* March 15, 1978, p. 15; "Social Security Issue Giving Lift to G.O.P.," ibid., April 9, 1978, p. 17; for Carter's position, see the transcript of his press conference, ibid., March 3, 1978, p.10.

24 Despite tentative support from the White House and praise from the *New York Times,* two powerful Democratic Louisiana legislators, Representative Joe Waggoner and Senator Russell Long (who chaired the Senate Finance Committee), effectively killed the idea by pointing out that such a move would hurt oil producers and make it harder to control future increases in social security benefits. See "White House Would Allot Oil Levy to Offset Social Security Tax Cut," *New York Times,* April 4, 1978, p. 1; "New Grease for the Oil Tax," ibid., April 6, 1978, p. 20.

25 The administration also recommended phasing out benefits for survivors' children between the ages of eighteen and twenty-one attending school and called for a provision granting parents pensions only for children under the age of sixteen, not eighteen as then permitted. See "Carter Plans Cuts in Social Security," *New York Times,* December 31, 1978, pp. 1, 11; and Joseph A. Califano, *Governing America* (New York: Simon & Schuster, 1981), ch. 9.

26 "Ullman: No Social Security Cuts," *New York Times,* January 8, 1979, p. 12.

27 "Breifcases," *New York Times,* January 8, 1979, sect. IV, p. 2; "Coalition Established to Oppose Trims in Social Security Benefits," ibid., January 25, 1979, sect. II, p. 2. Cruikshank quoted in Califano, *Governing America,* p. 397.

28 "Social Security Commissioner Calls Improvements in Benefits Unlikely," *New York Times,* July 17, 1979, p. 10.

29 On May 29, 1980, Congress passed legislation expected to reduce social security and welfare spending by $2.6 billion by fiscal year 1985. Most of the savings were to come from cuts in benefits to workers who became disabled after July 1, 1980. See "Social Security Disability," *Congressional Quarterly Almanac* 35(1979):504–5; ibid. 36(1980):434–7. Some reforms, moreover, actually led to new initiatives. See "1981 Low-Income Energy Assistance Program," *Social Security Bulletin, Annual Statistical Supplement* (1981), p. 52.

30 Califano, *Governing America,* p. 401.

31 See Dennis S. Ippolito, *Congressional Spending* (Ithaca, N.Y.: Cornell University Press, 1981); Aaron Wildavsky and Michael J. Boskin, eds., *The Federal Budget: Economics and Politics* (San Francisco: Institute for Contemporary Studies, 1982); Robert J. Myers, *Social Security,* 2nd ed. (Homewood, Ill.: Richard D. Irwin, 1981), pp. 230–2.

32 Quoted in Derthick, *Policymaking,* p. 411.

33 Quoted in Califano, *Governing America,* p. 391.

34 Califano was not alone. See Stanford Ross's views in "Outgoing Social Security Head Assails 'Myths' of System and Says It Favors the Poor," *New York Times,* December 2, 1979, p. 75. My interpretation of the senior policymakers' motives is based on interviews with Wilbur Cohen and Robert Ball.

35 J. Douglas Brown, *Essays on Social Security* (Princeton University: Industrial Relations Section, 1977), p. 15.

36 A striking difference still persists between the poverty thresholds used by the Census Bureau for *statistical* purposes and by the Department of Health and Human Services for *administrative* purposes. See "The 1984 Federal Poverty Income Guidelines," *Social Security Bulletin* 47(July 1984):24; data found in SOS Education Fund, *Supplemental Security Income* (Washington, D.C.: Save Our Security, June 1984), pp. 3–4; *Social Security Bulletin, Annual Statistical Supplement* (1982), pp. 63, 240. The same pattern exists when official poverty levels for the aged are compared with the size of the federal SSI payment a typical elderly beneficiary receives.

There is, in fact, little coordination among various antipoverty measures for the aged. Thus, paradoxically, changes in benefit rates or eligibility criteria have sometimes reduced the SSI program's attractiveness. Under existing regulations, for instance, all but the first $240 per year of "unearned income" (which includes social security benefits, railroad retirement pensions, veterans' benefits, and workers' compensation) is deductible from a recipient's SSI payments. For those at the margin, this has meant that an increase in social security benefits would give SSI recipients more money, but simultaneously make them ineligible for Medicaid or food stamps. Special legislation has been enacted to deal with this anomaly. For instance, a 1976 amendment to the Social Security Act preserved the Medicaid eligibility of recipients who became ineligible for SSI cash payments because of Title II COLA increases. Although the original legislation stipulated that SSI recipients would not be eligible for food stamps, the law now permits exceptions; as a result, most states ignore the "cash" value of food stamps and in-kind assistance in calculating state supplements to the federally guaranteed income. See Carroll Estes, *The Aging Enterprise* (San Francisco: Jossey-Bass, 1979); Gary Nelson, "Social Class and Public Policy for the Elderly," *Social Service Review* 56(January 1982):85–107; Bernice L. Neugarten, ed., *Age or Need?* (Beverly Hills: Sage Publications, 1983); Myers, *Social Security*, 2nd ed., pp. 606–7.

37 Stein, *Social Security*, pp. 141–2, 237.

38 U. S. Senate Special Committee on Aging, *Developments in Aging: 1982,* (Washington, D.C.: Government Printing Office, 1983), vol. 1, p. viii. See also William E. Oriol, " 'Modern' Age and Public Policy," *The Gerontologist* 21(February 1981):35–46; and Melinda Upp, "Relative Importance of Various Income Sources for the Aged, 1980," *Social Security Bulletin* 46(January 1983):3–10.

39 This included the disabled and their survivors before 1979. Statistics from *Social Security Bulletin, Annual Statistical Supplement* (1981), pp. 15, 234. The average monthly benefit paid in 1981 was $366.50.

40 Brown, *Essays*, pp. 72–5. Alicia Munnell, *The Future of Social Security* (Washington, D.C.: Brookings Institution, 1977), p. 51.

41 Carolyn L. Weaver, *The Crisis in Social Security* (Durham, N.C.: Duke Press Policy Studies, 1982), pp. 170–1; data on fluctuations in Myers, *Social Security*, 2nd ed., p. 79.

42 In February 1979, HEW Secretary Califano released "Social Security and Changing Roles of Men and Women," a 323-page report offering two ways to increase the protection of women in their later years. Ten months later, the seventh Quadrennial Advisory Council on Social Security issued a report that recommended sweeping changes in financing the OASDI system. In 1978 Carter had established the President's Commission on Pension Policy, which issued its final report three years later. While this commission was studying the nation's retirement, survivors, and disability benefits system, a nine-member National Commission on Social Security (not to be confused with the fifteen-member NCSSR of 1982–3) was convened under a provision in the 1977 amendments to the Social Security Act.

43 Two influential "liberal" critiques are Munnell, *Future of Social Security,* and Robert M. Ball, *Social Security: Today and Tomorrow* (New

York: Columbia University Press, 1978). For representative "conservative" analyses, see Robert S. Kaplan, *Financial Crisis in the Social Security System* (Washington, D.C.: American Enterprise Institute, 1976); and Rita Ricardo Campbell, *Social Security: Promise and Reality* (Stanford: Hoover Institution Press, 1977). For business views, see Committee for Economic Development, *Reforming Retirement Policies* (New York: CED, 1981). For the opinions of labor officials and the gray lobby, see Bert Seidman, "Concepts of Balance between Social Security (OASDI) and Private Pension Benefits," in *Social Security and Private Pension Plans,* ed. Dan McGill (Homewood, Ill.: Richard D. Irwin, 1977), pp. 778–93; and various editorials published after 1976 by the National Council on the Aging in *Perspectives on Aging* and by the National Retired Teachers Association/American Association of Retired Persons in *Modern Maturity.*

44 For instance, Martin Feldstein, a Harvard economist who became President Reagan's chief economic advisor in 1982, estimated that each dollar paid into the system by a worker and his or her employer corresponded to a reduction of $0.87 in private savings. Not surprisingly, Feldstein's argument provoked a spate of rebuttals, rejoinders, recalculations, and restatements. Feldstein first presented his case in "Social Security, Induced Retirement, and Aggregate Capital Accumulation," *Journal of Political Economy* 82(September/October 1974):905–26. He subsequently wrote articles for such prestigious journals as *The Public Interest* and official publications of the Federal Reserve Bank of Boston and the National Bureau of Economic Research.

45 Hence, critics such as Peter Ferrera resurrected arguments first set forth in the 1930s. See Ferrera's *Social Security: The Inherent Contradiction* (San Francisco: Cato Institute, 1980). Some economists called for "privatizing" social security. See Michael J. Boskin, "Social Security: The Alternatives Before Us," in *The Crisis in Social Security* ed. Michael J. Boskin (San Francisco: Institute for Contemporary Studies, 1977). A. Haeworth Robertson, who had served as chief actuary of the Social Security Administration between 1975 and 1978, proposed a "Freedom Plan," featuring optional retirement savings bonds and cost-of-living adjustments for private plans, to take effect on July 4, 1984. See Robertson, *The Coming Revolution in Social Security* (McLean, Va.: Security Press, 1981), chs. 27–30. See also "Social Security Commissioner Departs with Strong Views of System's Future," *Wall Street Journal,* December 31, 1979, p. 8.

46 Daniel Bell, *The Cultural Contradictions of Capitalism* (New York: Basic Books, 1976); James M. Buchanan and Richard E. Wagner, *Democracy in Deficit* (New York: Academic Press, 1977).

47 James O'Connor, *The Fiscal Crisis of the State* (New York: St. Martin's Press, 1973); see also the review of this literature in John Myles, *Old Age in the Welfare State* (Boston: Little, Brown, 1984).

48 Fred Hirsch, *Social Limits to Growth: A Twentieth Century Fund Study*

(Cambridge, Mass.: Harvard University Press, 1976); see also Jürgen Habermas, *Legitimation Crisis* (Boston: Beacon Press, 1975); and Ivan Illich, *Toward a History of Needs* (New York: Pantheon, 1977).

49 For more on this, see Janowitz, *The Last Half-Century,* ch. 1; Albert O. Hirschman, "The Welfare State in Trouble," *American Economic Review* 70(May 1980):113–16; and Henry Aaron, *The Economic Effects of Social Security* (Washington, D.C.: Brookings Institution, 1982).

50 See "Faulty Assumptions Led to Social Security Crisis," *New York Times,* January 4, 1983, pp. 1, 9. It should be noted that in making actual forecasts, the Social Security Administration generates figures based on "optimistic," "pessimistic," and two sets of "intermediate" assumptions. Even the worst-case scenario outlined in 1977 grossly underestimated how severe the 1980 recession would be.

51 Ippolito, *Congressional Spending,* pp. 245–6.

52 Peter N. Stearns, "Political Perspectives on Social Security Financing," in *Social Security Financing,* ed. Felicity Skidmore (Cambridge, Mass.: M.I.T. Press, 1981), p. 183. See also Robert J. Samuelson, "Busting the Budget: The Graying of America," *National Journal,* February 18, 1978, pp. 256–60. The gray lobby was dismayed by the "ageist" assumptions manifest in some commentaries, but there was no question that the aging of the population *would* affect the costs of federal programs. See Robert B. Hudson, "The 'Graying' of the Federal Budget and Its Consequences for Old-Age Policy," *The Gerontologist* 18(October 1978):428–40. Social security was not the only retirement plan in jeopardy. A variety of state and local public pensions were clearly in a precarious financial state. Furthermore, the bail-out provisions of ERISA meant that the federal government was potentially liable for millions of dollars in retirement benefits, benefits for which no adequate cash reserves could be maintained. See Chapter 7 in this volume.

53 The data and interpretation in this paragraph come from my reading of the National Commission on Social Security Reform, memorandum no. 13 (April 7, 1982), "Surveys of Public Confidence as to Financial Status of the Social Security Program." See also Louis Harris and Associates, *1979 Study of American Attitudes Toward Pensions and Retirement* (New York: Johnson & Higgins, 1979); National Council on the Aging, *Aging in the Eighties: America in Transition* (Washington, D.C.: National Council on the Aging, 1981); Peter D. Hart Research Associates, *A Nationwide Survey of Attitudes toward Social Security* (Washington, D.C.: National Commission on Social Security, 1981), p. S4.

54 Public opinion polls showed a dramatic decline, beginning in 1964, in Americans' trust in government. Surprisingly, the steepest drop was among those over sixty-five. Even so, most Americans thought that social security would provide a significant proportion of their retirement income. Harold R. Johnson et al., *American Values and the Elderly* (Ann Arbor: Institute of Gerontology, 1979), p. S-64.

55 Quoted in "Member of Congress and Aides Seeking Ways to Keep Social Security Solvent," *New York Times,* January 2, 1981, p. A11.

56 See "New Rules Drafted for Social Security," *New York Times,* April 8, 1981, p. 25; "Taking the Plunge on Social Security," ibid., April 12, 1981, sect. IV, p. 4; "Congress Expected to Seek Savings on Social Security for Short Term," ibid., April 27, 1981, p. 18. Under Dole's plan, benefit adjustments would depend on either the CPI or wage increases, whichever was lower.

57 A report by Reagan's advisory group on social security, prepared during the transition period between November 1980 and January 1981, had suggested making coverage under the program mandatory for new federal employees and changing the COLA formula. In March, however, President Reagan told congressional Republican leaders that he intended to keep a campaign promise *not* to change the formula for cost-of-living increases. See "Members of Congress and Aides Seeking Ways to Keep Social Security Solvent," *New York Times,* January 2, 1981, p. A11. Robert Myers and Mary Falvey Fuller, who later played key roles on the 1982–3 National Commission on Social Security Reform, were members of this transition task force. Another member, economist Michael Boskin, outlined his thoughts in "How to Reform Social Security," *New York Times,* January 11, 1981, p. 3. For Reagan's reaction, see "Reagan Challenges Congressional Budget Office Report on Budget for 1982," ibid., March 18, 1981, pp. 1, 22.

58 "Time for Surgery on Social Security," *New York Times,* May 10, 1981, sect. IV, p. 18.

59 "Schweiker Statement on Pensions," *New York Times,* May 13, 1981, p. A29.

60 "Reagan Backs Cuts For Some Programs in Social Security," *New York Times,* May 12, 1981, pp. 1, D22; "Reagan Social Security Plan Explained," ibid., May 13, 1981, pp. 1, A29.

61 "Interim Social Security Changes Approved," *Congressional Quarterly Almanac* 37(1981):118; "A Turning on Social Security," *New York Times,* May 13, 1981, p. A29. Tom Wicker, well known for his liberal views on social programs, had some nice things to say about the Reagan intiatives in his editorial "Smaller Is Necessary," ibid., May 15, 1981, p. 31.

62 "Coalition Plans Drive Against Move to Trim Social Security Benefits," *New York Times,* May 14, 1981, sect. B, p. 15. A policy analyst at the National Retired Teachers Association/American Association of Retired Persons told me in an interview that the telephone lines to Capitol Hill were busy for the rest of the week following Schweiker's announcement. He used this incident to support his thesis that the gray lobby could not possibly have mobilized forces so quickly; the aged themselves were clearly taking the initiative in reacting against the president's plan.

63 Moynihan quoted in the 1981 *Congressional Quarterly Almanac,* p.

284; see also "A.F.L.-C.I.O. President Assails Reagan Plan to Trim Social Security," *New York Times,* May 18, 1981, sect. IV, p. 12.

64   "Women's Benefits: Debate Is Rekindled," *New York Times,* June 4, 1981, sect. III, p. 3.

65   On May 19, the House Democratic Caucus unanimously adopted a resolution that called the entire package an "unconscionable breach of faith." The party solemnly vowed not to "destroy the program or a generation of retirees." O'Neill quoted in "Senate Rejects Reagan Bid to Trim Social Security," *New York Times,* May 21, 1981, p. B14; the House resolution is quoted in the 1981 *Congressional Quarterly Almanac,* p. 119. The Republican-controlled Senate, by a 96-to-0 voice vote, passed a resolution the next day maintaining that "Congress shall not precipitously and unfairly penalize early retirees."

66   "Senate Rejects," *New York Times,* May 21, 1981, pp. 1, B14. Armstrong quoted in the 1981 *Congressional Quarterly Almanac,* p. 118; see also "GOP Issues Views on Social Security," *New York Times,* May 11, 1981, p. 32. Some evidence suggests that the White House was eventually willing to admit that its initiatives had backfired. In an interview in December 1981, White House Chief of Staff James A. Baker III called the original plan to cut future benefits the administration's biggest mistake. See "Reagan Delays Move on Tax Rises," *New York Times,* December 23, 1981, sect. IV, p. 5.

67   Kennedy's comment appears in "Reagan Urges Pension Negotiation," *New York Times,* May 22, 1981, p. 16.

68   As Wilbur Cohen had noted in an interview a year earlier, "You can't change the rules of the game right in the middle, when people have made basic decisions about their futures. That would undermine people's faith in paying into the system." See "Social Security: Can Americans Afford It?" *New York Times,* April 6, 1980, sect. IV, p. 5.

69   See Martin Anderson, *Welfare* (Stanford: Hoover Institution Press, 1978). Anderson was the president's chief advisor on domestic social policy at the time. See also William Craig Stubblebein and Thomas D. Willett, eds., *Reaganomics* (San Francisco: Institute for Contemporary Studies, 1983). For a less charitable view, see Robert Lekachman, *Greed Is Not Enough* (New York: Pantheon, 1982).

70   Stockman's views at the time are reported at length in William Greider, "The Education of David Stockman," *The Atlantic* 248(December 1981):27–54.

71   Myers's criticism appeared in his December 1981 letter of resignation as deputy commissioner of the Social Security Administration. Part of the letter appeared in "Top Reagan Advisor on Social Security Quits," *New York Times,* December 19, 1981, p. 28. Nonetheless, the president soon afterward appointed Myers to be the NCSSR executive director.

72 The lack of contact with Dole is reported in the 1981 *Congressional Quarterly Almanac,* p. 119; the information on the others was confirmed in interviews with Representative Conable and senior staff members who worked for Representative Pickle and Senator Heinz. Heinz's criticism of the president's plan appears in "Reagan Accused of Overstating Social Security System's Woes," *New York Times,* June 18, 1981, p. 22.

73 Congress, for instance, agreed to eliminate the $122-per-month minimum benefit as part of the 1982 budget reconciliation bill (PL 97-35) passed on July 31. The public outcry over this "cut" was so great, however, that both the legislative and executive branches took steps to reinstate the minimum benefit for those on the roll and those becoming eligible before 1982. The House Ways and Means Subcommittee on Social Security wanted immediate action to shore up the system, but Speaker O'Neill, seeking political advantage from Reagan's blunder, would not permit his colleagues to bring in a financing bill that year. Robert Dole, chairman of the Senate Finance Committee, announced his intention to devise a proposal worthy of bipartisan support, but made little headway. See "Interim Social Security Changes Approved," *Congressional Quarterly Almanac* 37(1981):117–20; "In the Hurricane's Eye on Social Security Cuts," *New York Times,* June 6, 1981, p. 9; "Retirement at 68 is Gaining Favor as an Answer for Social Security," ibid., July 17, 1981, p. 13; "Congress Returning to Issue of Social Security Solvency," ibid., September 8, 1981, sect. II, p. 17; "Social Security Changes: Senator Bob Dole Bites the Bullet," ibid., September 16, 1981, p. 25; "Recipe for Crisis," *National Journal,* January 2, 1982, p. 35.

74 Henry J. Pratt, *The Gray Lobby* (University of Chicago Press, 1976); idem, "Symbolic Politics and White House Conferences on Aging," *Society* 15(July/August 1978):67–73.

75 "Aged at Parley Back Social Security View Espoused by Reagan," *New York Times,* December 2, 1981, pp. 1, B24; "White House Aging Parley Adopts Agenda for Decade," ibid., December 4, 1981, p. A18; White House Conference on Aging, *Final Report,* 3 vols. (Washington, D.C.: Government Printing Office, 1982). For a more favorable assessment than mine, see "Three Perspectives on the 1981 White House Conference on Aging," *The Gerontologist* 22(April 1982):125–8.

76 "Remarks [of President Reagan] Announcing Establishment of the Commission, December 16, 1981," in *Report of the National Commission on Social Security Reform* (Washington, D.C.: Government Printing Office, January 1983), appendix B.

77 Steven R. Weisman, "Reagan's Gains From Compromise on Bipartisan Social Security Accord," *New York Times,* January 17, 1983, p. 11. See also Jerome H. Skolnick, "The Violence Commission: Internal Politics and Public Policy," in *The Use and Abuse of Social*

Science, ed. Irving Louis Horowitz, 2nd ed. (New Brunswick, N.J.: Transaction Books, 1975), pp. 228–42; Hugh Sidey, "The Buck Stops Here," *Time* 121(May 30, 1983):14; Simon Rottenberg, "National Commissions: Preaching in the Garb of Analysis," *Policy Review* no. 23(Winter 1983):127–41; and Edward D. Berkowitz, "Commissioning the Future, Getting the Present," *Reviews in American History* 11(June 1983):294–9.

4 Social security gets a new lease on life

I drafted this chapter before reading Paul Light's *Artful Work* (New York: Random House, 1985), which is the fullest account to date of the policymaking activities that culminated in the 1983 amendments to the Social Security Act. Insofar as my account parallels his, it provides independent corroboration of his off-the-record interviews. Readers should be forewarned, however, that the differences between *Artful Work* and the present work go beyond academic quibbles. Light was an "insider." He worked as an American Political Science Congressional Fellow for Barber Conable and interacted regularly with NCSSR commissioners and staff throughout the period in question. Propinquity pays: Light's perspective was clearly shaped by his day-to-day experiences.

As an "outsider," I have been more dependent on published sources than Light, who provided minimal documentation for his behind-the-scenes reporting. Nonetheless, I found that most of the relevant information could be uncovered by mining the periodical literature and "official" documents: I cite quotations and "facts" that appeared in the *Congressional Quarterly, National Journal, New York Times,* and *Washington Post.* I also made considerable use of the *Final Report of the National Commission on Social Security Reform;* NCSSR memoranda, transcripts, and public minutes; and legislative publications, including the *Congressional Record* and House and Senate hearings. Press officers sent me all releases issued by Senators Howard Baker, Bob Dole, Edward Kennedy, and Daniel Moynihan, and by more than a dozen representatives, including Bill Archer, Speaker O'Neill, and Dan Rostenkowski. I was able to make better sense of this wealth of material after informal interviews with Larry Atkins, James A. Baker III, Robert M. Ball, Wilbur J. Cohen, Barber Conable, Edwin L. Dale, Jr., Suzanne Dilk, Elizabeth Duskin, Arthur Flemming, Mary Falvey Fuller, Alan Greenspan, Janice Gregory, Paul A. Kerschner, Martha Keys, Robert J. Myers, Claude Pepper, J. J. Pickle, Sylvester J. Schieber, Bert Seidman, Eric Shulman, Lawrence Smedley, David A. Stockman, James R. Swensen, Alexander B. Trowbridge, and Carolyn Weaver.

Roger Fisher and William Ury's *Getting to Yes* (New York: Penguin Books, 1983) served as a prime theoretical model in this chapter: NCSSR members, Congress, and White House staff employed many of the negotiating tactics the book describes. I have also tried to put the 1983 social security amendments into historical perspective. In this regard I have learned much from Graham T. Allison, *Essence of Decision* (Boston: Little, Brown, 1971); Albert O. Hirschman, *Exit, Voice, and Loyalty* (Cambridge, Mass.: Harvard University Press, 1970) and *Essays in Trespassing* (Cambridge University Press, 1981); Ernest May, *"Lessons" of the Past* (Oxford University Press, 1973); and Herbert A. Simon, *Reason in Human Affairs* (Stanford University Press, 1983).

1   "Benefit 'Indexing' Is Facing Scrutiny," *New York Times,* April 12, 1982, p. 1, and sect. D, p. 9; Dale Tate, "Senate Republicans, Reagan Press a New Budget Package," *Congressional Quarterly* 40(May 8, 1982):1038.

2   "Pension Meeting Ends in Conflict," *New York Times,* May 11, 1982, p. 17; "Reagan to Fight Cuts in Current Social Security Aid," *Washington Post,* May 11, 1982, p. A11.

3   "Social Security Funds: A 'New' Political Issue," *New York Times,* May 14, 1982, p. 18; "Social Security Issue Splits G.O.P As Senators Begin Budget Debate," *New York Times,* May 15, 1983, p. 46; Pamela Fessler, "Members Caught in an Election-Year Bind," *Congressional Quarterly* 40(May 15, 1982):1093.

4   A November 1981 Harris poll, released by the National Council on the Aging to coincide with the White House Conference on Aging, revealed that 92% of the sample disapproved of reducing benefits for present retirees, that 85% felt that those planning to retire should keep their benefits established under current law, and that 72% did not want a change in COLA entitlements. A May 1982 Gallup poll found that only 30% of the public thought that social security payments were "just about right"; 57% felt they were too low, and a mere 9% believed they were too high. See Louis Harris and Associates, Inc., *Aging in the Eighties: America in Transition* (Washington, D.C.: National Council on the Aging, 1981), p. 124; and Timothy B. Clark, "A Lesson in Politics," *National Journal,* May 22, 1982, p. 919.

5   This point was made by NCSSR members of both parties in off-the-record interviews. Note how well the commission's behavior in May satisfied several preliminary steps that some experts on the art of negotiating consider essential to reach a settlement. The NCSSR was making emotions explicit and acknowledging them as legitimate; each side was allowing the other to blow off steam, thereby making rational debate easier at a later time. And through efforts to defuse the issue, both sides were trying to establish a genuine working relationship. See Fisher and Ury, *Getting to Yes,* ch. 2.

6   Minutes of the fourth meeting of the National Commission on Social Security Reform, June 27, 1982, p. 3.

7   Transcript of the public meeting of the National Commission on Social Security Reform, November 13, 1982, p. 51.

8   Executive Director Myers wanted to base future adjustments in ben-

efits on increases in nationwide wage rates *minus* 1.5 percentage points, rather than on rises in the CPI, as the current law required. Robert J. Myers, memorandum no. 16, "Possible Method of Revising Social Security to a Self-Adjusting, Self-Stabilizing Basis," April 29, 1982. Greenspan considered Myers's proposal a way to reduce the system's long-term financing problems. Robert Beck saw the change as a "safety valve." The Democrats had mixed reactions to the idea. Lane Kirkland and Claude Pepper objected that the change could reduce beneficiaries' protection in periods of high inflation, just when they needed more money to cope with soaring prices. While acknowledging its possible disadvantages, Robert Ball did not reject the new indexing proposal in toto, "because in the long run, wages are expected to increase more than prices." See "Panel Considers Linking Increases In Social Security to Wage Levels," *New York Times,* August 9, 1982, sect. B, p. 5.

9   The proceedings at this stage thus conformed to the second step of the Fisher-Ury model – the need to focus on interests, not positions; see Fisher and Ury, *Getting to Yes,* ch. 3.

10 "Much Talk, Little of It Candid, on Social Security," *New York Times,* September 8, 1982, p. 10.

11 "G.O.P. Ad Crediting Reagan for Pension Rise Is Attacked," *New York Times,* July 7, 1982, p. A11.

12 "Unemployed Feel the Pain; Elderly Express the Worry," *New York Times,* October 24, 1982, sect. IV, p. 2.

13 "The Social Security Stew Simmers," *New York Times,* October 30, 1982, p. 13; "President Says 'Big Spenders' Forced Ban on School Prayers," *New York Times,* November 1, 1982, sect. D, p. 14. Although the Democrats captured twenty-six seats in the House on election day, it was hardly a resounding repudiation of the Republicans, who kept control of the Senate. A president's party traditionally loses ground in midterm elections. See "Democrats Victors in Key Races In a Wave of Reagan Discontent," ibid., November 3, 1982, p. 20.

14 "Pension Trust Fund Set To Borrow Money to Meet Payments," *New York Times,* October 18, 1982, p. 1.

15 "Leaders of Both Parties Facing Tough Choices on Social Security Problems," *New York Times,* November 7, 1982, sect. A, p. 18. As it turned out, Congress did meet in a lame-duck session in late 1982, but spent much of its time debating the Reagan administration's MX missile proposal. Because little of substance resulted from this special session, it is reasonable to suppose that it would have failed to produce a social security package even had it been called specifically for that purpose.

16 For a more detailed explanation of how Myers derived these estimates, see memorandum 57, "Reconciliation of Cost Estimates of CBO and SSA as to Amount of Additional Funding Needed by

OASDI Trust Funds in 1982–1985 in Order to Have Specified Fund Ratio at Beginning of 1986," October 14, 1982; and memorandum 62, "Amounts Needed in Short Run to Restore Financial Soundness of OASDI System Under 'More Realistic' Pessimistic Cost Estimates," November 5, 1982. The long-term estimates appear in the NCSSR *Final Report*, p. 2-2, and ch. 4, statement (7), p. 1. In order to provide an independent check on these estimates, Greenspan asked the Department of Commerce's Bureau of Economic Analysis to study the dynamics of social security financing, using its own econometric model. In public testimony, Myers affirmed that the Commerce Department and SSA estimates were consistent with each other (official transcript of the November 11, 1982, meeting of NCSSR, pp. 6–10, 31).

17 This was Heinz's characterization, quoted in Timothy B. Clark, " 'Social Security Ball in Your Court,' Greenspan Panel Tells Reagan, O'Neill," *National Journal*, November 20, 1982, p. 1989.

18 A revised version of the options (the "blue book") appears as Appendix K in the final commission report. The value of having such a set of options can hardly be overstated. Developing "objective criteria" promotes wise, amicable, and efficient agreements, according to Fisher and Ury. See *Getting to Yes*, ch. 5.

19 See "Assurance Urged on Social Security," *New York Times*, November 14, 1982, p. 31; "Social Security Panel Recesses But Leaders Offer Compromise," *Washington Post*, November 14, 1982, p. A1. Dole's reaction quoted in Clark, "Ball in Your Court," p. 1991. An authoritative administration source told me that the president himself rejected the package. If this is true, the president was involved in negotiations much earlier than reported at the time.

20 The Beck and Heinz compromises were explained to me in separate interviews with Larry Atkins, Robert Ball, Martha Keys, and James Swensen.

21 Armstrong's challenge appears in Pamela Fessler, "Greenspan Commission Seeks Reagan, O'Neill Involvement," *Congressional Quarterly*, November 20, 1982, p. 2879.

22 "Social Security Commission and Its Partisan Divisions," *New York Times*, December 20, 1982, sect. B, p. 17. See also "Social Security Panel to Go On," ibid., December 23, 1982, sect. II, p. 6; "A Debate: What to Do About Social Security," ibid., December 26, 1982, sect. IV, p. 5. Robert Myers recalled his grave doubts about the prospects for success in "Myers Optimistic, Realistic on Social Security Outcome," *NRTA News Bulletin* 24(June 1983):12.

23 Robert Dole, "Reagan's Faithful Allies," *New York Times*, January 3, 1983, p. 14.

24 Daniel Patrick Moynihan, "More Than Social Security Was at Stake," *Washington Post*, January 18, 1983, p. A17; "Dole Holds Meeting to Seek a Social Security Consensus," *New York Times*, January 5, 1983,

sect. D, p. 20. Conable has told me that he thought he was invited, at least in part, because of his partisan exchanges with Moynihan during the 1982 campaign.

25 In mid-December, Darman called on Ball for an off-the-record meeting. Ball told me that Darman left with a clearer sense of what was needed to satisfy the Democrats. Ball thinks this overture showed that the president's men preferred to negotiate at the commission level rather than to fight matters out on Capitol Hill.

26 These assertions were confirmed in several off-the-record interviews. By putting the issues this way, my informants portrayed Baker as employing a classic negotiating tactic: nurturing a mutual search for broader options while encouraging a look at the issues from a new perspective. More on this in Fisher and Ury, *Getting to Yes*, pp. 68–71. On another level, Baker was also asserting his role as an interested third party. According to Fisher and Ury, "a natural third party may be a participant whose interests on this issue lie more in effecting an agreement than in affecting the particular terms." Ibid., p. 121.

27 Ball figured that Kirkland's vote would be the hardest to obtain. Kirkland understood Ball's desire to reach a settlement within the commission, but the AFL-CIO leader also assumed that, in the end, the Democrats would have to turn the package down. Interviews with close associates of Kirkland suggest that he was demonstrating his skill at using his "best alternative to a negotiated agreement" (in this case, a compromise forged on the Hill) as a powerful tool to facilitate a compromise. Fisher and Ury, *Getting to Yes*, pp. 106–10.

28 Armstrong, Archer, and Waggoner did not go along; that meant that the president, Speaker O'Neill, and Senate majority leader Baker each had one dissenter among the group of five they had originally appointed to the panel. It was important that the business community see that their representatives on the panel concurred in the NCSSR's final recommendations. It remains a matter of speculation, however, whether or not Trowbridge or Fuller would have joined the majority if Beck had not done so. Beck, after all, was head of the country's largest life insurance company; his views counted – likewise his reservations. This is why Beck's vote, relatively speaking, mattered more than the votes of others.

29 Claude Pepper, "A Triumph of Bipartisan Negotiating," *New York Times,* January 23, 1983, sect. F, p. 2. Pepper's evaluation resonates with a classic negotiating ploy: "In searching for the basic interests behind a declared position," Fisher and Ury observe, "look particularly for those bedrock concerns which motivate all people." *Getting to Yes*, p. 49.

30 Although virtually everybody had reason to be uneasy with these major provisions, plausible defenses were available. Liberals and Democrats who did not like postponing benefits that had been auto-

matically indexed could claim that the actual economic effect of the COLA delay would be temporary and minimal if the rate of inflation fell as much as economists had forecast. Conservatives and Republicans deplored the use of general revenues to reduce social security, but at least this had been limited to one year (1984), and no increase in the payroll tax would be necessary during Reagan's presidency. Both sides, in short, could make a virtue out of necessity.

31 The panel recommended that only for single taxpayers with an adjusted gross income (AGI) of over $20,000 and couples with an AGI over $25,000 would 50% of social security benefits count as taxable income. These income ceilings, once established by law, were not to be adjusted. Assuming modest rates of inflation and continued income-bracket creep, this meant that more and more older people eventually would have to pay taxes on their benefits.

32 Even items for which no immediate or long-range savings were anticipated were intended to strengthen the financing of OASDI. To minimize the likelihood that there would be another funding crisis in the 1980s, for instance, interfund borrowing was permitted through 1987, at which time a "stabilizer" went into effect.

33 See *Final Report of the National Commission on Social Security Reform* (Washington, D.C.: Government Printing Office, 1983), ch. 4, Supplementary Statements 1 and 2.

34 See House Ways and Means Chairman Dan Rostenkowski's opening statement in U.S. Congress, House of Representatives, 98th Cong., 1st sess., *Recommendations of the National Commission on Social Security Reform,* hearings before the Committee on Ways and Means, February 1, 1983, p. 3. [Henceforth abbreviated as *1983 House Hearings.*] See also the comments by Senator Bob Dole in U.S. Senate, 98th Cong., 1st sess., *National Commission on Social Security Reform Recommendations,* hearings before the Subcommittee on Social Security and Income Maintenance Programs of the Committee of Finance, February 15, 1983, p. 2.

35 Interviews and testimony found in *1983 House Hearings,* part 2, February 9, 1983, p. 774; for Kuhn, see *1983 House Hearings,* part 1, p. 226.

36 See "Congress Avoiding Political Abyss," *National Journal,* p. 611, for business opposition. The special pleadings of the two interest groups cited appear in *1983 House Hearings,* part 1, pp. 133–49. See Chapters 5 and 7 in this volume for the resistance of labor groups to various provisions.

37 In separate interviews, both Ball and Greenspan recalled that immediately before the hearings they had worked out how they were going to respond to some of the anticipated questions. For self-conscious instances of Democrats speaking to Democrats, and Republicans speaking to Republicans, see the exchanges in *1983 House Hearings,* February 1, 1983, pp. 62–6.

38 This characterization of Fuller's position is based on her published remarks, particularly those appearing in Supplementary Statement 8 in the *NCSSR Report,* in her testimony in the *1983 House Hearings* (February 1, 1983, pp. 66–7), and in confidential interviews.

39 The assertions in this paragraph are based on my interviews with Representative Pepper, James Swensen of Prudential, two high-ranking labor officials, and Trowbridge and Flemming. See also *1983 House Hearings,* February 7, 1983, pp. 95–6, 102–16, 886, 915.

40 For an "official" account, see John A. Svahn and Mary Ross, "Social Security Amendments of 1983," *Social Security Bulletin* 46(July 1983):3–49. See also the amendments made by the Senate Finance Committee and Senator Dole's comments on the differences between the House and Senate versions in *Congressional Record* 129(March 16, 1983):S2999–S3025.

41 *Congressional Record,* March 9, 1983, p. H954.

42 Ibid., March 24, 1983, p. H1781.

43 Majorities of both Republicans and Democrats in both houses supported the measure. Neither chronological age nor seniority in Congress appears to have significantly influenced a legislator's vote. Controlling for race, gender, previous occupation, or religion uncovers no hidden relationships. Even knowing the proportion of older people in a legislator's constituency or the degree of his or her prior support for the elderly (as determined by the National Council of Senior Citizens) does not help predict a legislator's final vote. There is not even a strong correlation between an individual's vote on the measure before and after it went to conference. These statements are based on analyses using biographical and voting data gathered from the *Congressional Quarterly* and ratings published in the February 1983 issue (volume 6) of the NCSC's *Senior Citizen News.* I thank Michael Santos for his help in executing the computer runs.

44 The president waited to sign the amendments until Congress returned from its Easter recess, and then had to delay the ceremony a bit more because of a printing error: The House quietly had to pass H.R. 1900 a second time because the original version in several places read "Soviet Security" instead of "Social Security." See "Washington Briefs," *New York Times,* April 15, 1983, p. 18; "President, on Note of Bipartisanship, Signs Social Security Bill," *Washington Post,* April 21, 1983, p. A10.

45 For more on the pertinence of history to policy analysis, see my "Making of an Applied Historian: Stage Two," *The Public Historian* 5(Spring 1983), especially pp. 27–34.

46 The 1939 comparisons are taken from Berkowitz, "The First Crisis," p. 138; the 1983 figures are drawn from the supplementary statements by Senator William Armstrong (No. 7, p. 2) and by Senator Dole and Representative Conable (No. 5, p. 2) in the *NCSSR*

Report. Peter Peterson's scenario was even scarier. See his "The Salvation of Social Security," *New York Review of Books,* December 14, 1982, pp. 55–7. Significantly, Peterson's forecasts were often cited on the editorial pages of the *New York Times, Washington Post,* and *Wall Street Journal.*

47 Minutes of the third meeting of the National Commission on Social Security Reform, May 10, 1982, p. 3. See also "Remedies for Social Security; Retrenchments or New Revenues," *Washington Post,* May 8, 1982, p. A4.

48 See Robert Ball, *The Financial Condition of the Social Security Program,* mimeograph, April 1982 (a working paper for the Save Our Security coalition), and the SOS pamphlet *Social Security: A Sound and Durable System* Washington, D.C.: SOS, 1982).

49 Kirkland made this point in public testimony on November 12, 1982. See the official NCSSR transcripts, p. 36. Note also the partisan jockeying on pp. 111, 121–3.

50 See, for instance, the different numbers used and "guesses" made by Ball and Greenspan as well as the reference to Fuller's estimates in the House hearings on February 1, pp. 56–62, and by Greenspan in the Senate hearings, February 15, p. 102. Testifying before the Senate on February 15, Senator Armstrong (p. 74) and Representative Archer (p. 167) – who had opposed the NCSSR package – worried that "political judgements" were influencing actuarial estimates. Paul Light gives some evidence that would substantiate this "hunch," in "Social Security and the Politics of Assumptions," pp. 46–8. Light's paper was prepared for the 1983 American Political Science Association meetings.

51 Robertson's testimony appears in U.S. Congress, House of Representatives, 98th Cong., 1st sess., *Financing Problems of the Social Security System,* hearings before the Subcommittee on Social Security, February 8, 1983, pp. 456–7. For Bartlett, see ibid., part 2, February 9, 1983, pp. 543–5. For the GAO report, see ibid., p. 848. Social Security Commissioner John A. Svahn thought that the NCSSR solution left "little margin for error," particularly in 1985. See "Statement on Social Security Financing" by John A. Svahn, in the Senate Hearings, part 1, especially pp. 191–5 and 203, and his two letters to Senator Dole, especially pp. 214–15, 219.

52 Many called for fundamental changes, of course, but off-the-record interviews and my readings of published accounts lead me to think that only three people's ideas might have been supported by President Reagan (against his advisors' judgment) had he thought they could be enacted. The most salient "radical" positions were advanced by Stanford economist Michael Boskin, who at the August 1982 meeting of the NCSSR advocated "Personal Security Accounts" as a way to shift the cost of old-age retirement gradually from the public to the private sector; Martin Feldstein, who was Reagan's chief

economic advisor between 1982 and 1984; and Senator Jesse Helms (D–N.C.), who presented a scheme of his own on the Senate floor during debate over the NCSSR package. See Robert J. Myers, "Personal Security Accounts: A Proposal for Fundamental Social Security Reform by Boskin, Kotlikoff, and Shoven," NCSSR memorandum no. 47, September 1, 1982, p. 1. More on Reagan's personal views in Ronnie Dugger, *On Reagan* (New York: McGraw-Hill, 1983), ch. 3.

53 See how two highly placed social security lawyers diagnosed the system's ailments and prescribed solutions in "The Reserve Fund," *New York Times*, September 5, 1938, p. 14; and Thomas H. Eliot, "Funds for the Future," *Atlantic Monthly* 162(August 1938):225–32.

54 To meet a deadline established by powerful members of Congress and the president, Brown and seven of his colleagues worked as a subcommittee to develop a proposal. Though this group differed from the NCSSR's "gang of five" insofar as it included no incumbent lawmaker and never negotiated directly with the administration, it did create a set of recommendations reflecting the desires of those who later acted on the proposed amendments.

55 In this section I build on insights derived from Albert O. Hirschman's seminal *Exit, Voice, and Loyalty* (Cambridge, Mass.: Harvard University Press, 1970) and articles that amplify his theory in Hirschman, *Essays in Trespassing* (Cambridge University Press, 1981), especially chs. 9–10.

56 While recognizing this as plausible, Robert Ball nonetheless insisted on active negotiation. In an interview with me, Ball stressed that this disagreement reflected different emphases on strategy, a problem that did not have to be resolved among the Democrats. Note that the Democrats had by then determined their "best alternative to a negotiated agreement," which Fisher and Ury postulate as essential. See *Getting to Yes*, ch. 6.

57 In each instance, Trowbridge checked his facts and figures with Robert Myers. He also sought reactions from key members of the commission, including Greenspan, Ball, Dole, Heinz, and Moynihan, and with White House advisors. Mr. Trowbridge graciously permitted me to examine all of his package proposals. Details of the fourth revision, prepared on December 8, were reported in the press. See "Compromise Arises on Social Security," *New York Times*, December 9, 1982, p. 17. Robert Myers told me that Trowbridge's effort was a significant step toward the eventual compromise because he persisted despite the odds.

58 Ball and Trowbridge nonetheless did try to dovetail their schemes. In a long telephone conversation with Trowbridge on December 16, Ball recommended that the possibility of new taxes be incorporated into subsequent proposals by the NAM president (letter to the author

from A. B. Trowbridge, May 23, 1983). Ball told me flatly that without the taxation of benefits, there would have been no compromise advanced by the commission. Fisher and Ury characterize this procedure as inventing options for mutual gain. Rather than trying to eliminate differences in interests, "differences can also lead to a solution." See *Getting to Yes*, p. 76.

59 See "Panel Eyes Social Security Tax Plan As a Possible Way to Save System," *Washington Post*, January 7, 1983, p. A4; "Social Security Panel Fails to Compromise," ibid., January 9, 1983, p. A8.

60 This reconstruction of events is based on my interviews and details presented in the following *Washington Post* articles: "Social Security Talks Nearing Compromise," January 12, 1983, pp. A1, A8; "Social Security Accord Reported Near," January 13, 1983, p. A12; "Agreement Nears on Aid to Aged," January 14, 1983, p. A1; "Social Security Compromise Is Seen," January 14, 1983, p. A5; and "Dole, Domenici Predict Congress Will Pass Social Security Plan," January 17, 1983, p. A2.

61 See Arthur J. Altmeyer, *The Formative Years of Social Security* (Madison: University of Wisconsin Press, 1963), pp. 106–13.

62 *Congressional Record*, June 8, 1939, p. H6861. It took longer for the panel's recommendations to be translated into law in 1939 than it did in 1983. The House alone devoted forty-eight days to public hearings, which amounted to 2,500 pages of printed testimony from 164 witnesses. It was another six weeks before the Ways and Means Committee introduced legislation. Progress through the Senate was equally slow. See *Congressional Record*, June 9, 1939, pp. H6894, H6904; Mark Leff, *The Limits of Symbolic Reform* (Cambridge University Press, 1984), pp. 279–86.

63 Ibid., pp. H6849, H6964.

64 See ibid., June 8, 1939, pp. H6857, H6862; ibid., July 13, 1939, p. S9002.

65 For criticisms of the rule, see *Congressional Record* 129(March 9, 1983):949–50, 1003.

66 *Congressional Record* 129(March 23, 1983):S3776. See also ibid., March 17, 1983, pp. S3252–60; March 22, pp. S3610–20; March 23, p. S3729.

67 J. Douglas Brown, *Essays on Social Security* (Princeton, N.J.: Industrial Relations Section, 1977), appendix, p. 47.

68 "Reagan Signs Social Security Changes Into Law," *New York Times*, April 21, 1983, p. 9.

69 "Social Security Solves 2 Reagan Political Problems," *Pittsburgh Press*, January 17, 1983, p. 1; "Reagan's Gains from Compromising On Bipartisan Social Security Accord," *New York Times*, January 17, 1983, p. 11; see as well Baker's observations in "Managing the White House," *Princeton Alumni Weekly*, March 28, 1983, pp. 14–15. See also Lou Cannon, "White House Views Compromise as a Tonic,"

Washington Post, January 17, 1983, pp. A1, A3; and idem, *Reagan* (New York: Putnam, 1982), especially pp. 202–3, 297, 330–7, 374–81.

70 "Reagan Weighs Broadening Cost-of-Living Raise Delay," *Washington Post,* January 18, 1983, p. A1.

71 Munnell and Cohen were quoted in "The Pension Package," *New York Times,* January 18, 1983, p. 9.

72 "Reagan Voices Doubt on Funds of Pension Plan," *New York Times,* July 7, 1984, pp. 1, 7; "Reagan Criticized on Social Security," ibid., July 8, 1984, pp. 1, 11. Two months earlier, Treasury Secretary Donald T. Regan claimed that "we're going to have to revisit social security sometime in the late '80s." He was not referring to the imminent Medicare "crisis," but to the balance of equity maintained in Title II. See "Regan Says Benefits Need Reexamining," *Washington Post,* May 7, 1984, p. A3; "Why Stigmatize Social Security?" *New York Times,* May 8, 1984, p. 22.

5 Retirement under social security

In addition to the general works cited in Chapters 1–4 and the specific works mentioned in the notes that follow, those interested in this aspect of social security policymaking should mine Stuart Brandes's *American Welfare Capitalism* (University of Chicago Press, 1975) and Wilbur J. Cohen's *Retirement under Social Security* (Berkeley: University of California Press, 1958), which offer cogent summaries of trends in public and private retirement policies prior to the 1960s. Robert C. Atchley, *The Social Forces in Late Life,* 3rd ed. (Belmont, Calif.: Wadsworth Publishing, 1980); Herbert S. Parnes, ed., *Work and Retirement* (Cambridge, Mass.: M.I.T. Press, 1981); and James Schulz, *The Economics of Aging,* 3rd ed. (Belmont, Calif.: Wadsworth Publishing, 1985) provide instructive analyses of recent trends. I also recommend that readers comb recent articles in the *Journal of Human Resources, Monthly Labor Review,* and *Social Security Bulletin.*

1 New beneficiaries who retired at age sixty-two would receive checks reduced 25% in 2005 and 30% in 2022. Retirement benefits begun at age sixty-two are now reduced 20%.

2 *Report of the National Commission on Social Security Reform* (Washington, D.C.: Government Printing Office, 1983), pp. 2–5, 2–17, 2–18.

3 Commissioners Archer, Beck, Conable, Dole, Fuller, Greenspan, Heinz, and Trowbridge, "Supplementary Statement on Meeting the Long-Range Financing Requirements," in NCSSR *Final Report,* Statement (1), pp. 1–2.

4 Commissioners Ball, Keys, Kirkland, Moynihan, and Pepper, "Long-Term Financing and Issues of Special Concern to Women," ibid., Statement (2), p. 3.

5   European data based on interviews and proceedings at the Carnegie Corporation conference on "Aging in Western Societies," Bellagio, Italy, June 1984. See also Sara Rix and Paul Fisher, *Retirement-Age Policy: An International Perspective* (London: Pergamon, 1982), pp. xx, 29–40, 50–1.

6   The 1900–70 data in this paragraph are taken from W. Andrew Achenbaum, *Old Age in the New Land* (Baltimore: Johns Hopkins University Press, 1978), pp. 95–105. The 1981 figures are from U.S. Department of Labor, *Employment and Training Report to the President* (Washington, D.C.: Government Printing Office, 1982).

7   See also Chapter 6 in this volume.

8   Employees' working careers may actually have been prolonged as automation and new machines reduced the burdens and stress associated with certain jobs in industry and new opportunities were created in the service sector of the economy. See Henry D. Sheldon, *The Older Population of the United States* (New York: Wiley, 1958), pp. 55–6, 173; William G. Bowen and T. Aldrich Finegan, *The Economics of Labor Force Participation* (Princeton University Press, 1969), pp. 353–5, 373–4; Clarence D. Long, *The Labor Force under Changing Conditions of Income and Employment* (Princeton University Press, 1958), pp. 13, 159–61, 172–3; Peter M. Blau and Otis Dudley Duncan, *The American Occupation Structure* (New York: Wiley, 1967), pp. 428–9; and Daniel Bell, *The Coming of the Post-Industrial Society* (New York: Basic Books, 1973).

9   See Marjorie Shearon, "The Economic Status of the Aged," *Social Security Bulletin* 2(March 1983):5–16. The 1967 data come from James Schulz's *The Economics of Aging* (Belmont, Calif.: Wadsworth Publishing, 1976), p. 42. Social security data from Melinda Upp, "Relative Importance of Various Income Sources of the Aged, 1980," *Social Security Bulletin* 46(January 1983):3–14. Because older people often have multiple sources of income, the figures do not add up to 100%.

10 See Chapters 2 and 6 in this volume. For more details, see Murray Webb Latimer, *Industrial Pension Systems in the United States and Canada,* 2 vols. (New York: Industrial Relations Counselors, 1932); and Luther Conant, Jr., *A Critical Analysis of Industrial Pension Systems* (New York: Macmillan, 1922); Robert M. Fogelson, "The Morass: An Essay on the Public Employee Pension Program," *Social History and Social Policy,* eds. David J. Rothman and Stanton Wheeler (New York: Academic Press, 1981), pp. 145–73; Elmer A. Lews, comp., *Civil Service Retirement and Salary Classification Laws* (Washington, D.C.: Government Printing Office, 1927), pp. 1–5; and William Graebner, *A History of Retirement* (New Haven, Conn.: Yale University Press, 1980), ch. 3.

11 Testimony of Thomas Kennedy, *U.S. Senate Hearings on S. 1130, Economic Security Act* (1935), p. 1269. See also the testimony by Joseph

P. W. Weir in ibid., p. 989. For more on the contemporary association of the onset of old age with a specific number of years, see I. M. Rubinow, "Old Age," *Encyclopedia of the Social Sciences* (New York: Macmillan, 1933), vol. 11, pp. 454–60; and Abraham Epstein's "Where Will You Be at Sixty-Five?" in his respected work *Insecurity: A Challenge to America* (New York: Henry Holt & Co., 1934).

12 William Green, *Hearings on S. 1130*, p. 179; see also Wilbur J. Cohen, *Retirement under Social Security* (Berkeley: University of California Press, 1958), p. 20.

13. For the original wording of the House draft concerning a "retirement test," see U.S. Social Security Board, *Social Security Bill, Summary of Provisions, Comparison of Text of Original Bill, and Ways and Means Redraft, Compilation of Proposed Amendments, etc., for Committee on Finance* (Washington, D.C.: Government Printing Office, 1935), especially pp. 4–7, 23, 29.

14 Section 202(d) specified that "the old age benefit payable to such individual shall be reduced for each calendar month in any part of which such regular employment occurred."

15 A version of the Townsend plan was reintroduced into the House and defeated by a vote of 302 to 97. A proposal to reduce the qualifying age for old-age assistance was also defeated in the Senate during the social security debate. See *Congressional Record*, June 1, 1939, pp. 6524–5.

16 U.S. Congress, House Committee on Ways and Means, *Social Security Hearings Relative to the Social Security Act Amendments of 1939* (Washington, D.C.: Government Printing Office, 1939), p. 899.

17 Cohen, *Retirement*, p. 69; see also Chapter 1 in this volume.

18 Several members of the 1948 Advisory Council on Social Security appointed by the Senate Finance Committee recommended reducing the retirement age for working women from sixty-five to sixty, but Congress took no action that year. A proposal by Senator Olin Johnston (D–S.C.) in 1954 to reduce the eligibility criterion for Title II benefits from sixty-five to sixty in order to deal with the unemployment problem in his state's textile industry was defeated by voice vote; the Senate was persuaded that extending coverage to potential beneficiaries in the age group sixty to sixty-five would cost an exorbitant sum. See Arthur J. Altmeyer, *The Formative Years of Social Security* (Madison: University of Wisconsin Press, 1968), p. 163.

19 A working woman's pension would be reduced 20% at age sixty-two; a wife's spousal benefit would be reduced 25% at the same age. A potential beneficiary who was dually entitled – as both a wife (or widow) and a worker – could also choose the beneficiary status that would afford her the greatest income. For more on the rationale behind this amendment, see the next chapter.

20 Age grading was less pertinent to occupational roles in farming than in industry: Those unable to perform certain tasks simply did less physically demanding but equally necessary tasks. Hence, "retire-

ment" on a farm typically meant alleviation, not cessation, of work.

21 Gail Buchwalter King and Peter N. Stearns, "The Retirement Experience as a Policy Factor," *Journal of Social History* 14(Summer 1981):589–625.

22 Edwin E. Witte, *The Development of the Social Security Act* (Madison: University of Wisconsin Press, 1963), pp. 189, 209–10.

23 Nevertheless, some progress was made. The 1946 amendments to the Social Security Act permitted states with employee contributions under their unemployment insurance laws to use these funds to make payments for temporary disability payments. A limited program of aid to permanently and totally disabled recipients of public assistance was included in the 1950 amendments. See Altmeyer, *The Formative Years,* pp. 280–1.

24 For more on the history of the disability insurance program, see Chapter 2 in this volume.

25 Interview (1968) with Roswell B. Perkins, oral history collection, Butler Library, Columbia University, pp. 25–6. Perkins was assistant secretary of HEW in 1954.

26 See Martha Derthick, *Policymaking for Social Security* (Washington, D.C.: Brookings Institution, 1979), ch. 15. In 1954, Congress enacted a "disability freeze" whereby years of disability were excluded in calculating a worker's OASI eligibility and benefit. The 1956 amendments imposed a six-month waiting period before a worker could receive disability benefits, because an applicant's incapacity for work had to be verified. No such rule, however, regulated the shift from receipt of disability benefits to a retirement check at sixty-five.

27 See Deborah A. Stone, *The Disabled State* (Philadelphia: Temple University Press, 1984); and Jerry L. Mashaw, *The Bureaucratic State* (New Haven, Conn.: Yale University Press, 1983).

28 See U.S. Department of Health and Human Services, *Social Security Bulletin: Annual Statistical Supplement, 1980* (Washington, D.C.: Government Printing Office, 1981), p. 25. As noted in Chapter 4, the 1983 amendments reduce benefits by $1 for every $3 of earnings.

29 Members of the House Ways and Means Committee used this issue as a negotiating chip in their broader fight over benefit levels for all beneficiaries as well as in the debate over the most desirable moment to extend coverage to new constituencies. See Derthick, *Policymaking,* p. 48.

30 See Altmeyer, *The Formative Years,* pp. 203–4.

31 *Social Security Bulletin, Annual Statistical Supplement* (1980), p. 26.

32 See U.S. Congress, House Ways and Means Committee, *Report of the 1979 Advisory Council on Social Security* (Washington, D.C.: Government Printing Office, 1980), pp. 175–8, 238–9; President's Commission on Pension Policy, executive summary, *Coming of Age* (Washington, D.C.: Government Printing Office, 1981), p. 2.

33 National Commission on Social Security, *Social Security in America's*

Future (Washington, D.C.: Government Printing Office, 1981), pp. 120–4; three members of the panel dissented from this recommendation (pp. 330–4).

34 Committee for Economic Development, *Reforming Retirement Policies* (New York: CED, September 1981), pp. 8, 36–8, 62. The NCSSR research staff developed several scenarios in anticipation of a change. See National Commission on Social Security Reform, memorandum no. 22, "Increasing the Normal Retirement Age Under Social Security by an Automatic-Adjustment Method," June 4, 1982; idem, memorandum no. 29, "Cost Aspects of Increasing the Normal Retirement Age under Social Security by an Automatic-Adjustment Method," June 28, 1982.

35 The law currently bans mandatory retirement before age seventy for all workers in local, state, and private employment, except executives or persons in "high policymaking positions" who are entitled to employer-financed pensions exceeding $27,000 per annum. To allow colleges and universities to deal with their tenure problems, professors were also exempted from the provision until the early 1980s. See my *Shades of Gray* (Boston: Little, Brown, 1983), pp. 103, 117.

36 Malcolm H. Morrison and Victor S. Barocas, "The Aging Work Force – Human Resource Implications," unpublished paper presented at the September 1983 Mohonk Conference on the Older Worker, sponsored by the Carnegie Corporation of New York, pp. 7–11. See also George T. Menake, *Policy-making in the American System: The Case of the Manpower Development and Training Act* (Washington, D.C.: University Press of America, 1978).

37 U.S. Department of Labor, *Final Report to Congress on Age Discrimination in Employment Act Studies* (Washington, D.C.: Department of Labor, 1982). This chapter will demonstrate, however, that the existence of mandatory retirement provisions has had a less direct impact on retirement behavior than might be expected.

38 William M. Mercer, *Employer Attitudes: Implications of an Aging Work Force* (New York: William M. Mercer, 1981), pp. 12–19, 25, 29.

39 Beverly Jacobson, *Young Programs for Older Workers: Case Studies in Progressive Personnel Policies* (New York: Van Nostrand Reinhold, 1980); National Older Workers Information System, *NOWIS IDEAPAC: Personnel Practices for an Aging Work Force* (Ann Arbor, Mich.: Institute of Gerontology, 1983); and Lawrence S. Root, *Employee Benefits and an Aging Society* (Ann Arbor, Mich.: Institute of Gerontology, 1984).

40 Insofar as the computer revolution will eliminate many current jobs, it is not altogether clear that corporate America will need or be able to create adequate job opportunities for older people who want to work in existing jobs or be retrained for new positions. See Bowen and Finegan, *Economics,* pp. 274–5, 374; Harold L. Sheppard, "Work and Retirement," in *Handbook of Aging and Social Sciences,* eds. Rob-

ert H. Binstock and Ethel Shanas (New York: Van Nostrand Reinhold, 1976), pp. 286–309; Harrison Givens, Jr., "An Evaluation of Mandatory Retirement," *Annals of the American Academy of Political and Social Sciences* 438(July 1978):50–7; *The Future of Older Workers in America* (Scarsdale, N.Y.: Work in America Institute, Inc., 1980).

41 See Bert Seidman, *Pensions: The Public–Private Interplay* (Washington, D.C.: AFL-CIO, 1979); Larry Smedley, "Sound Financing for Social Security," *American Federationist* 51(January 1977):38–44. Kirkland's views were confirmed in interviews with three different eyewitnesses.

42 For a brilliant exposition of this point, see Peter N. Stearns, "Political Perspectives on Social Security Financing," in *Social Security Financing,* ed. Felicity Skidmore (Cambridge, Mass.: M.I.T. Press, 1981), especially pp. 193–202.

43 See Achenbaum, *Old Age in the New Land,* p. 118.

44 Wilbert E. Moore, "The Aged in Industrial Societies," in *Industrial Relations and the Social Order,* rev. ed., ed. Wilbert E. Moore (New York: Macmillan, 1951), p. 530. See also my *Shades of Gray,* pp. 60–1, 101–2.

45 Margaret Clark and Barbara G. Anderson, *Culture and Aging* (Springfield, Ill.: Charles C. Thomas, 1967); and Joseph Pechman, Henry J. Aaron, and Michael K. Taussig, *Social Security: Perspectives for Reform* (Washington, D.C.: Brookings Institution, 1968), pp. 120–4.

46 "National Council of Senior Citizens Sees End to 'Scare Stories' about Social Security," news release, March 25, 1983. A statement issued January 31, 1983, by the Leadership Council of Aging Organizations (LCAO), which represents seventeen independent organizations, also opposed raising the retirement age.

47 Margaret Kuhn, *Maggie Kuhn on Aging* (New York: Harper & Row, 1977). The National Council of Senior Citizens, however, does not consider this approach part of its overall strategy.

48 In adopting this view, the leadership of the American Association of Retired Persons has knowingly parted company with other elements of the gray lobby, according to AARP, "AARP Social Security Position in Brief," unpublished memorandum dated October 22, 1982; see also the statement of the American Association of Retired Persons before the Senate Finance Committee, February 23, 1983. It is significant that AARP chose *not* to endorse the January 31, 1983, statement of the Leadership Council of Aging Organizations, preferring instead to advance its own position.

49 See, for instance, Harold L. Sheppard, "The Issue of Mandatory Retirement," *Annals of the American Academy of Political and Social Sciences* 438(July 1978):40–50.

50 This general point is developed in a different way in Chapters 6 and 7.

51 *Social Security Bulletin, Annual Statistical Supplement* (1981), p. 115;

U.S. Department of Labor, *Final Report to Congress on Age Discrimination in Employment Act Studies* (Washington, D.C.: Government Printing Office, 1982), p. 9.

52 *Final Report on ADEA Studies,* p. 28; see also Willis J. Goudy, "Changing Work Expectations: Findings from the Retirement History Study," *The Gerontologist* 21 (December 1981):644–9; D. J. Ekerdt, R. Bosse, and J. M. Mogey, "Concurrent Change in Planned and Preferred Age for Retirement," *Journal of Gerontology* 35(March 1980):232–40.

53 Philip L. Rones, "The Labor Market Problems of Older Workers," *Monthly Labor Review* 106(May 1983):3–12; U.S. Senate, Special Committee on Aging, *Developments in Aging: 1982,* vol. 1, pp. 337–9; Morrison and Barocas, "The Aging Work Force," p. 5.

54 Robert C. Atchley, "Retirement as a Social Institution," *Annual Review of Sociology* 8(1982):283–4; Herbert S. Parnes, ed., *Work and Retirement* (Cambridge, Mass.: M.I.T. Press, 1981), pp. 155–97.

55 M. L. Stecker, "Why Do Beneficiaries Retire?" *Social Security Bulletin* 18(May 1955):3–12; Peter O. Steiner and Robert Dorfman, *The Economic Needs of the Aged* (Berkeley: University of California Press, 1957); Karen Schwab, "Early Labor Force Withdrawal," *Social Security Bulletin* 37(August 1974):24–38; and Parnes, *Work and Retirement;* Louis Harris and Associates, Inc., *Aging in the Eighties: America in Transition* (Washington, D.C.: National Council on the Aging, 1981), p. 53.

56 A. W. Pollman, "Early Retirement: A Comparison of Poor Health to Other Retirement Factors," *Journal of Gerontology* 26(January 1971):41–5; U.S. Department of Health, Education, and Welfare, *Limitations of Activity Due to Chronic Conditions, United States, 1970,* series 10, no. 80 (Washington, D.C.: Government Printing Office, 1973), tables 1, 3, 4, B; Robert C. Atchley, *The Social Forces of Late Life,* 3rd ed. (Belmont, Calif.: Wadsworth Publishing, 1980).

57 Joseph F. Quinn, "The Microeconomic Determinants of Early Retirements," *Journal of Human Resources* 12(Summer 1977):329–46.

58 Dena K. Motley, "Availability of Retired Persons for Work," *Social Security Bulletin* 41(April 1978):18–29.

59 Statistic from Robert L. Kahn, "Work and Leisure in the Year 2000," unpublished paper for the Mohonk Conference on the Older Worker, September 1983, p. 19. See also *Work in America: A Report of a Special Task Force to the Secretary of Health, Education, and Welfare* (Cambridge, Mass.: M.I.T. Press, 1973); R. P. Quinn and G. L. Staines, *The 1977 Quality of Employment Survey* (Ann Arbor, Mich.: Institute for Social Research, 1979); and Jack Barbash et al., eds., *The Work Ethic – A Critical Analysis* (Madison, Wisc.: Industrial Relations Research Association, 1983), ch. 5.

60 Joseph F. Quinn and Richard V. Burkhauser, "Influencing Retirement Behavior," *Journal of Policy Analysis and Management* 3(Spring 1983):4–6, 9–10.

61 Harris, *Aging in the Eighties,* pp. 63–71.

62 Ibid., pp. 53–5, 92.

63 Malcolm H. Morrison, "The Aging of the U.S. Population: Human Resource Implications," *Monthly Labor Review* 106(May 1983):16–18; *Older Americans: Data Tract 9* (Washington, D.C.: American Council of Life Insurance, 1982), pp. 17–18; Joseph F. Quinn, "The Extent and Correlates of Partial Retirement," *The Gerontologist* 21(December 1981):634–43.

64 Harris, *Aging in the Eighties,* p. 99; for more on the general point, see Robert L. Kahn, *Work and Health* (New York: Wiley, 1981), and Kahn's "Work and Leisure in the Year 2000," pp. 23–4.

65 For the impact of mandatory retirement on behavior, see Richard V. Burkhauser and Joseph F. Quinn, "Is Mandatory Retirement Overrated? Evidence from the 1970s," *Journal of Human Resources* 18(Summer 1983):337–59; on attitudes, see Louis Harris and Associates, *1979 Study of American Attitudes toward Pensions and Retirement* (New York: Johnson & Higgins, 1979), p. ix; and Harris, *Aging in the Eighties,* pp. 47–9.

66 David Horton Smith et al., *Participation in Social and Political Activities* (San Francisco: Jossey-Bass, 1980); George Gallup, "Volunteerism: America's Best Hope for the Future," *Voluntary Action Leadership* 5(Fall 1980):24–7.

67 Harris, *Aging in the Eighties,* pp. 95–7; Steven H. Sandel, "Older Americans: Issues, Research Findings and Possible Recommendations," unpublished summary for the National Commission for Economic Policy, June 1983, p. 10; Robert L. Kahn, "Productive Behavior: Assessment, Determinants and Effects," unpublished paper (June 1983) presented at the Mohonk Conference, pp. 5–6; Susan Maizel Chambre, "Is Volunteering a Substitute for Role Loss in Old Age?" *The Gerontologist* 24(June 1984):292–8.

68 Alan Pifer, "Put Out to Pasture Our Idea of Age 65," *New York Times,* February 7, 1984, p. 29.

69 Ibid.

6 Social security and the modern American woman

Carl Degler's *At Odds* (Oxford University Press, 1980) and Ralph E. Smith, ed., *The Subtle Revolution: Women at Work* (Washington, D.C.: Urban Institute, 1979), provide good introductions to the history of the modern American woman. For a range of opinion concerning social security's impact on women, see Marilyn R. Flowers, *Women and Social Security* (Washington, D.C.: American Enterprise Institute, 1977), and Richard V. Burkhauser and Karen C. Holden, eds., *A Challenge to Social Security* (New York: Academic Press, 1982). The Department of Health, Education, and Welfare published two useful studies for reconstructing shifts in policy: *Report of the HEW Task Force on the Treatment of Women under Social Security* (Washington, D.C.: n.p., 1978) and *Social Security and the Changing Roles of Men and Women* (Washington, D.C.: Government Printing Office, 1979). I suspect that the *Report on Earnings Sharing Implementation Study* (Washington, D.C.: Government Printing Office, 1985) issued by the House Ways and Means Committee in February of 1985 will become the basis for future policy initiatives in this area.

1   J. Douglas Brown, *Essays on Social Security* (Princeton, N.J.: Industrial Relations Section, 1977), p. 20.

2   Sar A. Levitan, William B. Johnston, and Robert Taggart, *Still a Dream* (Cambridge, Mass.: Harvard University Press, 1975), pp. 220–1; Dorothy K. Newman et al., *Protest, Politics, and Prosperity* (New York: Pantheon Books, 1978), pp. 241–2; James D. Williams, ed., *The State of Black America 1983* (New York: National Urban League, 1983), pp. 48, 65–70; Jacqueline Johnson Jackson, *Minorities and Aging* (Belmont, Calif.: Wadsworth Publishing, 1980), pp. 139–43; Karin Stallard, Barbara Ehrenreich, and Holly Sklar, *Poverty in the American Dream: Women and Children First* (New York: Institute for New Communications, 1983), pp. 14, 17, 19; Andrew Hacker, ed., *U/S: A Statistical Portrait of the American People* (New York: Penguin Books, 1983), p. 18.

3   Burkhauser and Holden, *A Challenge to Social Security*, pp. 10–11, 31, 103–7; U.S. Senate, Special Committee on Aging, *Developments in Aging: 1982* (Washington, D.C.: Government Printing Office, 1983), vol. 1, pp. 8, 20–1; James H. Schulz, *Economics of Aging*, 2nd ed. (Belmont, Calif.: Wadsworth Publishing, 1980), pp. 38–9, 46–7; Evelyn M. Kitagawa and Philip M. Hauser, *Differential Mortality in the United States* (Cambridge, Mass.: Harvard University Press, 1973); 1971 White House Conference on Aging, *Toward a National Policy on Aging, Final Report* (Washington, D.C.: Government Printing Office, 1973), vol. 2, pp. 177–96.

4   U.S. Bureau of the Census, "Some Demographic Aspects of Aging in the United States," *Current Population Reports,* series P-23, no. 43 (Washington, D.C.: Government Printing Office, 1973), pp. 5–7; Paul C. Glick, "Updating the Life Cycle of the Family," *Journal of Marriage and the Family* 39(February 1977):3–15; Stallard et al., *Poverty in the American Dream*, p. 7; Diane Pearce, "The Feminization of Poverty: Women, Work and Welfare," *Urban and Social Change Review* 11(February 1978):28–36; and Barbara Ehrenreich and Frances Fox Piven, "The Feminization of Poverty," *Dissent* (Spring 1984):162–70. Although I shall be concentrating on the needs of older women in this chapter, I certainly do not want to underplay the desperate plight of female-headed families. Here and abroad, children living in single-parent families are particularly vulnerable to growing up poor. See Sheila B. Kamerman and Alfred J. Kahn, "Income Transfers and Mothers-only Families in Eight Countries," *Social Service Review* 57(September 1983):448–64; "56 Million Fathers," *New York Times,* June 17, 1984, p. E22.

5 Report of the Advisory Council to the Committee on Economic Security, reprinted in U.S. Senate, 74th Cong., 1st sess., *Hearings on Economic Security Act, S. 1130*, p. 234.

6 Probably the best overview of women's relationships in the American family, and the tensions that women historically have faced in pursuing their own interests and in dealing with their kin, is Carl Degler's *At Odds*. Despite the recent extraordinary interest in women's history and family history, no one (to the best of my knowledge) has yet written a social history of American motherhood.

7 Committee on Economic Security [CES], *Social Security in America* (Washington, D.C.: Government Printing Office, 1937), pp. 239–44, 248. See also Title IV, *Social Security Act*, 49 Stat. 620 (1935).

8 CES, *Social Security in America*, pp. 259, 270; see also Title V of the Social Security Act for the administrative and financial particulars.

9 *Congressional Record*, July 13, 1939, p. 9012. For more on the 1939 amendments, see Chapters 1 and 4 in this volume.

10 See Leslie Woodcock Tentier, *Wage-Earning Women* (Oxford University Press, 1979); Lois Scharf, *To Work and to Wed* (Westport, Conn.: Greenwood Press, 1980); Winifred D. Wandersee, *Women's Work and Family Values* (Cambridge, Mass.: Harvard University Press, 1981).

11 Gail Buchwalter King, "The Changing Roles of Women and Their Implications for Social Security Policy," PhD dissertation, Carnegie-Mellon University, 1983, pp. 19, 75.

12 *Social Security Bulletin, Annual Statistical Supplement* (1981), p. 158; Karen C. Holden, "Supplemental OASI Benefits to Homemakers," in Burkhauser and Holden, *A Challenge to Social Security*, p. 51.

13 The 1946 amendments, for instance, altered the stringent marital-status eligibility criteria and permitted a widowed mother who had been married to an insured worker for three years to get benefits. Four years later, benefits were extended to divorced or widowed survivors *under age sixty-five* of retired-worker beneficiaries who were caring for an eligible child. Husbands and widowers over sixty-five who were dependent on insured women workers also became eligible for benefits. Amendments enacted in 1957, 1958, and 1960 further liberalized definitions of "marriage" so that more women qualified for spousal benefits. *Report of the HEW Task Force*, pp. 106–11; Wilbur J. Cohen and Robert J. Myers, "Social Security Act Amendments of 1950: A Summary and Legislative History," *Social Security Bulletin* 13(October 1950):3–14.

14 Secretary Hobby's testimony is excerpted in King, "Changing Roles," pp. 91–3. Insured women workers retiring between the ages of sixty-two and sixty-four received benefits reduced $\frac{5}{9}$% for each month under age sixty-five. Wives of retired workers could receive at age sixty-two benefits reduced $\frac{25}{36}$% for each month they were under the age of sixty-five. Widows over sixty-two, on the other hand, received

full-rate benefits (at 75% of their husbands' primary insurance amounts – the rate established in the 1939 amendments for widows over age sixty-five). For a careful description of the legislation, see Charles I. Schottland, "Social Security Amendments of 1956: A Summary and Legislative History," *Social Security Bulletin* 19(September 1956):3–15ff.

15 Gaston V. Rimlinger, "Social Security, Incentives, and Controls in the U.S. and U.S.S.R.," *Comparative Studies in Society and History* 4(1961–2):108–9.

16 See *Social Security Bulletin, Annual Statistical Supplement* (1981), pp. 18–20; *Report of the HEW Task Force,* pp. 111, 116–18.

17 In order to circumvent state laws that banned alimony payments, thereby making it difficult for many women to prove their "dependency," Congress in 1972 eliminated the support requirements for divorced wives, divorced widows, and surviving divorced mothers. See *Social Security Bulletin, Annual Statistical Supplement* (1981), pp. 19, 21; *Report of the HEW Task Force,* pp. 111–13, 117.

18 Betty Friedan, *The Feminine Mystique* (New York: Norton, 1963).

19 Goldberg v. Kelly, 397 U.S. 254 (1970).

20 Weinberger v. Wiesenfeld, 420 U.S. 636 (1975); for a sharply worded criticism of the Court's reasoning, see Brown, *Essays,* pp. 16–18.

21 Mathews v. DeCastro, 429 U.S. 181, 189 (1976).

22 In two 1977 cases, *Califano v. Goldfarb* and *Califano v. Silbowitz,* the Supreme Court struck down gender-based dependency tests as unconstitutional. While liberals, feminists, and civil rights activists praised the decisions, fiscal conservatives noted that these rulings made it possible for federal workers who did not contribute to social security to receive their own civil service pensions as well as 50% of their deceased spouses' Title II benefits. Some experts predicted that this change would cost $220 million in 1977 and $540 million in 1978. U.S. House of Representatives, 95th Cong., 1st sess., *Hearings before the Subcommittee on Social Security on President Carter's Social Security Proposals,* serial 95-27, pp. 571ff.

23 See, among others, the articles in the *Social Security Bulletin* by Ella J. Polinskyu, "The Position of Women in the Social Security System" 32(July 1969):3–19; Robert W. Weise, Jr., "Housewives and Pensions: Foreign Experience" 39(September 1976):37–44ff; Lucy C. Mallan, "Women's Worklives and Future Social Security Benefits" 39(April 1976):3–12; and John C. Henretta and Angela M. O'Rand, "Labor-Force Participation of Older Married Women" 43(August 1980):10–15.

24 In response to the 1977 social security amendments, which required a study "of proposals to eliminate dependency as a factor in the determination of entitlement to spouse's benefits and of proposals to bring about equal treatment for men and women under the program," the Department of Health, Education, and Welfare created two special panels to assess various policy options advanced by fem-

inists, social security experts, and congressional leaders. See *Report of the HEW Task Force,* p. 120; "Task Force Report on Treatment of Women Under Social Security," *Social Security Bulletin* 41(May 1978):37–9; U.S. Department of Health, Education, and Welfare, *Social Security and the Changing Roles of Men and Women* (Washington, D.C.: Government Printing Office, 1979).

25   See, for instance, Flowers, *Women and Social Security;* a four-essay section entitled "Women and Aging" in *The Gerontologist* 19(June 1979):236–63; and Karen C. Holden, "Spouse and Survivor Benefits," *Research on Aging* 1(September 1979):301–18.

26   This conclusion was quoted in the 1977 House of Representatives hearings of the Subcommittee on Social Security (serial 95-27), p. 571.

27   *Report* of the 1979 Advisory Council on Social Security (Washington, D.C.: Government Printing Office, 1980), p. 86.

28   National Commission on Social Security [NCSS], *Social Security in America's Future* (Washington, D.C.: Government Printing Office, 1981), p. 225.

29   This phrase appears in Mary Falvey Fuller's supplementary statement (no. 9, p. 1). See also the position taken by Democrats in their supplementary statement (no. 2, pp. 5–8) and the commission recommendations on pp. 2-5, 2-12, 2-13, all in the *Report of the National Commission on Social Security Reform* (Washington, D.C.: Government Printing Office, 1983). [Hereafter, NCSSR *Report.*]

30   This proposal led to the publication of a 632-page document, U.S. House of Representatives, Committee on Ways and Means, *Report on Earnings Sharing Implementation Study* (Washington, D.C.: Government Printing Office, 1985). It presents cost–benefit analyses of "generic earnings sharing," a "modified generic earnings sharing plan," and a "no-loser earnings sharing" scheme. Although the report made no formal recommendations, the Reagan administration's initial reaction was cool because of the financial implications of adopting any of these plans.

31   The analysis in this section is influenced by my understanding of what Albert Hirschman characterizes as the "loyalty," "exit," and "voice" modes of political-economic reform in *Exit, Voice, and Loyalty* (Cambridge, Mass.: Harvard University Press, 1970). This model seems particularly apt here, for Hirschman is concerned with how people respond to institutions or products in the public and private sectors that no longer satisfy current demands.

32   Robert J. Myers, "Incremental Change in Social Security," in Burkhauser and Holden, *A Challenge to Social Security,* p. 245.

33   Robert M. Ball, "Women and Social Security: Adapting to a New Era," in U.S. Senate Special Committee on Aging, *Task Force on Women and Social Security* (Washington, D.C.: Government Printing Office, 1975), pp. 16–17.

34   Ball proposed raising the primary benefits for all workers by 12.5%

and lowering the dependent spouse's benefit from 50% to 33⅓% of the worker's benefit. The former commissioner's plan was endorsed by the Task Force on Women and Social Security in its 1975 report to the U.S. Senate Special Committee on Aging. Changing the rates by these amounts would not only solve the issues Ball was address-ing but also increase the likelihood that a working spouse would qualify for a higher benefit on the basis of his or her earnings rec-ords. But because this formula change would increase overall costs and worsen the plight of separated spouses and divorced wives, it did not get very far. See *Report of the HEW Task Force,* pp. 21, 38–9.

35   To support this suggestion, Myers points out that the House had advanced the same idea, but in the final draft of the 1977 amend-ments, the marriage-duration criterion was reduced only from twenty to ten years. Myers's recommendation has the virtue of picking a number less than the average duration of marriages that end in divorce – the median in 1979 was 6.8 years. See Hacker, *U/S,* p. 109.

36   Myers, "Incremental Change," p. 241.

37   This benefit is designed to help workers with lengthy service in low-paying jobs. It is paid only if it yields more than the regular formula. The commission proposed that workers with children under the age of six not earning enough to gain regular credits toward social secu-rity could receive up to a maximum of ten years' credit for child care. No one would lose benefits under this plan; pensions would increase for about 20% of all retired women and 5% of all retired men. See NCSS, *Social Security in America's Future,* pp. 231–8.

38   Edith U. Fierst, "Supplemental OASI Benefits to Homemakers: Discussion," in Burkhauser and Holden, *A Challenge to Social Secu-rity,* pp. 70–1; Sheila B. Kamerman, "Child-care Services: A National Picture," *Monthly Labor Review* 106(December 1983):35–9.

39   For a sample of plans that conform to this principle, see 1979 Advis-ory Council *Report,* pp. 78–82; *Final Report* of the National Com-mission on Social Security, pp. 37–43. For a fuller discussion of issues, see Alicia H. Munnell and Laura E. Stiglin, "Women and a Two-Tier Social Security System," in Burkhauser and Holden, *A Challenge to Social Security,* pp. 101–24; and Jennifer L. Warlick et al., "The Double-Decker Alternative for Eliminating Dependency under Social Security," in ibid., pp. 131–61.

40   For SSA models, see Jerry R. Cates, *Insuring Inequality: Administra-tive Leadership in Social Security, 1935–54* (Ann Arbor: University of Michigan Press, 1983), pp. 71–5.

41   More recent "liberal" support for a two-tier system can be found in Joseph A. Pechman, Henry J. Aaron, and Michael K. Taussig, *Social Security: Perspectives for Reform* (Washington, D.C.: Brookings Insti-tution, 1968); and Alicia H. Munnell, *The Future of Social Security*

(Washington, D.C.: Brookings Institution, 1977). For "radical" conservative schemes, see Peter Ferrera, *The Inherent Contradiction* (San Francisco: Cato Press, 1980); and A. Haeworth Robertson, *The Coming Revolution in Social Security* (Reston, Va.: Reston Publishing, 1981).

42 Henry Aaron, "Women and a Two-Tier Social Security System: Discussion," in Burkhauser and Holden, *A Challenge to Social Security*, p. 127. It is worth noting that by the 1980s, Aaron had reversed his earlier support for this idea.

43 *Report of the HEW Task Force*, pp. 21, 41–3. Campbell, a Stanford University economist, headed the 1975 Advisory Council's Subcommittee on the Treatment of Men and Women Under Social Security and has served as an official consultant and informal expert on domestic policy matters for Ronald Reagan.

44 Eliminating spousal and survivors' benefits would mean that the married wage earner with the lower average covered wages would no longer have to choose between entitlements based on marital status or prior earnings record. Nor would one-earner couples still receive higher replacement rates than single workers with the same earnings.

45 Partly for these reasons, but largely because it placed such a heavy emphasis on the principle of "equity," the Campbell plan gained influential supporters. The American Association of Retired Persons, for instance, joined with the National Retired Teachers' Association in endorsing the plan at a 1981 hearing of the National Commission on Social Security. See King, "Changing Roles," pp. 126, 129.

46 Statistics from the 1979 Advisory Council on Social Security *Report*, p. 89.

47 See *Report of the HEW Task Force*, p. 24; King, "Changing Roles," p. 31. The National Commission on the Observance of International Women's Year (1976) and the National Women's Conference (1977) also endorsed the idea of homemaker credits.

48 *Report of the HEW Task Force*, pp. 53–4, 69; 1979 Social Security Advisory Council *Report*, pp. 121–2.

49 "Earnings sharing" was first broached in Congress by Representative Donald Fraser (D–Mich.) in 1976; by the end of 1977, a plan coauthored by Fraser and Representative Martha Keys (D–Kans.) had sixty sponsors. The staff of the Justice Department's Task Force on Sex Discrimination (1977–8) developed a plan. The 1979 Advisory Council on Social Security *Report* considered the sharing of earnings "the most promising approach," though it was not prepared to endorse any specific version of the scheme. The President's Commission on Pension Policy (1981) also went on record as supporting the concept. Though the National Commission on Social Security rejected the idea because it "would not support a proposal which reduced benefits to some people and increased them for oth-

ers," it did propose that "couples who want their Social Security benefits to reflect the principle that marriage is an economic partnership" should be permitted to receive separate but equal retirement checks. See NCSS, *Social Security in America's Future*, pp. 229–30, 243; King, "Changing Roles," p. 127. Mary Falvey Fuller and Martha Keys (with the support of her Democratic colleagues) kept referring to this option in the course of NCSSR deliberations.

50 The examples in this paragraph are drawn from Nancy Gordon, "Institutional Responses: The Social Security System," in *The Subtle Revolution*, pp. 239–55; and *Report of the HEW Task Force*, pp. 57–64.

51 In Burkhauser and Holden, *A Challenge to Social Security*, see Robert Lampman and Maurice MacDonald, "Concepts Underlying the Current Controversy," pp. 24–5; and Francis P. King, "Occupational Pension Plans and Spouse Benefits," pp. 213–18. Community-property rules currently prevail in eight states and Puerto Rico. Seven states have adopted the Uniform Dissolution of Marriage Act, which puts community-property laws into effect at divorce settlements, though common-law property arrangements normally prevail. Elsewhere the situation is less clear-cut: In twelve states and the District of Columbia, only that property acquired and jointly held in marriage will be divided at a divorce settlement; in the other twenty-three states, courts are empowered to make "equitable" or "reasonable" distributions, but there are no clear guidelines.

52 Smith v. Lewis, 13 Cal. 3d 349, 530 P. 2d 589 (1975).

53 Virginia Reno, "Earnings Sharing Discussion," in Burkhauser and Holden, *A Challenge to Social Security*, pp. 95–8; NCSS, *Social Security in America's Future*, pp. 229–31. Applying the earnings-sharing formula to disability insurance raises another set of issues about "equity" vs. "adequacy."

54 People whose benefits would vary according to which way they were calculated would surely be accorded the right to a maximum claim. "Grandfathering" current beneficiaries is a venerable social security tradition.

55 Gordon, "Institutional Responses," in *The Subtle Revolution*, p. 255.

7 Universal coverage: an either/or proposition?

Neil Gilbert, *Capitalism and the Welfare State* (New Haven, Conn.: Yale University Press, 1983); Robert J. Lampman, *Social Welfare Spending* (New York: Academic Press, 1984); and James H. Schulz, *The Economics of Aging*, 3rd ed. (Belmont, Calif.: Wadsworth Publishing, 1985), provide a good introduction to the public and private dimensions of social insurance. The Employment Benefit Research Institute (EBRI), a Washington-based policy center, has emerged as a major source of data and ideas about the changing nature of American retirement policies. Here I relied heavily on the EBRI publications by Dallas L. Salisbury, ed., *Retirement Income and the Economy: Policy Directions for the 80s* (1981), and Sylvester J. Schieber and Patricia M. George, *Retirement Income Opportunities in an Aging America* (1981). The President's Commission on Pension Policy, *Coming of Age* (Washington, D.C.: Government Printing Office, 1981), and articles in the *Monthly Labor Review* are useful. Besides the data in the *Social Security Bulletin,* researchers should consult *Pension Facts,* an annual report issued by the American Council of Life Insurance.

1   Because the panel doubted that there were constitutional grounds for requiring nonfederal public employees to participate in the program, the commission did not try to effect broader coverage in this area. The Supreme Court's 1976 decision in *National League of Cities v. Usery* (426 U.S. 833), many claimed, did not allow Congress to "displace the States' freedom to structure integral operations in the areas of traditional governmental functions." The commission expressed concern over the "windfall" benefits received by retirees who spent most of their careers in noncovered employment but became eligible for Title II benefits after contributing to the social security system for a short period of time. Hence, the panel recommended that a new formula be adopted for calculating the social security benefits claimed by former government employees who had already earned pension rights under public retirement programs. See *Report of the National Commission on Social Security Reform* (Washington, D.C.: Government Printing Office, January 1983), ch. 2. The anticipated savings were calculated on the basis of data in Table A on p. 2–5.

2   "Social Security Rescue Plan Wins Final Hill Approval," *Congressional Quarterly* 41(March 26, 1983):596–7; see also notes 48 and 52 in op. cit., p. 645.

3   Social Security Board for the Committee on Economic Security, *Social Security in America* (Washington, D.C.: Government Printing Office, 1937), p. 209.

4   Ibid., p. 208. See also Edwin E. Witte, *The Development of the Social Security Act* (Madison: University of Wisconsin Press, 1963), pp. 152–6; and Secretary Morgenthau's testimony in 74th Cong., 1st sess., House of Representatives, *The Economic Security Act,* Hearings on H.R. 4120, pp. 901–2.

5   J. Douglas Brown, *Essays on Social Security* (Princeton, N.J.: Industrial Relations Section, 1977), p. 58.

6   Social Security Administration, *Annual Statistical Supplement* (1981), pp. 10, 56. These figures are lower than the ones typically cited because I have defined "coverage" to count only those *contributing* part of their wages to the system. My statistics thus do not include nonworkers who would be eligible for benefits through their relationship to a covered employee, nor do they include those workers

(such as groups of state and local employees) who elected *not* to contribute to the system at various times.

7   Eisenhower administration officials pressed to extend coverage to federal workers. Advisory Councils regularly called for disinterested analyses; a special presidential committee was convened to study retirement policies for federal personnel. Elizabeth M. Heidbreder, "Federal Civil-Service Annuitants and Social Security," *Social Security Bulletin* 32(July 1969):20–33; Martha Derthick, *Policymaking for Social Security* (Washington, D.C.: Brookings Institution, 1979), p. 265.

8   A Universal Social Security Coverage Study Group, mandated under the 1977 amendments, blandly noted that "the desirability of expanding Social Security coverage depends on one's perspective." See "Report of the Universal Social Security Study Group: Executive Summary," *Social Security Bulletin* 43(June 1980):25. The 1975 and 1979 Social Security Advisory Councils, the National Commission on Social Security (1981), and the President's Commission on Pension Policy (1981), however, all recommended coverage of all new federal, state/local, and nonprofit employees, and better coordination between social security and public-employee plans until universal coverage was complete. Prestigious task forces in the private sector, such as the Business Roundtable and the Committee on Economic Development, made similar pleas. Salisbury, *Retirement Income and the Economy: Policy Directions for the 80s,* pp. 291–2; Brown, *Essays,* p. 64; and CED, *Reforming Retirement Policies* (New York: Committee on Economic Development, 1981), p. 9; Business Roundtable, *Pensions, Social Security Benefits: Levels, Costs and Issues* (New York: Business Roundtable, August 1979), p. 4.

9   Lane Kirkland, for example, supported the whole NCSSR package except for the mandatory social security coverage provisions, which threatened to jeopardize the interests of public employees within the AFL-CIO. The Fund for Assuring an Independent Retirement (FAIR), a coalition of more than two dozen organizations, mobilized grassroots opposition among more than 6 million active and retired federal and postal employees. To counter charges that the commission had not thought through the economic consequences of universal coverage, Robert J. Myers prepared a series of memoranda documenting expected short-range and long-term savings in government expenditures and indicating possible ways to modify the Civil Service Retirement System to accommodate the changes in social security. See "Supplementary Statement on Mandatory Coverage of Public Employees by Lane Kirkland," in the NCSSR *Report,* statement (10), pp. 1–2. "Federal Workers Will Fight Social Security Coverage Plan," *Congressional Quarterly* 41(January 22, 1983):161. Myers's testimony and accompanying memoranda in House Committee on Ways and Means, *Hearings on the Recommendations of the National Commission on*

Social Security Reform, 98th Cong., 1st sess., serial 98-3 (February 2, 1983), pp. 198–211; and Senate Subcommittee on Social Security and Income Maintenance Programs, *Hearings on the National Commission on Social Security Reform Recommendations,* 98 Cong., 1st sess. (February 24, 1983), pp. 386–414.

10 Senate Special Committee on Aging, *Social Security Financing: Background Material on the Recommendations of the National Commission on Social Security Reform,* reprinted in ibid., part 3 of 3, pp. 270–1.

11 See Senate Special Committee on Aging, *Developments in Aging: 1982* (Washington, D.C.: Government Printing Office, 1983), vol. 1, pp. 170–1.

12 Under the Railroad Retirement Act of 1974, employees with more than ten years of service receive a two-tier benefit, the first part based on earnings record and work history (including employment covered by social security), and the rest reflecting total years of railroad service. In 1981, because of the declining relative number of railroad employees, only 477,000 workers paid into the system. Yet $3.1 billion was paid out to 447,000 beneficiaries who met the stipulated age, service, and disability criteria; another $2.3 billion was distributed to 559,000 dependents and survivors. See American Council of Life Insurance [ACLI], *Pension Facts* (Washington, D.C.: ACLI, 1983), p. 29; Senate Special Committee on Aging, *Developments in Aging: 1982,* p. 176.

13 Robert J. Myers, *Social Security,* 3rd ed. (Homewood, Ill.: Richard D. Irwin, 1985), p. 933; William Graebner, *A History of Retirement* (New Haven, Conn.: Yale University Press, 1980), p. 80; ACLI, *Pension Facts,* p. 28. Benefits are computed on the basis of years of service and an average of the highest three consecutive years of earnings, automatically indexed for inflation.

14 Quoted in Les Aspin, "The Burden of Generosity," *Harper's* 243(December 1976):24; James R. Storey and Gary Hendricks, *Retirement Income in an Aging Society* (Washington, D.C.: Urban Institute, 1979), p. 26. At a time when the annual defense budget is the target of critics who want to cut expenditures in order to reduce the federal deficit, there is a certain irony in the fact that a large proportion of the department's seemingly "uncontrollable" budget is earmarked for retired personnel, not new weaponry.

15 Ross A. Marcou, "Comparing Federal and Private Employer Benefits," *Civil Service Journal* (October–December 1978):12–18.

16 This interpretation of the Clark amendment is based on my reading of Witte, *Development,* pp. 105–8; Brown, *Essays,* p. 59; and Arthur J. Altmeyer, *The Formative Years of Social Security* (Madison: University of Wisconsin Press, 1968), pp. 40–2. Representatives of the Senate Finance Committee and House Ways and Means Committee convened early in 1936 but took no action on the amendment. Insurance companies and large corporations lost interest. They concluded

that the new social security measure would not reduce the growing market for private pensions and annuities, as they had initially feared. They also realized that for their individual plans to gain government approval for exemption from social security contributions would require complicated administrative guidelines and strict federal controls over pension investments and financing.

17 See ACLI, *Pension Facts,* p. 34; William P. Greenough and Francis P. King, *Pension Plans and Public Policy* (New York: Columbia University Press, 1976), pp. 59–63.

18 Sylvester J. Schieber, *Social Security* (Washington, D.C.: EBRI, 1982), p. 47; James H. Schulz, *The Economics of Aging,* 3rd ed. (Belmont, Calif.: Wadsworth Publishing, 1985), p. 125; see also Peter F. Drucker, *The Unseen Revolution* (New York: Harper & Row, 1976), pp. 6–7.

19 Solomon Barkin, "Union Policies and the Older Worker," in *The Aged and Society,* ed. Milton Derber (Champaign: Industrial Relations Research Association, 1950), pp. 75–92.

20 John J. Corson and John W. McConnell, *Economic Needs of Older People* (New York: Twentieth Century Fund, 1956), pp. 476–80; Margaret S. Gordon, "Aging and Income Security," in *Handbook of Social Gerontology,* ed. Clark Tibbitts (University of Chicago Press, 1960), p. 578; ACLI, *Pension Facts,* pp. 34–5.

21 See Robert L. Tilove, *Pension Funds and Economic Freedom* (New York: The Fund for the Republic, 1959).

22 President's Committee on Corporate Pension Funds and Other Private Retirement and Welfare Programs, *Public Policy and Private Pension Programs* (Washington, D.C.: Government Printing Office, 1965), p. 11. The committee viewed private pension plans as a key element in the nation's total retirement security system. Hence, it recommended that more uniform and equitable vesting standards be employed. The panel also stressed that more rigorous standards for adequate funding needed to be set if pension commitments were to be honored.

23 U.S. Senate, 93rd Cong., 1st sess., *Private Pension Plan Report,* no. 93-383 (August 1973); Alfred M. Skolnik, "Pension Reform Legislation of 1974," *Social Security Bulletin* 37(December 1974):35–44; Schulz, *Economics,* p. 139.

24 Salisbury, *Retirement Income and the Economy,* p. 121. For a thoughtful analysis of ERISA from the president of a leading actuarial firm, see Robert D. Paul, "The Impact of Pension Reform on American Business," *Sloan Management Review* 18(Fall 1976):59–71. For a less sanguine view, see Norman B. Ture, *The Future of Private Pension Plans* (Washington, D.C.: American Enterprise Institute, 1976). On recent efforts, see Senate Special Committee on Aging, *Developments in Aging: 1983,* pp. 170–84.

25 Senate Special Committee on Aging, *Developments in Aging,* p. 260.

Representative Eugene J. Keogh (D–N.Y.) sponsored the original legislation.

26 Schieber, *Social Security*, p. 62.

27 "Text of the President's Message on Private Pension Plan," reprinted in the *1971 Congressional Quarterly Almanac*, pp. 101A, 103A.

28 Surprisingly few people initially took advantage of the tax breaks that resulted from establishing an IRA; only 11% of those eligible to create an account in 1977 actually did so. This statement comes from a 1981 Employment Benefit Research Institute study quoted by Schieber in *Social Security*, p. 63.

29 Sylvester J. Schieber and Patricia M. George, *Retirement Income Opportunities in an Aging America* (Washington, D.C.: Employment Benefit Research Institute, 1981), p. 109; and Business Roundtable, *Social Security Benefits*, p. 23.

30 Robin C. DeMagistris and Carl J. Palash, "Impact of IRAs on Saving," *Federal Reserve Bank of New York Quarterly Review* 7(Winter 1982–3):24–32; "IRAs Are Poor Substitute for Pension, Social Security Study Says," *Pittsburgh Press*, July 10, 1984, p. C4.

31 For blacks, social security constitutes an even greater percentage of the total income available; in 1981, the figures were 47% and 62%, respectively.

32 Senate Special Committee on Aging, *Developments in Aging*, p. 18. See also Melinda Upp, "Relative Importance of Various Income Sources of the Aged, 1980," *Social Security Bulletin* 46(January 1983):9–10.

33 Ibid. That earnings represent a decreasing share of the financial resources available to older Americans results from two historical trends: During the twentieth century there has been a striking decline in the labor-force participation rates among elderly men, and most women over the age of sixty-five have never relied on current earnings to meet their financial needs. See Chapters 5 and 6 in this volume.

34 No single figure is commonly accepted. The percentages cited in the literature range from a low of 42% to a high of nearly 70%. Several factors account for such extreme variance. Some commentators cite the latest published statistics, whereas others rely on the most recent national commission's estimates. No government-sponsored analysis or official commission report thus far has indicated that more than 50% of the employees in the private sector are covered. No study conducted by or for a pension-consulting firm or life insurance company has found that less than two-thirds of the population is covered. See Harrison Givens, Jr., "Coverage Gaps Under the Retirement System," in *Arranging the Pieces: The Retirement Income Puzzle*, ed. Dallas L. Salisbury (Washington, D.C.: Employment Benefit Research Institute, 1980), pp. 30–3; Daniel J. Beller, "Cov-

erage Patterns of Full-Time Employees Under Private Pension Plans," *Social Security Bulletin* 44(July 1981):3–22. Analysts at the Employment Benefit Research Institute (EBRI) claim that in May 1979, 68% of the work force was eligible for pensions – a figure that fits ERISA criteria.

35 Walter W. Kolodrubetz, "Employee-Benefit Plans, 1972," *Social Security Bulletin* 37(May 1974):15–21; Kolodrubetz and Donald M. Linday, "Coverage and Vesting of Full-Time Employees under Private Retirement Plans," *Social Security Bulletin* 36(November 1973):20–36; Schultz, *Economics*, pp. 127–8; Schieber and George, *Retirement Income Opportunities*, p. 49.

36 As a result of various amendments to the Social Security Act during the past two decades, the percentage of the population over age seventy-two entitled to some sort of benefit is higher than the figure for the elderly population as a whole. The figure for non-social-security pension families would be lower if the entire population over sixty-five were counted, because the percentage of all retired workers whose employment histories qualify them for pensions is smaller than for the subset under the age of sixty-eight. See Senate Special Committee on Aging, *Developments in Aging*, pp. 17, 155.

37 The Employment Benefit Research Institute, whose judicious assessment of this issue has been widely cited in congressional and executive reports, makes similar projections. See Schieber and George, *Retirement Income Opportunities*, pp. 23–5. William C. Greenough, the former chairman of TIAA/CREF who served on the President's Commission on Pension Policy, dissented from the official report and cited data calculated by EBRI. See his remarks in Salisbury, *Retirement Income*, p. 54.

38 Most firms, however, have adopted a ten-year/100% vesting option, which means that an employee who changes jobs before finishing the requisite decade of continuous employment loses all pension credits associated with that period of employment. Some public-employee plans impose even stiffer standards; an employee very often must complete at least fifteen years of service before vesting begins.

39 Gayle B. Thompson, "Pension Coverage and Benefits, 1972: Findings from the Retirement History Study," *Social Security Bulletin* 41(February 1978):3–17. The Labor Department estimated in 1978 that the median tenure for men was 4.5 years on the current job; the median for women was even lower, 2.6 years. Although this gross statistic is biased downward by the job mobility of younger workers, the median tenure of workers between the ages of fifty-five and sixty-four was only 13.5 years for men and 8.4 years for women. And insofar as the long-term trend has been toward shorter tenure in employment, it is likely that a significant portion of men, and an even larger percentage of women, will not meet minimum vesting requirements. See Stephan Crystal, *America's Old-Age Crisis* (New

York: Basic Books, 1982), pp. 118–22. The proliferation of multiemployer pension plans has made it easier for some workers to
"carry" their retirement credits from one job to the next as long as
the plan offered by the new employer belongs to the same centralized fund.

40 See Schulz, *Economics,* pp. 134–5.

41 James H. Schulz, Thomas Leavitt, and Leslie Kelly, "Private Pensions Fall Far Short of Preretirement Income Levels," *Monthly Labor
Review* 102(February 1979):28–32.

42 See Alfred M. Skolnik, "Private Pension Plans, 1950–74," *Social
Security Bulletin* 39(June 1976):3–17; Bankers Trust Company, *1975
Study of Corporate Pension Plans* (New York: Bankers Trust Com-
pany, 1975); Martha R. Yohalem, "Employee-Benefit Plans," *Social
Security Bulletin* 40(November 1977):19–38; Robert Frumpkin and
Donald Schmitt, "Pension Improvements Since 1974 Reflect Infla-
tion – New U.S. Law," *Monthly Labor Review* 102(March 1979):32–
7.

43 Alicia Munnell, *The Economics of Private Pensions* (Washington, D.C.:
Brookings Institution, 1982), pp. 184–5; William J. Mischo, Sook-
Kuen Chong, and Eugene J. Kasten, *Corporate Pension Plan Study: A
Guide for the 1980s* (New York: Bankers Trust Company, 1980).

44 Whereas only 36.8% of those earning between $5,000 and $9,999
were participating in supplementary plans, roughly 80% of those
earning more than $20,000 were covered. The affluent are clearly
overrepresented. See Schieber, *Preserving Social Security,* p. 63; President's Commission on Pension Policy, *Coming of Age* (Washington,
D.C.: Government Printing Office, 1981), p. 35.

45 Senate Special Committee on Aging, *Developments in Aging,* p. 17;
cf. Lawrence S. Root, *Fringe Benefits* (Beverly Hills, Calif.: Sage
Publications, 1982).

46 See Schieber and George, *Retirement Income Opportunities,* p. 49; Salisbury, *Retirement Income and the Economy,* p. 45.

47 David L. Birch, *The Job Generation Process* (Cambridge, Mass.: M.I.T.
Program on Neighborhood and Regional Change, 1979), pp. 23,
31–7, 41. See also idem, *Firm Behavior as a Determinant of Economic
Change: Final Report* (Springfield, Va.: National Technical Information Service, 1981), pp. 25–42 and appendices B and C.

48 President's Commission on Pension Policy, *Coming of Age,* p. 31.
See also Robert L. Tilove, *Public Employee Pension Funds* (New York:
Columbia University Press, 1976); James H. Schulz, *The Economics
of Aging,* 2nd ed. (Belmont, Calif.: Wadsworth Publishing, 1980),
p. 147.

49 ERISA requires that all plans created after 1974 be fully funded to
meet pension obligations within thirty years; plans predating ERISA
have four decades to develop full funding.

50 To illustrate the confusion: An "unfunded actuarial liability" does

not refer to the same thing as an "unfunded past service liability" under ERISA; yet the two terms are used interchangeably. Similarly, definitions are not always consistent with the terminology adopted by the SEC and IRS. Such confusion spawns legitimate differences of opinion; the result is widely differing levels of funding. Government studies have issued warnings about the precarious status of several large pension funds. See 'The Arithmetic Doesn't Look Good for Industry-Wide Pension Plan," *National Journal* 9(December 17, 1977):1955; Paul A. Gewirtz and Robert C. Phillips, "Unfunded Pension Liabilities: The New Myth," *Financial Executive* (August 1978):18–24; Francis X. Burkhardt, "ERISA Problems and Programs," *Labor Law Journal* 28(December 1977):747–51; Alvin D. Lurie, "The Once and Future Pension Reform," *Business Week* (April 21, 1980):25ff; "Federal Pension Insurance System Teetering on the Financial Brink," *National Journal* 15(September 15, 1983):1776–83.

51 Senate Special Committee on Aging, *Developments in Aging: 1982*, pp. 141–2; Pension Benefit Guaranty Corporation, *1981 Annual Report* (Washington, D.C.: Government Printing Office, 1982), p. 34; "Pension Agency Warns Its Solvency Threatened by Wave of Bankruptcies," *National Journal* 14(June 26, 1982):1137–9; "Established to Resolve Crisis, Federal Pension Corporation Finds Itself in Financial Straits," ibid. 16(March 10, 1984):559–63.

52 Drucker, *Unseen Revolution;* Edward S. Herman, *Corporate Control, Corporate Power* (Cambridge University Press, 1981); Robert B. Reich, *The Next American Frontier* (New York: Times Books, 1983), p. 260.

53 "Raiding Pension Plans," *New York Times,* September 25, 1983, sect. 3, p. 1; "Pension Managers Terminate Plans, then Grab Surplus Assets," *National Journal* 16(March 24, 1984):566–9. To cite just one example down the road, Occidental Petroleum Corporation alone could get back $400 million if pending modifications of its pension plans are approved.

54 Quoted in "ERISA's Roadblocks to Pension Politics," *Business Week* (December 4, 1978):64.

55 See data reported in Crystal, *America's Old-Age Crisis,* pp. 106–7. See also Munnell, *Economics of Private Pensions,* ch. 3.

56 Crystal, *America's Old-Age Crisis,* p. 103; ACLI, *Pension Facts,* p. 9.

57 Kreps's testimony before the U.S. Special Committee on Aging hearings on "The Economics of Aging" is quoted in Robert Clark, *The Role of Private Pensions in Maintaining Living Standards in Retirement* (Washington, D.C.: National Planning Association, 1977), p. 11.

8 Federal health care programs and social security

Essential reading for reconstructing the development of health care policies for the elderly in the United States are Robert J. Myers, *Medicare* (Homewood, Ill.: Richard D. Irwin, 1970); Theodore R. Marmor, *The*

Politics of Medicare (Chicago: Aldine Publishing, 1973); Bruce C. Vladeck, *Unloving Care* (New York: Basic Books, 1980); Paul Starr, *The Social Transformation of American Medicine* (New York: Basic Books, 1982); and Carroll L. Estes, Lenore E. Gerard, Jane Sprague Zones, and James S. Swan, *Political Economy, Health, and Aging* (Boston: Little, Brown, 1984). To understand recent trends, readers should turn to the 1984 Advisory Council on Social Security, *Medicare: Benefits and Financing* (Washington, D.C.: Government Printing Office, 1984); Duncan Yaggy, ed., *Health Care for the Poor and Elderly* (Durham, N.C.: Duke Press Policy Studies, 1984); as well as special issues of *Annals of the American Academy of Political and Social Sciences* 468(July 1983); and *Milbank Memorial Fund Quarterly* 62(Spring 1984). I relied heavily on reports issued by the U.S. Special Committee on Aging (especially its annual volumes, *Developments in Aging*) and on publications of the Congressional Budget Office. Besides consulting the periodical literature cited in the first four chapters, I monitored ideas disseminated in the *Hastings Center Reports, Health Care Financing Review,* and *New England Journal of Medicine.*

1   Statistics from *Report of the National Commission on Social Security Reform* (Washington, D.C.: Government Printing Office, 1983), p. 3-1 [hereafter, NCSSR *Report*]; Senate Special Committee on Aging, *Prospects for Medicare's Hospital Insurance Trust Fund* (Washington, D.C.: Government Printing Office, 1983), pp. 2–4; idem, *Developments in Aging: 1983* (Washington, D.C.: Government Printing Office, 1984), vol. 1, p. 380.

2   Senate Special Committee on Aging, *Developments in Aging: 1982,* vol. 1, pp. 391, 396. See also Bruce C. Vladeck and James P. Firman, "The Aging of the Population and Health Services," *Annals of the American Academy of Political and Social Sciences [AAAPSS]* 468(July 1983):146; and Judith R. Lave and Herbert A. Silverman, "Financing the Health Care of the Aged," ibid., p. 169.

3   U.S. House of Representatives, 98th Cong., 1st sess., *Recommendations of the National Commission on Social Security Reform,* hearings before the Committee on Ways and Means, February 3, 1983, p. 225. See also "The Medicare Tradeoff," *National Journal* 15(March 12, 1983):544–7; "Major Change in Medicare Hospital Payment System Is on Fast Track in Congress," *Congressional Quarterly* 41(March 5, 1983):455–7; "Who Says Congress Can't Move Fast? Just Ask Hospitals About Medicare," *National Journal* 15(April 2, 1983):704–7.

4   A Prospective Payment Assessment Commission, to be established in 1984 for a three-year period, was to recommend further ways to recalibrate the DRG provisions as well as to make procedures underwritten by the federal government safer and more cost-effective. Capital expenses (until October 1, 1986) and medical education expenses were specifically excluded from the prospective payment system. See Title VI of Public Law 98-21.

5   Senate Special Committee on Aging, *Developments in Aging: 1983,*

pp. vii–viii. Heinz and Glenn were, respectively, majority and minority leaders of this committee. Cf. John Svahn and Mary A. Ross, "Social Security Amendments of 1983: Legislative History and Summary of Provisions," *Social Security Bulletin* 46(July 1983):45–6. See also Congressional Budget Office, *Changing the Structure of Medicare Benefits: Issues and Options* (Washington, D.C.: Government Printing Office, March 1983); and Senate Special Committee on Aging, *Prospects for Medicare's Hospital Insurance;* Committee for Economic Development, *Social Security: From Crisis to Crisis* (New York: CED, 1984), pp. 3–4; Paul B. Ginsburg and Marilyn Moon, "An Introduction to the Medicare Financing Problem," *Milbank Memorial Fund Quarterly* [*MMFQ*] 62(Spring 1984):167–82.

6	David Rothman, *The Discovery of the Asylum* (Boston: Little, Brown, 1971); Barbara G. Rosenkrantz, *Public Health and the State* (Cambridge, Mass.: Harvard University Press, 1972); Susan Reverby and David Rosner, eds., *Health Care in America* (Philadelphia: Temple University Press, 1979); David Rosner, *The Once Charitable Enterprise* (Cambridge University Press, 1982).

7	"Report of the Committee on Medical Economics," *New York State Journal of Medicine* 25(1925):789. See also Ronald L. Numbers, *Almost Persuaded* (Baltimore: Johns Hopkins University Press, 1978); Daniel S. Hirshfeld, *Lost Reform* (Cambridge, Mass.: Harvard University Press, 1970). See also Chapter 1 in this volume.

8	Estes et al., *Political Economy, Health and Aging,* p. 53.

9	The committee nevertheless stressed that "the medical benefits of health insurance have been furnished through the private practice and not through the 'socialized' practice of medicine." See I. S. Falk, *Security Against Sickness* (Garden City, N.Y.: Doubleday, 1936), pp. 7–9, 48–9, 286.

10	Initially Baylor agreed to provide 1,500 schoolteachers with up to twenty-one days of hospital care per year at a cost of $6 per person per day. Michael M. David and C. Rufus Rorem, *The Crisis in Hospital Finance* (University of Chicago Press, 1932), pp. 211–13; Odin W. Anderson, *Blue Cross Since 1929* (Cambridge, Mass.: Ballinger Publishing, 1975), ch. 1.

11	U.S. Department of Labor, *The Cost of American Almshouses,* bulletin no. 386 (Washington, D.C.: Government Printing Office, 1925); idem, *Care of Aged Persons in the United States,* bulletin no. 489 (Washington, D.C.: Government Printing Office, 1929); Harry Evans, *American Poor Farm* (Des Moines: Royal Order of the Moose, 1926); Marjorie Shearon, "Economic Status of the Aged," *Social Security Bulletin* 1(March 1938):6, 15. Two fine secondary sources are Ethel McClure, *More Than a Roof* (St. Paul: Minnesota Historical Society, 1968); and Carole Haber, *Beyond Sixty-Five* (Cambridge University Press, 1983). For more on the care provided for the aged in mental institutions, see Barbara G. Rosenkrantz and Maris A.

Vinovskis, "The Invisible Lunatics," in *Aging and the Elderly*, eds. Stuart F. Spicker et al. (Atlantic Highlands, N.J.: Humanities Press, 1978), pp. 95–125; and New York State Commission on Lunacy, *Annual Report* 12(1900):29–30.

12 See G. Perrott and Selwyn D. Collins, "Relation of Sickness to Income and Income Change in 10 Surveyed Communities," *Public Health Reports* 50(May 3, 1935):622; W. F. Walker, "Analysis of Public Health Expenditures by Geographic Subdivisions," *American Journal of Public Health* 25(July 1935):851–6.

13 FDR signaled his doubts about including health insurance in a social security bill in his November 14, 1934, address to a conference sponsored by the Committee on Economic Security. See *The Public Papers and Addresses of Franklin Delano Roosevelt*, comp. Samuel I. Rosenman (New York: Random House, 1938), vol. 3, pp. 452–5. See also Edwin E. Witte, *The Development of the Social Security Act* (Madison: University of Wisconsin Press, 1963), pp. 173–89; and Arthur J. Altmeyer, *The Formative Years of Social Security* (Madison: University of Wisconsin Press, 1968), pp. 14, 27–8, 115–16, 146–8.

14 The analysis in this paragraph is based on my reading of the comments on health insurance in the January 15, 1935, report of the Committee on Economic Security to FDR, reprinted in Falk, *Security Against Sickness*, pp. 365–7; Committee on Economic Security, *Social Security in America* (Washington, D.C.: Social Security Board, 1937), pp. 13–15; and the CES's letter of transmittal (dated November 6, 1935) and summary, reprinted in Witte, *Development of the Social Security Act*, pp. 205–10.

15 Philip R. Lee and Carroll L. Estes, "New Federalism and Health Policy," *AAAPSS* 468(July 1983):95; Herman M. Somers and Anne R. Somers, *Medicare and the Hospitals* (Washington, D.C.: Brookings Institution, 1967), p. 4.

16 "Message on the State of the Union," January 11, 1944, in *The Public Papers and Addresses of Franklin Delano Roosevelt*, ed. Samuel I. Rosenman (New York: Harper & Bros., 1950), vol. 13, p. 41. On the impact of World War II on health care initiatives, see Richard Polenberg, *War and Society* (Philadelphia: Lippincott, 1972); and Geoffrey Perrett, *Days of Sadness, Years of Triumph* (Baltimore: Penguin Books, 1973).

17 Paul Starr, *Social Transformation of American Medicine* (New York: Basic Books, 1982), pp. 347–51; Bruce C. Vladeck, *Unloving Care* (New York: Basic Books, 1980), pp. 39–40.

18 Starr, *Social Transformation*, pp. 290–331.

19 Richard Harris, *A Sacred Trust* (New York: New American Library, 1966), pp. 55, 69–72; Theodore R. Marmor, *The Politics of Medicare* (Chicago: Aldine Publishing, 1973), pp. 14–20.

20 Wilbur J. Cohen and Robert J. Myers, "Social Security Act Amendments of 1950," *Social Security Bulletin* 13(October 1950):3–14.

21 Ewing and his associates did not provide nursing home benefits because their definition of "insurance" eschewed long-term care. A copy of Ewing's statement at the June 25, 1951, press conference in which the plan was released is in Official File 7, Harry S Truman Papers, Truman Library, Independence, Missouri.

22 Charles I. Schottland, "Social Security Amendments of 1956," *Social Security Bulletin* 19(September 1956):3–15; Martha Derthick, *Policymaking for Social Security* (Washington, D.C.: Brookings Institution, 1979), p. 319.

23 See Karen Davis, "Medicare Reconsidered," in *Health Care for the Poor and Elderly,* ed. Duncan Yaggy (Durham, N.C.: Duke Press Policy Studies, 1984), p. 81; Harris, *Sacred Trust,* chs. 14–15; Glenn R. Markus, *Nursing Homes and the Congress,* report 72-224 (Washington, D.C.: Library of Congress, 1972).

24 See Vladeck, *Unloving Care,* pp. 30, 42–4.

25 For more on the original links to Blue Cross and Blue Shield, see Jonathan H. Sunshine, "Medicare: Past, Present and Future," *National Journal* 14(June 5, 1982):1030; and John K. Iglehart, "Will Medicare's Success Spoil Its Chance to Survive Spending Cuts?" in ibid. 14(May 1, 1982):774.

26 Mills's comments appear in the *Congressional Record,* October 3, 1964, p. 24015. Robert J. Myers, who was social security's chief actuary in 1965, explains some of the problems in estimating health care benefit costs in his *Medicare* (Homewood, Ill.: Richard D. Irwin, 1970), ch. 4. See also Derthick, *Policymaking,* pp. 327–33; Carolyn L. Weaver, *The Crisis in Social Security* (Durham, N.C.: Duke Press Policy Studies, 1982), p. 156. Representative Barber Conable recalls this moment in his comments about the current Medicare crisis in *Social Security: The Long View,* ed. Mary Gardiner Jones (College Park, Md.: Center for Business and Public Policy, 1983), p. 55.

27 "Devising New Medicare Payment Plan May Prove Much Easier than Selling It," *National Journal* 14(November 20, 1982):1981.

28 Joseph A. Califano, Jr., "The Challenge to the Health Care System," in Yaggy, *Health Care for the Poor and Elderly,* p. 48; Vladeck, *Unloving Care,* pp. 32, 51; Starr, *Social Transformation,* p. 374.

29 Vladeck, *Unloving Care,* pp. 50–1, 56–7; Harris, *Sacred Trust,* pp. 188–9.

30 Message to Congress on January 7, 1965, in *Public Papers of the Presidents of the United States: Lyndon B. Johnson, 1965* (Washington, D.C.: Government Printing Office, 1966), vol. 1, p. 13. See also S. E. Berki, "Health Care Policy," *AAAPSS* 468(July 1983):232; and Judith Feder et al., "Health," in *The Reagan Experiment,* eds. John L. Palmer and Isabel V. Sawhill (Washington, D.C.: Urban Institute, 1982), p. 273.

31 Arthur R. Jacobs and Richard B. Froh, "Significance of Public Law 89-749," *New England Journal of Medicine* 279(December 12,

1968):1314; Ephraim H. Mizruchi, "Aspirations and Poverty," *The Sociological Quarterly* 8(Autumn 1967):338–51.

32 *Social Security Bulletin, 1982 Supplement,* p. 32; Vladeck, *Unloving Care,* pp. 67–8.

33 For the HMO's early history, see John K. Iglehart, "The Federal Government as Venture Capitalist," in *Politics and Health Care: Milbank Reader 6,* ed. John B. McKinlay (Cambridge, Mass.: M.I.T. Press, 1981), pp. 158–98; Harold Luft, "How Do Health Maintenance Organizations Achieve Their Savings?" *New England Journal of Medicine* 298(June 5, 1978):1137; and Spitz Brown, "When a Solution Is Not a Solution," *Journal of Health Politics, Policy and Law* 14(Winter 1979):513.

34 During the Nixon presidency, influential lobbying groups, such as the Committee of One Hundred chaired by Walter Reuther of the United Auto Workers, pressed for universal national health insurance. The American Medical Association advocated a federal tax deduction for health insurance premiums in order to stimulate the growth of more comprehensive private plans. Pivotal members of Congress introduced new legislation: The Long-Ribicoff-Wagner bill offered a "catastrophic illness" plan for the general population and increased benefits for the poor and medically indigent; the Kennedy-Cornman bill proposed a government monopoly of health insurance without cost sharing. For more details, see Theodore R. Marmor and Jon B. Christianson, *Health Care Policy* (Beverly Hills, Calif.: Sage Publications, 1982), ch. 6.

35 U.S. Senate Finance Committee, 91st Cong., 1st sess., *Medicare and Medicaid: Problems, Issues, and Alternatives* (Washington, D.C.: Government Printing Office, 1970), p. 62; John K. Iglehart, "The Rising Costs of Health Care," *National Journal* 8(October 16, 1976):1460; *Congressional Quarterly Almanac* 23(1977):500.

36 Paul Starr, "Transformation in Defeat," in Ronald L. Numbers, ed., *Compulsory Health Insurance* (Westport, Conn.: Greenwood Press, 1982), p. 134; Hale Champion, "Medicare: Retrospect and Prospect," in Jones, *Social Security: The Long View,* pp. 61–2.

37 The Medicare and Medicaid Antifraud and Abuse Amendments of 1977 were designed to remedy the situation. See Vladeck, *Unloving Care,* pp. 70, 161, 174–81.

38 For more on the plans and options discussed during the Carter years, see Joseph A. Califano, *Governing America* (New York: Simon & Schuster, 1981), ch. 4; Judith Feder, Jack Hadley, and John Holahan, *Insuring the Nation's Health* (Washington, D.C.: Urban Institute, 1981); Mark V. Pauly, ed., *National Health Insurance* (Washington, D.C.: American Enterprise Institute, 1980); Starr, *Social Transformation,* pp. 411–17; and *Congressional Quarterly Almanac* 26(1980):462.

39 Senate Special Committee on Aging, *Developments in Aging: 1983,* vol. 1, p. 381.

40   See Lee and Estes, "New Federalism and Health Policy," p. 98; Judith
R. Lave and Herbert A. Silverman, "Financing the Health Care of
the Aged," *AAAPSS* 468(July 1983):157–63; Feder et al., "Health,"
in Palmer and Sawhill, eds., *The Reagan Experiment,* pp. 291–305;
David A. Stockman, "Personal Perspective," *Business and Health*
1(November 1983):44; Donald F. Reilly, "Public Policy Report,"
Perspectives on Aging 12(May/June 1983):28–30. By June 1985, the
New York Times editorial board was endorsing these initiatives.

41   Davis, "Medicare Reconsidered," in Yaggy, *Health Care for the Poor
and Elderly,* p. 111. Other criticisms by Davis and Califano appear
in ibid., pp. 51–2, 85. There has been sharp debate, moreover,
whether or not DRGs – the most original solution enacted during
Reagan's first term – will actually save money and improve efficiency without affecting the quality of health care. See Senate Special Committee on Aging, *Developments in Aging: 1983,* vol. 1, pp.
389–94, 404–6; "Diagnosis Related Groups," *University of Pennsylvania Center for the Study of Aging Newsletter* 6(December 1983):6–8;
Bruce C. Vladeck, "Comment on 'Hospital Reimbursement under
Medicare'," *MMFQ* 62:269–78.

42   Although racial and income-determined disparities in amounts and
levels of use of resources persist, their relative sizes have decreased
over time. See Lave and Silverman, "Financing Health Care," pp.
155–6; Regina Loewenstein, "Early Effects of Medicare on the Health
Care of the Aged," *Social Security Bulletin* 34(April 1971):3–20; Martin Ruther and Allen Dobson, "Equal Treatment and Unequal Benefits," *Health Care Financing Review* 2(Winter 1981):55–83.

43   See Lee and Estes, "New Federalism," p. 89; Vladeck and Firman,
"Health Services," p. 143; Starr, *Social Transformation,* p. 380; Lave
and Silverman, "Financing Health Care," pp. 152–3; Congressional
Budget Office, *Changing the Structure,* pp. 9–10. See also Charles R.
Fisher, "Differences by Age Groups in Health Care Spending," *Health
Care Financing Review* 1(Spring 1980):65–90; Senate Special Com-
mittee on Aging, *Health Care Expenditures for the Aging* (Washing-
ton, D.C.: Government Printing Office, 1982), pp. iii, 6–8. For
criticisms of Medicare, see Robert R. Alford, *Health Care Politics*
(University of Chicago Press, 1975), pp. 8–9; Robert H. Binstock,
"Federal Policy Toward the Aging – Its Inadequacies and Its Politics," *National Journal* 10(November 11, 1978):1838–9; Laura Katz
Olson, *The Political Economy of Aging* (New York: Columbia University Press, 1982), pp. 137, 149, 155.

44   Because poverty rates are sensitive to economic conditions and
demographic circumstances, people move above and below "official" levels. And although it is true that Medicaid pays a large proportion of the nation's nursing home costs, it is also worth mention-
ing that states finance different types of facilities. In addition,
institutions supported by public taxes conform in varying degrees

to divergent standards of "quality." Data on Medicare/Medicaid administration from Califano, "The Challenge," p. 49; John C. Beck, "Response," in Yaggi, *Health Care for the Poor and Elderly*, p. 131; and Vladeck, *Unloving Care*, pp. 8–9, 133–8, 252.

45 The incidence of chronic disability increases with age, but only a minority of those under eighty-five experience health problems severe enough to restrict at least one major activity. Senate Special Committee on Aging, *Developments in Aging: 1983*, vol. 1, p. 42. Furthermore, most of those within the over-sixty-five group perceive their health to be "good" or "excellent"; 71% think that old people are healthier now than they were a decade ago. There are important variations in these optimistic perceptions, however. Positive health ratings decline with advancing years. The incidence of poor health varies directly with low income. Nearly two-thirds of all blacks and Hispanics over sixty-five consider their health "only fair" or "poor." See Louis Harris and Associates, *Aging in the Eighties* (Washington, D.C.: National Council on the Aging, 1981), pp. 134–6. The NCOA study reports that somewhat fewer women assess their health as favorably as men, but the published data do not give age- or race-specific breakdowns. See also Paul W. Newacheck et al., "Income and Illness," *Medical Care* 18(December 1980):1165–70.

46 On the average, sickness and disability limit the activities of older Americans nearly forty days per year, compared with nineteen days of restricted activity for the population as a whole.

47 Senate Special Committee on Aging, *Developments in Aging: 1983*, pp. 43, 47; Vladeck and Firman, "Health Services," pp. 134, 140.

48 Congressional Budget Office, *Changing the Structure*, pp. 9, 17, 31; for an independent analysis that reports slightly different results, see Yaggi, ed., *Health Care for the Poor and Elderly*, pp. 80, 101. The aged and disabled enrollees use different mixes of Hospital Insurance (HI) and Supplementary Medical Insurance (SMI) services; the latter require more per capita outpatient hospital services and are more likely to demand kidney dialysis. Consequently, although the distribution of Medicare expenditures to hospitals and physicians remained fairly constant during the 1970s, nursing home and administrative expenses became relatively smaller, and outlays for "other services" rose. This generalization, however, masks an important regional variation: Medicare lengths of stay consistently run 50% higher in the Northeast than in the Far West, even after controlling for age, sex, and ailment.

49 See Senate Special Committee on Aging, *Developments in Aging: 1983*, pp. 43–4, 54–5; Vladeck, *Unloving Care*, pp. 13–16, 220.

50 See David E. Rogers, "Providing Medical Care to the Elderly and Poor," in Yaggi, ed., *Health Care for the Poor and Elderly*, p. 6. See also David E. Rogers et al., "Who Needs Medicaid?" *New England Journal of Medicine* 307(July 1, 1982):13–18; Vladeck, *Unloving Care*,

p. 24; Vladeck and Firman, "Health Services," pp. 145–6; and U.S. Senate, 98 Cong., 1st sess., *Hearings on the Future of Medicare,* April 13, 1983, p. 20. Medicaid expenditures for nursing homes reported in the literature range from 15% to 40%; this apparent discrepancy reflects different definitions of "nursing home."

51 Victor R. Fuchs, "Reflections on Aging, Health, and Medical Care," *MMFQ* 62(Spring 1984):164. In light of such trends, the 1984 Advisory Council on Social Security agreed that "in principle, a comprehensive range of long term care services is covered by Federal programs." See the council's *Medicare: Benefits and Financing* (Washington, D.C.: Government Printing Office, 1984), p. 55. For an opposing view by Robert N. Butler, former director of the National Institute on Aging, see "Still No Federal Policy on Aging," *National Journal* 14(July 31, 1982):1344–6.

52 "Development of effective and affordable systems of chronic care as the core of the health care system is the central task for health policy in the coming decades," claim Vladeck and Firman in "Health Services and the Aging," p. 148. Among other things, this will require more attention to the elderly's drug abuse, depression, and suicide. Because long-term care is not synonymous with Medicare, policymakers will have to distinguish more rigorously among alternative institutional care provisions for various segments of the aged population. They will also have to establish more precise guidelines for the use of "heroic" measures for terminally ill patients. See Senate Special Committee on Aging, *Developments in Aging: 1983,* vol. 1, pp. 54, 412, 421; comments by Tom Nesbitt and Eli Ginzburg in Yaggi, ed., *Health Care for the Poor and Elderly,* pp. 40, 42.

53 I doubt that it is the *cost* of more health care that really worries policymakers and the public at large. Failure to allocate more money for the elderly's well-being, I suspect, reflects the pervasiveness of ageism in the United States.

54 A fuller exposition of the ethical issues at stake has appeared in the *Hastings Center Reports* and the writings of some of its associates, especially Daniel Callahan, Robert Veatch, and H. R. Moody. The three-volume National Science Foundation study, *Social Ethics, Social Policy, and an Aging Society,* eds. Bernice Neugarten and Robert Havighurst (Chicago: Committee on Human Development, University of Chicago, 1976–7), and *Summing Up,* a volume issued by the President's Commission for the Study of Ethical Problems in Medical and Biomedical and Behavioral Research (Washington, D.C.: Government Printing Office, 1983), are also useful. For cross-cultural and historical background, see Leo W. Simmons, *The Role of the Aged in Primitive Societies* (New Haven: Yale University Press, 1945); Simone de Beauvoir, *The Coming of Age* (New York: Putnam, 1972); and Phillipe Ariès, *The Hour of Our Death* (New York: Random House, 1982).

55 Victor R. Fuchs's *Who Shall Live? Health, Economics and Social Choice* (New York: Basic Books, 1974) is both a useful source for the early experiences under Medicare and Medicaid and an incisive statement of the issues at stake. See also Kenneth Arrow, "Uncertainty and the Welfare Economics of Medical Care," *American Economic Review* 53(September 1963):946; Victor R. Fuchs, ed., *Essays in the Economics of Health and Medical Care* (New York: National Bureau of Economic Research, 1972), ch. 2; and Louise B. Russell, "Inflation and the Federal Role in Health," in John B. McKinlay, ed., *Politics and Health Care* (Cambridge, Mass.: M.I.T. Press, 1981), pp. 120–39.

56 Senate Special Committee on Aging, *Developments in Aging: 1983,* vol. 1, pp. 392, 399–400; "When a Booming Population of Old Vets Checks in for VA Health Care, Look Out," *National Journal* 16(June 2, 1984):1091–3.

57 See the comments by David Hamburg, president of the Carnegie Corporation, in Yaggi, ed., *Health Case for the Poor and Elderly,* pp. 71, 137. See also "Relative Responsibility," *National Journal* 15(May 21, 1983):1073; "Study Says Added Health Aids Could Help Aged," *New York Times,* May 6, 1984, p. 21; and Gary A. Tobin's *Social Planning and Human Service Development in the Voluntary Sector,* to be published by Greenwood Press.

58 Some contend that Americans are obsessed with a "technological fix," relying too much on "heroic intervention." Others stress the tremendous gains wrought by technology and note that many useful inventions in the biomedical sciences still have not been applied in geriatric care. According to the 1984 Advisory Council on Social Security, new technology accounted for only about 21% of hospital expenditure increases between 1970 and 1981. See the council's *Medicare,* p. 80; also the comments by David Mechanic and David Hamburg in Yaggi, ed., *Health Care for the Poor and Elderly,* pp. 37, 136.

59 Advisory Council on Social Security, *Medicare,* especially pp. 1–17 and appendix G.

60 The similarities were intentional. Chapter 8 of the council's report, for instance, analyzes the NCSSR's proposals, indicating that the two panels' recommendations were generally complementary.

61 The decision to raise the Medicare eligibility age, for instance, was justified in light of the 1983 social security amendment that stipulated sixty-seven as the retirement age by 2027.

62 Even if policymakers do not abandon the OASDI model, critics may still dismiss the council's report. They are likely to cite undue deference to health care professionals and to decry the lack of input from Medicare beneficiaries. See "The Additional Views of Stanford Arnold and Alvin Heaps," in Advisory Council on Social Security, *Medicare,* pp. 113–20. Two bills introduced in the spring of 1984 will gain supporters. In their "Medicare Solvency and Health Care Financing Act," Senator Edward Kennedy and Representative

Richard A. Gephardt (D–Mo.) hoped to capitalize on the strengths of competition and of regulation by expanding DRGs, discouraging hospitals from increasing Medicare admissions, and providing a 2% Medicaid bonus to states that develop plans to moderate increases in hospital costs. Senator John Heinz advocated incentives for physicians who accept Medicare rates as payment in full for outpatient services; he wanted a fee schedule that encouraged preventive and primary care. On Kennedy-Gephardt, see 98th Cong., 2nd sess., H.R. 4870, introduced February 21, 1984; and Richard A. Gephardt, "Creative Regulation Designed to Stimulate Competition," *Business and Health* 1(April 1984):19–20. Heinz unveiled his "Medicare Incentives Reform Act" proposal in a speech before the National Council on the Aging on April 5, 1984.

63   This scenario has been suggested by several "insiders" I interviewed, including Barber Conable, who served on the NCSSR. See Conable's remarks in Jones, *Social Security: The Long View*, pp. 50–1.

64   Senate Special Committee on Aging, *Present Problems – Future Options*, Wichita, Kans., April 20, 1984, pp. 18–20, 44–5, 78–9; and idem, *Developments in Aging: 1983*, vol. 1, pp. 383–5.

65   Alain Enthoven, "Consumer Choice Health Plan," *New England Journal of Medicine* 30(March 30, 1978):710–14; idem, *Health Plan: The Only Practical Solution to the Soaring Cost of Medical Care* (Reading, Mass.: Addison-Wesley, 1980). For a stinging criticism, see Mark Rushefsky, "A Critique of Market Reform in Health Care," *Journal of Health Politics, Policy and Law* 5(Winter 1981):736.

66   See Advisory Council on Social Security, *Medicare*, p. 8; Judith R. Lave, "Hospital Reimbursement under Medicare," *MMFQ* 62:251–68. Others want to increase the role that "Medigap" insurance plays in reducing public expenditures and mitigating direct consumer costs. Such a tack could build on the TEFRA requirement that employers offer workers over sixty-five and their spouses a choice between Medicare and another health plan. Yet Donald MacNaughton, the former president of Prudential, and other insurance executives contend that Medigap is not profitable: The industry must make up losses in this area with profits from life insurance premiums. MacNaughton's comments appear in Yaggi, ed., *Health Care for the Poor and Elderly*, p. 63. See also "Coming: Help in Funding a Medigap Policy That Makes Sense," *Changing Times* 35(February 1981):14; Davis, "Health Care Policies and the Aged," p. 7; Jones, *Social Security: The Long View*, p. 105; and Congressional Budget Office, *Financing Medicare*, p. 38.

67   Ginzberg, "The Financial Support of Health Care," especially pp. 21–3; Theodore R. Marmor, "Canada's Path, America's Choices," in Numbers, ed., *Compulsory Health Insurance*, pp. 77–96. See also Rosemary Stevens, *American Medicine and the Public Interest* (New

Haven: Yale University Press, 1971), pp. 540–1; John G. Goodman, *National Health Care in Great Britain: Lessons for the U.S.A.* (Dallas: Fisher Institute, 1980), ch. 11; Jack Hadley, "How Should Medicare Pay Physicians?" *MMFQ* 62:279–99; U.S. House of Representatives, Select Committee on Aging, *World Health Systems: Lessons for the U.S.* (Washington, D.C.: Government Printing Office, 1984), pp. 26–7.

68 Vladeck, *Unloving Care,* pp. 211, 218–41; also Davis, "Medicare Reconsidered," in Yaggi, ed., *Health Care for the Poor and Elderly,* p. 92; Senate Special Committee on Aging, *Developments in Aging: 1983,* p. 416; 1984 Advisory Council on Social Security, *Medicare,* p. 227.

69 Karen Davis, "Health Care Policies and the Aged," in Robert H. Binstock and Ethel Shanas, eds., *Handbook of Aging and the Social Sciences,* 2nd ed. (New York: Van Nostrand Reinhold, 1985).

70 Howard S. Zuckerman, "Industrial Rationalization of a Cottage Industry," *AAAPSS* 468(July 1983):221, 229; see also Starr, *Social Transformation,* pp. 441, 448.

71 For differences between medical and other markets, see Donald Cohodes, "Where You Stand Depends on Where You Sit: Musings on the Regulation/Competition Dialogue," *Journal of Health Politics, Policy and Law* 7(Spring 1982):54–79.

72 Henry J. Aaron, "Comment on 'Alternative Medicare Financing'," *MMFQ* 62(Spring 1984):350.

73 Wilbur J. Cohen, "A Postscript on the Future," in Numbers, ed., *Compulsory Health Insurance,* p. 156.

9 A vision renewed: individual needs and mutual responsibility

1 Marie L. Dallach, "Old Age, American Style," *New Outlook* 162(October 1933):50; see also Warren S. Thompson and P. K. Whelpton, "A Nation of Elders in the Making," *American Mercury* 19(April 1930):392–5; Arthur S. Y. Chen, "Social Significance of Old Age," *Sociology and Social Research* 23(July–August 1939):519–27; and Ralph Linton, "Age and Sex Categories," *American Sociological Review* 7(August 1942):592–601.

2 See Joseph A. Califano, *Governing America* (New York: Simon & Schuster, 1981), p. 398; Robert J. Samuelson, "Busting the Budget: The Graying of America," *National Journal* 10(February 18, 1978):256–60; and Robert B. Hudson, "The 'Graying' of the Federal Budget and Its Consequences for Old-Age Policy," *The Gerontologist* 18(October 1978):428–40.

3 Phillip Longman, "Taking America To The Cleaners," *Washington Monthly* 14(November 1982):26.

4 Nancy Foner, *Ages in Conflict* (New York: Columbia University Press, 1984).

5   Samuel H. Preston, "Children and the Elderly in the U.S.," *Scientific American* 251(December 1984):44–9; "Florida's Generations Split over Social Security," *Washington Post,* February 12, 1985, pp. A1, A4.

6   This essay, which first appeared in the June 1938 issue of *The Record* of the American Institute of Actuaries, is reprinted with comments stressing its historical significance in *Social Security: Program, Problems, and Policies,* eds. William Haber and Wilbur J. Cohen (Homewood, Ill.: Richard D. Irwin, 1960), pp. 61–3. Although considerations of "adequacy" took precedence over strict claims of "equity" in the pivotal 1939 amendments, social security's own policymakers expressed reservations at the time about the wisdom of increasing the elderly's benefits dramatically. "The only result," Edwin Witte confided in a memorandum to Wilbur Cohen, "may be that the present younger workers are taxed for the increased benefits to the older people without any assurance whatsoever that they will get similar benefits when they are old." Witte to Cohen, July 3, 1939, in the "Chairman's Files," National Archives, Record Group 47,095. The risk of future intergenerational inequities, however, seemed less important than building a floor of support for needy members of the population.

7   This recommendation will be opposed if it appears to hurt the very people who need the most help. To date, minimum benefits have provided the cushion vital to "welfare" under social insurance. But if SSI serves as a "safety net" for all age groups, the specter of systemic intergenerational inequities can be eliminated. By taking full advantage of SSI's welfare role, beneficiaries should be guaranteed a higher standard of living than if they had to rely exclusively on the lowest Title II monthly pension or the benefits given to "transitional" workers over the age of seventy-two.

8   George Masnick and Mary Jo Bane, *The Nation's Families* (Boston: Auburn House Publishing, 1980); Joseph Califano, "The Four-Generation Family," *Annals of the American Academy of Political and Social Sciences* 438(July 1978):96–107; Ethel Shanas, "The Family as a Social Support in Old Age," *The Gerontologist* 19(April 1979):169–74.

9   Sheila B. Kamerman and Cheryl D. Hayes, eds., *Families That Work: Children in a Changing World* (Washington, D.C.: National Academy Press, 1982); Alan Pifer, "Perceptions of Childhood and Youth," *Annual Report Essays* (New York: Carnegie Corporation of New York, 1983), pp. 157–67; U.S. Department of Health and Human Services, *Child Support Enforcement* (Washington, D.C.: Government Printing Office, 1983), pp. 18, 28; "Increase Found In Child Poverty In Study by U.S.," *New York Times,* May 23, 1985, pp. 1, 14; U.S. House of Representatives, *Children in Poverty* (WMCP 99-8) (Washington, D.C.: Government Printing Office, 1985).

10 Irwin Garfinkel, "The Role of Child Support Insurance in Antipov-

erty Policy," *Annals of the American Academy of Political and Social Sciences* 479(May 1985):119–31; see also Robert J. Lampman, *Balancing the Books* (Washington, D.C.: National Conference on Social Welfare, 1985), p. 13.

11 Sar A. Levitan, William B. Johnston, and Robert Taggart, *Still a Dream* (Cambridge, Mass.: Harvard University Press, 1975), pp. 220–1; and Dorothy K. Newman et al., *Protest, Politics, and Prosperity* (New York: Pantheon Books, 1978), pp. 241–2.

12 James D. Williams, ed., *The State of Black America, 1983* (New York: National Urban League, 1983), p. 48. Other data come from pp. 65, 69–70.

13 Between the ages of thirty-five and sixty-five, the unemployment rate among Hispanics exceeds that among whites, though it is lower than that among blacks. Hispanics on the average earn less than their white peers. Jacqueline Johnson Jackson, *Minorities and Aging* (Belmont, Calif.: Wadsworth Publishing, 1980), pp. 8, 139–45.

14 George F. Will, *Statecraft as Soulcraft* (New York: Simon & Schuster, 1983), p. 45; see also Morris Janowitz, *The Reconstruction of Patriotism* (University of Chicago Press, 1983).

15 Robert J. Samuelson, "The Great Postwar Prosperity," *Newsweek*, May 20, 1985, p. 57.

16 Congressional Panel on Social Security Organization, *A Plan to Establish an Independent Agency for Social Security* (Washington, D.C.: House Committee on Ways and Means, 1984), p. 5. In its formative years, the Social Security Board was an independent agency. It is now a part of the Department of Health and Human Services.

17 The President's Commission on Pension Policy, *Coming of Age* (Washington, D.C.: Government Printing Office, 1981), p. 38.

18 See transcript of President Reagan's press conference reprinted in *New York Times,* July 25, 1984, p. 10; "Senate Votes Plan to Guarantee Increase in Social Security Benefits," ibid., July 27, 1984, p. 8; Terry Hartle, "Election-Year Strategy: Pandering to the Elderly," *Buffalo Evening News,* July 28, 1984, p. B-3.

19 "Regan Says Benefits Need Reexamining," *Washington Post,* May 7, 1984, p. A3; "Regan's Benefit-Curb Remark Blasted," ibid., May 8, 1984, p. A1; "Why Stigmatize Social Security?" *New York Times,* May 8, 1984, p. 22.

20 Robert J. Myers, "Money's Worth Comparison for Social Security Benefits," NCSSR memorandum no. 45, dated August 12, 1982, p. 5. For a fuller discussion that includes the impact of the 1983 amendments, see Robert J. Myers and Bruce D. Schobel, "A Money's-Worth Analysis of Social Security Retirement Benefits," *Transactions of the Society of Actuaries* 87(1983):533–61.

21 Chapters 6 and 7 in this volume.

22 Elements of this proposal have been advanced by several commissions and various thoughtful commentators. See Senate Special

Committee on Aging, *Developments in Aging: 1983* (Washington, D.C.: Government Printing Office, 1984), vol. 1, pp. 252, 267. For a discussion of the broader connections between tax policy and the aged, see Gary M. Nelson, "Tax Expenditures for the Elderly," *The Gerontologist* 23(October 1983):471–8; and President's Commission on Pension Policy, *Coming of Age,* pp. 1, 45.

23 Evelyn R. Kay, *Participation in Adult Education, 1981* (Washington, D.C.: National Center for Education Statistics, 1982), p. 6.

24 On McDonald's effort (and why they think it so important), see House of Representatives, 97th Cong., 1st sess., *New Business Perspectives on the Older Worker,* hearings before the Select Committee on Aging, October 28, 1981, pp. 56–67. On ARCO, see Corporate Employee Relations, *Making the Right Decision* (Los Angeles: Atlantic Richfield Co., 1982); Blair A. Hyde, manager of Senior Worker Policies and Programs, kindly permitted me to read internal memoranda about the ways ARCO seeks to utilize retired employees.

25 It is beyond the scope of this work to say more on the subject here. But see the thoughtful recommendations advanced by Robert M. Fogelson in *The Morass* (New York: Columbia University Press, 1984).

26 Hale Champion, "Medicare: Retrospect and Prospect," *Social Security: The Long View,* ed. Mary Gardiner Jones (College Park, Md.: Center for Business and Public Policy, 1983), p. 68.

27 Ibid., p. 70; see also Joseph Califano and Karen Davis's endorsements of the idea in *Health Care for the Poor and Elderly,* ed. Duncan Yaggy (Durham, N.C.: Duke Press Policy Studies, 1984), on pp. 56 and 92, respectively.

28 This dialogue is not fictional; it appears in Edward D. Berkowitz, "Disability Insurance and the Social Security Tradition," unpublished paper, 1985, pp. 22–3.

Index

Abzug, Bella, 138
actuarial assumptions, 45, 72, 75, 92–
93, 128, 235n16, 239n50
erroneous, 127–128, 228n50
after 1983 Social Security amendments, 6
actuarially reduced benefits, 129, 153
acute care, 173–174, 194
adequacy:
as concept, 30–36, 49–50, 216n40
in health care, 165, 167–168
as social priority, 41, 55, 183–184,
188
of SSI, 71–72
of Title I benefits, 22
of Title II benefits, 34, 72, 73
as unfulfilled goal, 184
adequacy/equity, as conflicting social
policy objectives:
balance in social security, 2, 46, 57,
73–74, 123, 130, 137, 183–184,
186, 242n72, 256n53
decoupling, in social security, 135–
137, 255n45
issue confounded by technical jargon, 94
in original act, 22–23, 183
shifts due to 1939 amendments, 3,
32, 34–37, 276n6
should not be compartmentalized,
185
strain in 1970s, 71–74
Administration on Aging (U.S.), 175
adult education, 192
advisory boards, need for, 193
advisory councils on social security,
see Social Security Advisory Councils

AFDC see Aid to Families with
Dependent Children
Affluent Society, The, 48
age, as category, 25, 27, 33–34, 44,
46, 53, 109–110, 175–176
see also intergenerational relations;
transgenerational theme, in discussing social security
aged:
attitudes of, 118–121
as consumers of health care, 173–
174, 176–178
fears of, 1, 51–52, 82
heterogeneity of, 173, 182
images of, 76, 105, 116–117, 166
increased choices of, 120, 192
poverty among, 53–54
self-images of, 119, 120, 271n45
status of, 116-117, 166-169
as volunteers, 121
as workers, 103, 107, 108–109,
110–111, 115, 120–121, 191–192
see also dependency in old age;
elderly; old-old
Age Discrimination in Employment
Act, 113, 114, 118
age discrimination in employment
policies, 51, 113–114, 121, 191
age grading, 244n20
ageism, 75–76, 115, 191, 228n52,
272n53
age-specific vs. life course perspectives, 132–133, 182
aging society, 182
see also graying of America
Aid to Families with Dependent
Children (AFDC) (Title IV):
current scope of, 4, 184, 186

279